Performance Management in Healthcare

From Key Performance Indicators to Balanced Scorecard

Second Edition

Performance Management in Healthcare

From Key Performance Indicators to Balanced Scorecard

Second Edition

Bryan P. Bergeron, MD

CRC Press
Taylor & Francis Group
Boca Raton   London   New York

CRC Press is an imprint of the
Taylor & Francis Group, an **informa** business

A PRODUCTIVITY PRESS BOOK

CRC Press
Taylor & Francis Group
6000 Broken Sound Parkway NW, Suite 300
Boca Raton, FL 33487-2742

Productivity Press is an imprint of Taylor & Francis Group, an Informa business

No claim to original U.S. Government works

Printed on acid-free paper

International Standard Book Number-13: 978-1-1381-0452-5 (Hardback); 978-1-138-10453-2 (Paperback)

Library of Congress Cataloging-in-Publication Data

Names: Bergeron, Bryan P., author.
Title: Performance management in healthcare : from key performance indicators to balanced scorecard / Bryan Bergeron.
Description: Second edition. | Boca Raton : Taylor & Francis, 2018. | "A CRC title, part of the Taylor & Francis imprint, a member of the Taylor & Francis Group, the academic division of T&F Informa plc." | Includes bibliographical references and index.
Identifiers: LCCN 2017020974| ISBN 9781138104525 (hardback : alk. paper) | ISBN 9781138104532 (paperback : alk. paper) | ISBN 9781315102214 (ebook)
Subjects: LCSH: Health services administration. | Health facilities--Personnel management. | Medical personnel--Rating of. | Performance--Management.
Classification: LCC RA971 .B43 2018 | DDC 362.1068/3--dc23
LC record available at https://lccn.loc.gov/2017020974

Visit the Taylor & Francis Web site at
http://www.taylorandfrancis.com

and the CRC Press Web site at
http://www.crcpress.com

For Hamad

Contents

Preface

Performance Management, variably referred to as corporate performance management (CPM), business performance management (BPM), or enterprise performance management (EPM), is a strategy that can be used to achieve an optimum mix of solvency, quality, safety, and patient satisfaction. The basis of Performance Management (PM) is the effective use of resources, as measured by quantifying processes and outcomes using Key Performance Indicators (KPIs)—core measures that gauge the performance of the organization in particular areas.

Performance Management isn't something your organization can just buy, install on the cloud, and forget. It's a process that involves behavior change, leadership, and vision. As part of the process, performance indicators must be selected or developed and then maintained with the utmost care. Business intelligence (BI) tools that support the process, such as Online Analytical Processing (OLAP), data marts and data warehouses, analytics, and graphics applications, must be selected or developed with equal care amid emerging standards, uncertain best practices, and unknown tool longevity. Furthermore, it is essential to view BI tools as enabling technology in support of the process and not solutions in themselves.

Since the publication of the first edition of this book in 2005, innumerable articles, books, and websites have been developed to explain how Performance Management can be used to achieve significant results in venues ranging from relatively small group practices to expansive healthcare enterprises. This heightened interest in Performance Management stemmed from increased penetration of the EMR at every level of practice, fueled by carrot-and-stick legislation. EMR adoption has more than doubled since 2005.* However, despite what many glossy brochures would have you believe, regardless of the venue, there is more to Performance Management than selecting a few KPIs from a list and feeding the corresponding data into a pre-formatted graphical display or dashboard.

Enabling the chief executives, department chairs, and practice group managers with the ability to glance at their smartphones for a graphical dashboard that shows up-to-the-minute data on operations, utilization, financial, and clinical performance is a significant challenge for everyone in the organization. As detailed in this book, achieving the increased quality, safety, and other outcomes promised by Performance Management may start with selecting a suite of BI tools, but it certainly doesn't end there. A properly executed Performance Management Initiative touches everyone, from the janitors to the department chairs.

This second edition of *Performance Management in Healthcare: From Key Performance Indicators to Balanced Scorecard*, similar to the first edition, was created as a practical resource and reference for healthcare information technology (IT) executives and professionals. This book assumes a

---

* Office of the National Coordinator for Health Information Technology. Office-Based Physician Electronic Health Record Adoption, Health IT Quick-Stat #50. dashboard.healthit.gov/quickstats/pages/physician-ehr -adoption-trends.php. December 2016.

CIO to IT managerial-level reader who is knowledgeable of the IT operation of a healthcare organization of virtually any size, but who may be unfamiliar with the spectrum of challenges associated with the clinical, financial, and cultural issues associated with a Performance Management Initiative. After completing this book, you will be equipped with the knowledge necessary to start a Performance Management Initiative. Of course, Performance Management is just one tool in your arsenal. It's up to you to provide the leadership and vision to carry the initiative to a successful completion.

Much has happened in the US healthcare system since the first edition of this book was published. Meaningful Use is now in vogue. Many of the quality organizations listed in the appendix of the first book are no longer in existence, and there are new organizations to fill the void. Both patients and their physicians look to portals for the latest creditable information. And computing, including Internet connectivity, is ubiquitous. However, as we all know, automating a bad process simply accelerates the rate at which things get worse. Similarly, simply handing a physician a tablet computer doesn't make that physician technologically savvy. Any primate can operate a tablet computer.

Organization of this Book

Performance Management in Healthcare includes a high-level survey of the key financial and clinical performance indicators. Performance Management tools, including statistical process control (SPC) methods, managerial strategies, and graphical displays that support Performance Management, such as the dashboard and balanced scorecard, are also discussed. An extensive, updated glossary and references to indicate sources are provided for readers new to applying quality tools in a healthcare organization.

This book is structured as stand-alone chapters connected by the theme of Performance Management. Relevant BI technologies are identified as their application areas are discussed, and real-world examples illustrate key concepts and challenges. This organization is intended to facilitate the reader's access to relevant information in a particular area of Performance Management.

Chapter 1. Overview
This chapter considers the various promises and practical realities of a Performance Management Initiative in the modern healthcare organization, whether the organization is a small group practice or a sprawling medical research facility.

Chapter 2. Performance Management Strategies
This chapter looks at general and healthcare-specific strategies to developing a Performance Management Initiative.

Chapter 3. Meaningful Use
An overview of Meaningful Use as it pertains to a Performance Management Initiative.

Chapter 4. The Performance Management Cycle
Performance Management is a continuous cycle of measurement, analysis, and action. This chapter provides a roadmap through the cycle, from self-assessment, performance indicator selection, and implementation to report generation and analysis.

Chapter 5. Key Performance Indicators
This chapter discusses the role of KPIs in Performance Management and the challenges associated with the selection and use of indicators.

Chapter 6. Nonclinical Indicators

This chapter introduces the key financial, operational, and utilization performance indicators. Indicators in the areas of Capacity and Utilization, Capital Structure, Liquidity, Patient and Payer Mix, Pricing Strategies, Productivity and Efficiency, and Revenues Expenses and Profitability are defined computationally and described in terms of their ability to support decision making.

Chapter 7. Clinical Indicators

This chapter reviews the clinical performance indicators established by major quality organizations. Included in the discussion are indicators from the Agency for Healthcare Research and Quality (AHRQ), National Committee for Quality Assurance (NCQA), Centers for Medicare and Medicaid Services (CMS), Joint Commission on Accreditation of Healthcare Organizations (JCAHO), and England's National Health Service (NHS). Drivers for clinical performance indicators are discussed, including safety and the demand for best practices decision support tools.

Chapter 8. Benchmarks

Objective, industry-wide metrics provide decision makers with a basis for assessing the competitiveness of their organization. Sources of commercial and governmental benchmarks are discussed, as well as the limitations of relying on benchmarks to assess performance.

Chapter 9. Reporting

Performance Management relies on the ability of decision makers to assess performance indicators and respond accordingly. The interface between decision makers and indicator values—that is, reporting—defines the effectiveness and efficiency with which managers can interpret data. This chapter reviews performance indicator reporting formats, from spreadsheets to graphical dashboards, and discusses the types of data appropriate for each format. It also introduces the balanced scorecard, a strategy based on combining clinical and nonclinical performance indicators with "soft" measures, such as patient satisfaction.

Chapter 10. Behavior Change

Action in the form of positive behavior change is the major contribution of Performance Management to an organization's success. As detailed in this chapter, convincing decision makers and frontline clinicians to change their work habits to reflect new information is often a demanding task.

Chapter 11. Statistics

Statistical analysis of indicators values and the data that contribute to performance indicators is a cornerstone of Performance Management. This chapter provides a review of basic statistical methods that apply to selecting, validating, and interpreting performance indicators.

Appendix A. Healthcare Quality Organizations

A list of the top healthcare quality organizations worldwide with URLs.

Appendix B. Summary of AHRQ Quality Indicators

A summary of the AHRQ Quality Indicators available in the areas of prevention, inpatient, patient safety, and pediatrics.

Appendix C. AHRQ Toolkits

A summary of toolkits freely available from the Agency for Healthcare Research and Quality (AHRQ), with the target audience identified.

Appendix D. AHRQ QI Toolkit Components

A summary of the AHRQ QI Toolkit components, a set of tools available free of charge from the AHRQ website.

Appendix E. AHRQ National Healthcare Quality and Disparities Report Measures
> A summary of the measures used in the AHRQ's report, including measures of access, affordability, care coordination, effective treatment, and healthy living.

Appendix F. Health Plan Employer Data and Information Set (HEDIS) Measures for Physicians
> A summary of the HEDIS measures available for physicians.

Appendix G. OASIS-Based Outcomes Measures
> A summary of the OASIS-based outcomes measure descriptions.

Appendix H. OASIS-Based Process Measures
> A summary of the OASIS-based process measure descriptions.

Appendix I. NHS England Statistics (Measures)
> Indicators developed by NHS Service Trusts that have potential applicability to US hospitals and physicians.

Appendix J. Highlights of the Australian National Safety and Quality Health Service (NSQHS) Standards
> Established healthcare standards with potential applicability to US hospitals and physicians.

Acronyms
> The major acronyms readers are likely to encounter in a Performance Management Initiative.

Glossary
> One of the greatest hurdles for IT executives working with administrative, financial, clinical, and operational processes in a healthcare organization is communicating with the appropriate vocabulary. This glossary is intended to help bridge the vocabulary gap.

Acknowledgments

Special thanks to John Glaser, PhD, senior vice president, Cerner; Hamad Al-Daig, CEO, Carelink; Bashar Horanieh, director, Application and Health Informatics Division, King Faisal Specialist Hospital and Research Centre (KFSH&RC); and Osama Alswailem, MD, CIO at KFSH&RC. Thanks also to Lyle Berkowitz, MD, director of Innovation at Northwestern Medicine; Michael Bailin, MD, chairman of Anesthesia at Baystate Medical Center; Jim McClay, MD, MPH, director, Great Plains Clinical & Translational Research Biomedical Informatics Core; and Jeffrey Blander, PhD, chief innovation officer at Eurekalabs and US Department of State, Office of the Global AIDS Coordinator, for their invaluable assistance.

Author

Bryan P. Bergeron, MD, a fellow of the American College of Medical Informatics, is the author of numerous books, articles, software packages, and patents. He has practiced medical informatics at Massachusetts General Hospital in Boston and taught medical informatics, as well as more traditional medical courses, in the Health Sciences and Technology Division of Harvard Medical School and MIT for nearly three decades. This book reflects his experiences with Performance Management ranging from initiatives within the Harvard-affiliated teaching hospitals to the Data Warehouse project at King Faisal Specialist Hospital and Research Centre in Saudi Arabia.

Chapter 1

Overview

Despite decades of well-meaning effort, delivering *quality* healthcare remains an increasingly complex and costly proposition. Not only is there a long-standing tension between practitioners, political parties, hospital administrators, third-party payers, and patients, but much of the healthcare industry is at odds with fundamental free market business constraints. For example, there is the economic jolt to a once modest electronic medical record (EMR) market, thanks to the Health Information Technology for Economic and Clinical Health (HITECH) component of the American Recovery and Reinvestment Act (ARRA) of 2009 that at first enticed and then prodded physicians to "meaningfully" adopt electronic health records. Then, there is the enactment of the Affordable Care Act in 2010, through which millions of patients have come to view healthcare as an entitlement, immune to the law of supply and demand.

In many respects, the US healthcare industry is being squeezed to provide high-quality, low-cost healthcare to all, akin to FedEx offering guaranteed overnight delivery for the price of a first-class postage stamp, with pickup kiosks on every corner. This despite the fact that, in business, it is commonly accepted that improving the performance of an organization by increasing quality or availability is necessarily associated with a greater cost. It's for this reason that most successful businesses define a niche for themselves by offering products and services that compete on the basis of quality, cost, *or* availability (speed)—mutually orthogonal characteristics. For example, FedEx enjoys a brisk business from well-heeled procrastinators by providing guaranteed overnight delivery across the country for 20 times what the US Postal Service charges for regular delivery.

Unlike many other industries, US healthcare has never really achieved steady state, but has instead maintained a more or less constant state of turmoil. Consider just some of the disruptors:

- An aging population
- The long-standing, worldwide economic slowdown
- The increasing dependence on expensive, complex technology
- The overhead of Health Insurance Portability and Accountability Act (HIPAA) compliance
- The financial implications of the HITECH Act surrounding Meaningful Use
- Rising patient expectations
- Utter lack of political consensus on the future of healthcare at the federal level

- Expansion of the electronic health record (EHR) to include not only the hospital-derived EMR, but the insurer-derived patient health record (PHR)
- Evolving Medicare and Medicaid programs, with varying state and federal components
- Diminishing physician job satisfaction with cookbook medicine becoming the norm
- A long-standing belief among clinicians that financial issues should not interfere with what is best for their patients

Despite the turbidity caused by these divergent perspectives, it's clear that every healthcare organization can benefit from compiling the metrics required by management to make informed decisions. With the need of hospitals to demonstrate not only EMR adoption but also Meaningful Use, defining and measuring the appropriate indicators are becoming even more critical for institutions dependent on Medicare and Medicaid payments.

The metrics that apply to most healthcare organizations, referred to variably as Key Performance Indicators (KPIs), Quality Indicators (QI), or simply indicators, have been defined by performance-promoting organizations such as the Joint Commission on Accreditation of Healthcare Organizations (JCAHO), Centers for Medicare and Medicaid Services (CMS), and the Agency for Healthcare Research and Quality (AHRQ). The purpose of these indicators ranges from simply securing full Medicare and Medicaid reimbursements to actually helping management more effectively direct the use of their healthcare organization's resources, maximizing patient safety, and promoting clinical best practices, to increasing patient satisfaction with their healthcare provider.

1.1 Performance Management

It is impossible for management to have low-cost access to unlimited quantities of high-quality indicator data—that is, without a disruptive technology, process, or strategy. One such strategy is Performance Management. The basis of Performance Management is the effective use of resources, as measured by quantifying processes and outcomes using indicators that gauge the performance of an organization in particular areas. The strategy relies in part on properly leveraging myriad information technologies, from database management systems' high-speed networks to software and hardware for data analysis and display.

As noted above, cost, availability, and quality are orthogonal qualities in virtually every healthcare organization (see Figure 1.1, left). It is up to management, within physical, economic, and legal constraints imposed on the organization, to define the compromise between the three variables. For example, if management decides that availability—rapid access to care—is the organization's highest priority, then the cost of care will likely increase and quality may suffer, all else being equal. To achieve this higher availability figure, the director of the emergency room (ER) department may decide to add additional full-time ER physicians on every shift, thereby increasing cost. If, instead, the additional staff are primarily residents from other clinical services, then the cost increase should be less dramatic, but the quality of care may suffer.

The diagram on the left illustrates the constraints that apply to most business organizations, modeled as the apices of a triangle. As shown in the right diagram, the introduction of a disruptive technology, process, or strategy may reduce the interdependent constraints on each variable, modeled as contracted triangles. An increased focus on quality, cost, or availability incurs less of a deficit in the other two variables. The effect may be symmetrical (1) or asymmetrically favor availability (2), quality (3), or cost (4). Note that the models before and after the introduction of a disruptive technology, process, or strategy in Figure 1.1 are not to scale.

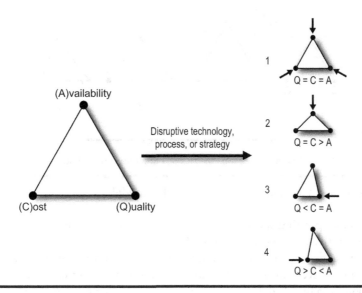

Figure 1.1   Mutually orthogonal constraints of availability, cost, and quality.

In Figure 1.1 (1), there is a symmetrical contraction of the availability, cost, and quality triangle. In (2), quality and cost remain constant, but availability increases. In (3), quality is improved, while cost and availability remain constant. In the last example, cost is diminished, with no change in quality or availability. The change in cost, availability, and quality is a function of the degree to which the introduction of a disruptive technology, process, or strategy improves the organization's operation. Furthermore, the shift takes time, and the changes in availability, cost, and quality may not be in sync. For example, shifting from paper-based medical records to an EMR may increase cost acutely, but result in increased access to and quality of patient data. Chronically, cost may gradually decline to a value less than the original cost of maintaining paper records. Using the model introduced in Figure 1.1, the disruptive effects of the technology can be visualized as contraction of the triangle in response to the EMR's introduction.

Before we delve deeper into the admittedly simplistic model, it's important to acknowledge my bias. If you note the last sentence above, I unconsciously narrowed the definition of the disruptive agent to a technology. Taking the perspective of an information technology (IT) specialist, every problem calls out for an IT solution. Presuming a reader with an IT background, it's important to at least recognize the potential bias toward technology solutions, and to be mindful of disruptive processes and strategies. Overreliance on IT technology in a Performance Management Initiative is akin to a clinician's overindulgence on diagnostic technology. We're all aware of the ranking of US healthcare worldwide, despite spending the most on healthcare and the associated clinical technologies. So, from here onward, when I mention disruptive technology, keep in mind that the statement generally applies to disruptive processes and strategies as well.

Of course, contraction of the axes of the model with the introduction of the disruptive technology, process, or strategy describes the best-case scenario. The disruptive technology might permanently increase overall cost of patient care; may not scale as anticipated, resulting in decreased availability; or may introduce errors in the data, decreasing quality. As depicted by the model, initially, all three bounds of the original triangle expand, as in Figure 1.2. In this sequence, drawn to scale, access, cost, and quality initially suffer after the introduction of a disruptive technology (from 1 to 2). Introducing the new technology disrupts the normal operation, patient access, and

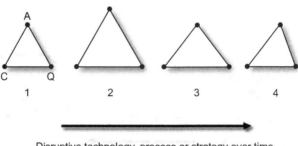

Figure 1.2 **Dynamics of availability, cost, and quality model.**

because the system is operating at decreased efficiency, quality often suffers (3). With time, quality improves, but the initial cost increase remains (4).

In my experience, the sequence depicted in Figure 1.2 is the norm instead of the exception. For example, when linear accelerators were first used in cancer treatment centers, a single treatment might take an hour or more. Today, the radiation can be delivered to a patient accurately, within a matter of minutes, thanks to optimization software and upgraded radiation delivery hardware. As a result, many more patients can be treated per day using customized treatment plans that more accurately target tumor tissue. Both quality and access are improved. The new linear accelerators and software, while more efficient and effective, are more expensive than their predecessors. Patient throughput has to be kept high in order to make the cost differential acceptable.

1.2 Performance Management in Action

For a practical illustration of how a Performance Management strategy can redefine the constraints of cost, availability, and quality of healthcare offered by a healthcare organization, consider the following scenario. The administration of a capital-constrained hospital, under quality pressure from the community and financial pressure from the federal government—in terms of Meaningful Use regulations tied to Medicare and Medicaid payments—decides to implement a modest EMR and computerizes its pharmacy services. Management also has a vision for additional quality and performance enhancing initiatives over 5 years, including radio-frequency identification (RFID) patient tracking, a fully integrated computerized physician order entry (CPOE) system, organization-wide wireless access, and digital picture archiving and communication system (PACS). This vision is also keyed to responding to patient demands and expectations as well as meeting specific stage requirements of the Medicare and Medicaid EMR incentive programs.

A key concern of hospital administration is patient safety, especially surrounding medication errors. In our hypotetical hospital, medication errors associated with prescriptions written by the hospital's physicians' account for 10% of clinic visits. Of these patients, 10% suffer from life-threatening adverse drug events that must be referred to the ER. Continuing with our example, it's reasonable to assume that a significant percentage of errors are attributed to poly-pharmacy, given that older patients are typically on multiple drugs that may interact, and that the remainder of errors are made in medication ordering.

To reduce clinic and ER visits secondary to medication errors, the hospital's senior executives commission the creation of a Performance Management Committee staffed with representatives from IT, clinical department heads, and clinicians. The Performance Management Committee, tasked with identifying and addressing the source of medication errors, works with clinicians and clinical workflow experts to develop a paper-based questionnaire for the physicians working in the clinics. The result is a high-level map of the medication ordering process, starting with the patient–physician encounter and ending with medication administration.

As shown in Figure 1.3, the physician collects data directly from the patient and reviews the patient's clinical history, including current medications, using the EMR. The physician makes a provisional diagnosis, records the findings in the EMR, and then writes a prescription for medication on a prescription pad. The patient then walks the prescription down to the pharmacy, where it is transcribed and the medication order keyed into the stand-alone pharmacy system. The pharmacy system generates a report that directs the pharmacy staff to prepare the appropriate medicine. Finally, the medicine is administered (or handed) to the patient, and the transaction is documented in the pharmacy system.

The IT infrastructure shown in Figure 1.3 does not support rapid data gathering for day-to-day reporting of transactions or the correlation of clinic visits with the number or kind of medication errors. Reports are generated, but they entail the batch processing of pharmacy and EMR data. As a result, the reports represent activity weeks to months after the relevant clinical events.

The reports, which establish a benchmark for later work, indicate that the greatest single source of error in our hypothetical hospital is the prescription step, which accounts for 39% of medication errors (see Figure 1.4). Administration and documentation together account for 38% of errors, with the balance attributed to transcription and medication preparation.

With the error sources identified at a high level, the committee decides to address the errors attributed to the prescription process. Many technological solutions are available to address the data collection challenge. One solution is to create a data warehouse and executive decision support system, as shown in Figure 1.5. The data warehouse is a central repository for selected clinical and nonclinical data from the pharmacy system, EMR, and other systems throughout the hospital. It enables decision makers with the appropriate security clearance to quickly access the performance indicator data through a variety of predefined reports and free-form data mining tools.

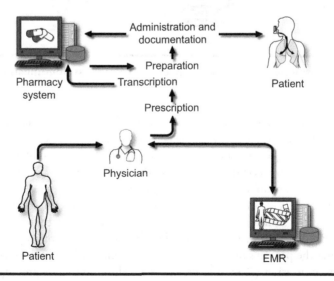

Figure 1.3   Original medication ordering process (based on data culled from printed question-naires completed by physicians prescribing medications in the hospital clinic).

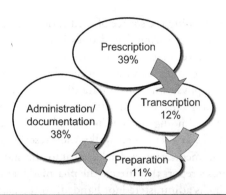

Figure 1.4 Initial analysis of error rates contributing to medication errors.

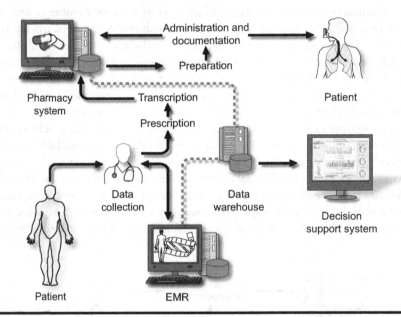

Figure 1.5 Data warehouse and executive decision support system illustrating medication ordering.

The system allows timely assessment of the medication ordering process, including correlation of physician ordering activity with admissions related to medication errors.

The Performance Management Committee works with a clinical data flow expert to identify key indicators that should reveal error sources within the prescription process. Several indicators are defined and the committee member from the IT department sees to it that the corresponding data are automatically extracted daily from the various hospital systems and stored in the data warehouse.

Three months later, by analyzing one of the new daily medication error reports, the committee members learn that the 39% error rate attributed to the initial prescription process breaks down as follows: obtaining the patient's history (7%); documenting medication history (12%); making the diagnosis-therapy decision (5%); and writing the order down on a prescription pad (15%), as shown in Figure 1.6. The largest contributor—writing the order—is addressed with a CPOE system.

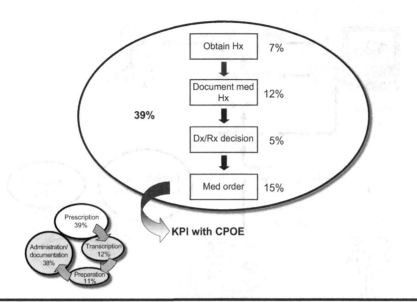

Figure 1.6   Breakdown of the 39% error rate associated with the prescription process.

In following the hospital's mission, the Performance Management Committee decides to reduce overall medication errors by requiring the clinics' physicians to verify patient response to drugs. It also commissions the development of web-based patient educational materials for the hospital's patient information portal that describe the importance of complying with prescriptions.

In addition to addressing patient behavior, the committee also decides to address the physician behavior that contributes to the 15% of errors that occur during medication ordering. Along with a physician education program, the IT representative convinces management to implement a CPOE system, in part because it was already part of the hospital's long-term IT plan. The CPOE implementation schedule is bumped up and the Performance Management Committee identifies a team to define the most appropriate indicators to monitor the effectiveness of CPOE in further reducing medication errors.

Two months after introduction of the CPOE system, the medication errors attributed to orders are down from 15% to 3%, well below the target defined by the Performance Management Committee. The CPOE system also obviates the transcription step of the overall process. The new error breakdown is as follows:

■ Prescription, 27%
■ Preparation, 16%
■ Administration and documentation, 57%

Figure 1.7 shows the medication ordering process (left) and error rates (right) after the introduction of CPOE as part of the Performance Management Initiative. The contribution of prescription errors has been reduced, and the translation step has been eliminated. The education program for physicians working in clinics and their patients has similar beneficial results.

The Performance Management Committee decides to focus on the process of documenting a medical history, which now accounts for 12% of medication errors. Because physicians are typically tasked with recording patient history in the EMR, they will bear the burden of extra work

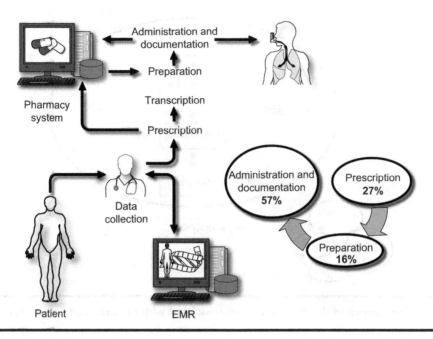

Figure 1.7   Medication ordering process (left) and error rates (right) after CPOE implementation.

associated with keying in additional history data. Given the EMR, no additional IT infrastructure is needed. The committee acquires an additional representative from the clinical staff to make certain they have buy-in to the initiative. Based on feedback from the representative, the committee agrees to incentivize physicians to contribute to the project.

1.2.1 Postmortem

In reviewing the above scenario, it is important to note that the data warehouse and decision support system do not make clinical decisions. Instead, they are part of the information infrastructure that provides decision makers with data needed to make informed decisions. It is up to the Performance Management Committee to decide which indicators to monitor and to establish acceptable ranges of indicator values, to analyze the data, and to act based on their analysis. The scenario also illustrates how data acquisition is rarely simply a matter of moving data from one computer system to the next. Often, the data have not been captured, and new acquisition mechanisms, from machine-readable paper questionnaires to modified applications, must be devised.

The decisions makers' perspectives influence the selection of performance indicators. For example, the criteria established by a chief financial officer (CFO) for what constitutes an acceptable medication error rate might be less than 10 lawsuits per quarter or less than $250K in settlements over a reporting period. In contrast, the chair of the department of medicine might be content when less than five patients suffering from medication errors are admitted to the ER per month. However, no indicator or perspective is perfect. The number of lawsuits may be influenced by seemingly extraneous factors, such as the unemployment rate. In addition, only a small percentage of patients on inappropriate medication may feel sick enough to travel to the clinic or ER. As is often the case, patients experiencing medication problems may decide instead to discontinue the medicine on their own. The result is often deterioration of the patient's health and much greater cost for urgent care if the patient's untreated condition becomes potentially life threatening.

As the scenario illustrates, there may be unintentional consequences associated with solving one problem identified through a Performance Management approach. For CPOE to be implemented sooner than previously planned, other work has to be bumped from the timeline and additional resources have to be put into place. The total cost of this decision, in direct and indirect costs, may be significant.

The scenario above also illustrates how the challenge of reducing medication errors was taken on one component at a time. It would have been unreasonable and unworkable to have an initial goal of reducing medication errors to zero. By taking on the largest contributor first, it was possible to monitor and, if necessary, modify the intervention. Had the Performance Management Committee attempted to address all or most known sources of error at once, the result would have certainly been failure. Moreover, it would have been impossible to identify, with certainty, which intervention(s) were successful and which contributed to the failure.

It's important to note that I haven't seen a paper prescription pad used in a hospital in decades. Fortunately, I live and work in a healthcare tech bubble in which hospitals routinely spend $5–$10M annually on IT projects. Even though you may work in a similar environment, it's important to keep in mind that, nationwide, this is the exception rather than the rule. Moreover, despite this lavish spending on IT, I don't know of a single hospital in this or any other high-tech bubble with zero medication errors. This strongly suggests that more time and energy need to be spent looking at process and strategy solutions to medication errors and other clinical challenges, as opposed to relying totally on technology.

1.3 Further Thinking

Performance Management is one of many management solutions available to the executive management of healthcare organizations. Although it is not the final word in quality management, when properly executed, Performance Management appears to be better than many of the alternatives. From a pragmatic perspective, there is no way to avoid many of the activities associated with the strategy, given the backing by accrediting and regulatory agencies that facilitate and promote quality healthcare. Even so, readers should be aware of the limitations of Performance Management:

Performance Management is largely intangible. Performance Management isn't a software package that can be purchased from a vendor, set up, and then left running in an equipment closet or the cloud. A Performance Management strategy can be supported and enabled with technology, but management and change are up to the people in the organization.

Change takes time. Behavior change is the cornerstone of an effective Performance Management Initiative. People change slowly, even with the best programming (training) and intentions. Your timeline and training resource planning should reflect this reality.

There may be multiple explanations for significant variation in QIs. Significant QI findings do not necessarily point to flawed processes or the need for new algorithms for handling clinical cases. A single clinician who unintentionally codes patients differently from his peers may account for the majority of nonrandom variability in a clinical system, for example. Expect more errors and variability when new clinicians enter or transfer into the healthcare delivery system, either through mergers and acquisitions or from normal hiring.

Performance Management is evolving. If the trend in other industries holds in healthcare, Performance Management will evolve to incorporate many of the techniques traditionally associated with Knowledge Management. Expect other evolutionary changes as well, in response to financial and political pressures.

The underlying technology is imperfect. The tools supportive of a Performance Management Initiative are not yet commodity products. There are no industry-wide standards for graphical dashboards, data warehouses, and other healthcare infrastructure and data management technologies—only snapshots of evolving technology in time.

Resource requirements may be significant. A Performance Management Initiative generally requires significant upfront capital and time investment. Once the basic system is in place, there will be costs associated with training decision makers, in devising new performance indicators, and in creating new reports. There are also the usual software maintenance costs, which average about 30% of the annual purchase price.

There are always unintended consequences. Ideally, a well-executed Performance Management Initiative enjoins the clinical faculty with the administration. However, without the proper groundwork, including incorporating clinician feedback at all levels of design and development, a Performance Management Initiative may instead reduce morale. Clinicians who have not bought in to the Performance Management Initiative, but who know their work is under a microscope, may work more carefully but less efficiently. As a result, quality of care may increase, but at an unacceptable marginal cost. Similarly, unintended behaviors, such as gaming the system to satisfy indicators at the expense of patients, for example, may result in cost savings but substandard quality of care.

It is easy to go overboard. There is often a temptation to use too many indicators initially and to use short-term financial "lag" indicators. However, the number and nature of indicators necessarily evolve with the time. Beginning with more than perhaps a dozen indicators is a recipe for disaster, regardless of the organization's size and available resources.

Sources and Further Reading

10 Patient Safety Tips for Hospitals: Evidence-based tips to prevent adverse hospital events. AHRQ Publication No. 10-M008, Dec 2009. Agency for Healthcare Research and Quality, Rockville, MD. *www.ahrq.gov/patients-consumers/diagnosis-treatment/hospitals-clinics/10-tips/index.html*

Amato, M.G., Salazar, A., Hickman, T.T. et al. Computerized prescriber order entry-related patient safety reports: Analysis of 2522 medication errors. *J Am Med Inform Assoc* 2016, 24(2): 316–22.

Bates, D. Frequency, consequences and prevention of adverse drug events. *J Qual Clin Pract* 1999, 19(1): 13–7.

Bates, D. et al. Incidence of adverse drug events and potential adverse drug events. Implications for prevention. ADE Prevention Study Group. *JAMA* 1995, 274(1): 29–34.

Bergeron, B., *Essentials of Knowledge Management*. 2003. New York: John Wiley & Sons.

Bergeron, B. and P. Chan, *Biotech Industry: A Global, Economic, and Financial Overview*. 2004. New York: J. Wiley & Sons.

Briere, R., ed. *Crossing the Quality Chasm: A New Health System for the 21st Century*. 2001. Washington, DC: National Academy Press.

EMR 2016: The Market for Electronic Medical Records. Kalorama Information Publication No. KLI5971507, April 16, 2016. Rockville, MD: Kalorama Information. *www.kaloramainformation.com/EMR-Electronic-Medical-10009693*

Graban, M. *Lean Hospitals*. 2016. Milwaukee: ASQ.

Harry, M. et al. *Practitioner's Guide to Statistics and Lean Six Sigma for Process Improvements.* 2010. New York: John Wiley & Sons.

Implementation Guidance for ISO 9001:2015. 2015. Geneva: International Organization for Standardization.

Levett, J. and R. Burney. *Using ISO 9001 in Healthcare, 2nd Edition.* 2014. Milwaukee: ASQ Press.

Meaningful Use Regulations. *www.healthit.gov/policy-researchers-implementers/meaningful-use-regulations.* Accessed April 7, 2017.

Quality Indicator Empirical Methods (Revised by Truven Health Analytics, Stanford University (prime contractor), under Contract No. HHSA290201200003I). 2014. Rockville, MD: Agency for Healthcare Research and Quality.

U.S. Census Bureau. *www.census.gov.*

van Doormaal, J.E. et al. The influence that electronic prescribing has on medication errors and preventable adverse drug events: An interrupted time-series study. *J Am Med Inform Assoc* 2009, 16: 816.

Wittich, C.M. et al. Medication errors: An overview for clinicians. *Mayo Clin Proc* 2014, 89: 1116.

Chapter 2

Performance Management Strategies

Performance Management promotes the effective use of resources by quantifying processes and outcomes. Potential upsides to the approach include better use of financial resources, improved utilization, better clinical outcomes, enhanced patient safety, and more satisfied patients. As illustrated in the previous chapter's medication error scenario, these benefits ultimately come about because of behavior change—patients increasingly complied with prescriptions and physicians fully utilized the computerized physician order entry (CPOE) system.

2.1 General Strategies

Performance Management is one of the many business strategies available to healthcare organizations tasked with increasing the quality of their services while containing costs. Strategies relevant to Performance Management that have been applied with variable success in healthcare include Statistical Process Control, Total Quality Management, Customer Relationship Management, Activity-Based Costing, Knowledge Management, and ISO 9000/ISO 9001:2015. These strategies are introduced below.

2.1.1 Statistical Process Control

The goal of Statistical Process Control (SPC) is to determine whether a process is functioning within statistical norms. That is, statistical analysis is used to determine whether observed changes in a variable are attributed to random variation or to some other factor. Six Sigma, an extension of SPC pioneered at Motorola, aims to eliminate nonrandom variation to the point that the likelihood of an error is six standard deviations (sigma's) from the mean—approximately three errors per million.

SPC has been used successfully in manufacturing since it was introduced in the early twentieth century. The challenge of relying on SPC in a healthcare Performance Management Initiative is related to its treatment of outliers. Changing a process in response to data as a result of random variation or "common cause variation" can create an unstable process. Conversely, if nonrandom variation is mistakenly interpreted as random variation, the process will become increasingly unstable, as the factor contributing to the variability becomes more prominent.

In the SPC vernacular, common cause variation is attributed to randomness inherent in the process or system. Nonrandom or special cause variation, in contrast, is unusual, unpredictable, unstable, and arises from factors outside of the process. See Chapter 11 for a review of the basic statistical methods that can be used to differentiate random from nonrandom variation.

2.1.2 Total Quality Management

Total Quality Management (TQM) is a strategy based on a commitment to perpetual improvement. The strategy aims to improve the system, instead of simply identifying and addressing the outliers, by focusing on the underlying processes. TQM is also customer focused, in that the customer—the patient in the case of healthcare—determines whether the quality of service is sufficient.

During the 1990s, many organizations embraced TQM as a means of saving money by cutting employees from their payrolls. System improvements invariably reduced the number of employees needed to provide the same level of service. As a result, employees at risk—nearly everyone— eventually resisted the strategy.

As word spread that TQM was a resizing strategy in disguise, employee resistance to the strategy was so great that management eventually found it impossible to even discuss a TQM initiative with their employees. The lesson is that if a Performance Management Initiative is sold as a resizing initiative, it will eventually be met with vehement resistance from employees and their labor unions. For an excellent overview of TQM, including the underlying eight principles, see the American Society for Quality (ASQ) website: asq.org/learn-about-quality/total-quality -management/overview/overview.html.

2.1.3 Customer Relationship Management

Customer Relationship Management (CRM) is a strategy that manages the organization's relationship with customers—patients and potential patients in the healthcare space. CRM advocates the promotion of mutually beneficial business and shuns unprofitable business. For example, older, sicker people who require more healthcare resources are not encouraged to enroll in a particular managed care plan. In contrast, young, healthy individuals are actively recruited to the plan. This form of cost containment, while bordering on moral and legal fringes, was nonetheless increasingly common in healthcare before the enactment of the Affordable Care Act, which made it impossible for insurers dissuade or turn away patients with preexisting conditions.

The contribution of CRM to a Performance Management Initiative is in information gathering practices and technologies used to profile potential patients. CRM relies on profiles of preferences and past behaviors to predict future behavior. A potential patient who engages in extreme sports, for example, is more likely to appear in the ER with a fractured arm than is someone of the same age and sex who spends their time in front of a video game console. CRM techniques and technologies can be used to gauge patient satisfaction, to determine how to best attract new patients, and to uncover behavior patterns that can be used to predict outpatient and inpatient loads.

2.1.4 Activity-Based Costing

Activity-Based Costing (ABC) is not a business strategy in the strictest sense but is a form of cost accounting that generates more accurate cost and performance information than is available through a traditional cost accounting approach. ABC achieves this accuracy by focusing on the costs of performing specific processes rather than on the aggregate cost at the department or division level. Because ABC provides management with process-level costs, it is easier to determine costs associated with the changes in process resulting from a Performance Management Initiative.

Consider that, in a hospital using traditional accounting methods, there may be no direct way to determine the cost of modifying the prescription process. As a result, the full cost of modifying the process by introducing CPOE or other technology may not be available. This reality reflects the long-standing frustration many chief information officers (CIOs) face in trying to prove the return on investment (ROI) of an information technology (IT) initiative using traditional accounting methods.

The general ledger and other traditional accounting methods reveal the contractual cost of the vendor-supplied CPOE system. However, not shown is the added "hidden" cost of internal IT support, which may be absorbed by the IT department in the form of a new hire. The diminished workload of a pharmacy clerk who no longer transcribes handwritten or e-mailed prescriptions may not result in reduced wages or cost savings. In contrast, assigning a cost to each step in the medication order process before and after any process changes are made allows management to quantify the financial burden borne by IT and pharmacy.

2.1.5 Knowledge Management

Knowledge Management (KM) is a deliberate, systematic business optimization strategy that involves the selection, distillation, storage, organization, packaging, and communication of information. See Figure 2.1 for a map of typical KM operations. KM is practiced to some degree in every successful knowledge-intensive organization, including the data-driven healthcare enterprise.

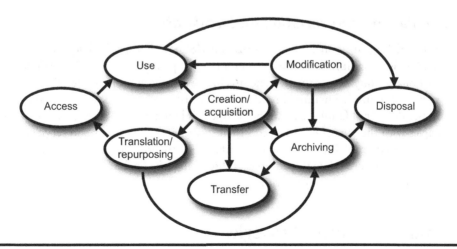

Figure 2.1   KM operations.

One of the contributions of KM to Performance Management is in the way KM treats intellectual capital as a major organizational asset. KM defines four types of intellectual capital:

■ **Human**—includes the knowledge, skills, and competencies of the clinical staff, managers, and other employees in the organization. Without a KM strategy in place, when key personnel leave the organization, they take their skills, competencies, and knowledge with them. For example, when the best cardiac surgeon leaves your institution for the competition, there is a vacuum of knowledge that may be impossible to fill, even with a national search for talent.
■ **Customer**—the value of the organization's relationships with its patients. Because patients often form bonds with their clinician, the organization and the clinical staff typically jointly own customer capital.
■ **Structural**—the process, structures, information systems, financial relations, and intellectual properties that are independent of the staff and managers who create them. The IT infrastructure typically takes years to build, and even more years to tune to the changing needs of the healthcare enterprise.
■ **Intellectual property**—patents, licenses, trademarks, and copyrights. KM treats intellectual capital as an asset that can be tracked, measured, and analyzed with performance indicators, just like any other clinical or nonclinical variable. Unlike customers and staff, IP can be readily bought and sold and locked away in a safe.

The primary challenge of fully realizing the benefits of KM is that few healthcare organizations are sufficiently evolved to take advantage of the strategy. KM is primarily concerned with documenting "what is," whereas a major focus of Performance Management and most other quality initiatives is identifying "what should be." As a result, preserving intellectual capital organization-wide makes sense only after processes have been optimized, not during a Performance Management Initiative, which is a driver for change. Even so, many of the tools and techniques developed for KM are directly applicable to a Performance Management Initiative. Knowledge audits, structured collaboration, development of practice communities, knowledge mapping, and social network analysis can be directly applied to the Performance Management cycle's measurement or information gathering phase. This is discussed in more detail in Chapter 3.

2.1.6 International Organization for Standardization

The International Organization for Standardization (ISO), a worldwide federation of national standards bodies, is recognized worldwide as a promoter of quality initiatives. The ISO 9000 family of international quality management standards focuses on the appropriate activities performed in a consistent and controlled manner in order to meet customer needs. ISO 9001:2015, the only standard in the ISO 9000 family that can be certified, is based on a number of quality management principles with the aim of ensuring consistent good quality products and services. Perhaps the greatest contribution of ISO's voluntary standards to Performance Management is that the standard has raised the level of quality awareness throughout the healthcare industry, from medical device manufacturing to delivery of care.

2.2 Healthcare-Specific Strategies

Performance Management Initiatives have been established in healthcare by dozens of private and public organizations (See Appendix A for a list of organizations and their URLs).

The most influential organizations include the Joint Commission on Accreditation of Healthcare Organizations (JCAHO), the Centers for Medicare and Medicaid Services (CMS), the Agency for Healthcare Research and Quality (AHRQ), and England's National Health Service (NHS). ISO has also become influential in the healthcare industry with its ISO 9000 and ISO9004:2000 standards.

Most US healthcare organizations abide by or at least acknowledge accreditation standards established by JCAHO, CMS, and the AHRQ. In addition, these organizations often work together to minimize hospital data collection efforts. For example, JCAHO has worked with CMS to standardize the collection of data required to report acute myocardial infarction and heart failure quality measures.

2.2.1 *Joint Commission on Accreditation of Healthcare Organizations*

JCAHO's ORYX initiative integrates performance indicators into its accreditation process. JCAHO defines performance in terms of outcome parameters, most of which are hard, objective measures of efficiency, appropriateness, availability, timeliness, effectiveness, continuity, safety, and respect for caring. US healthcare organizations seeking JCAHO accreditation are required to select outcome indicators from lists maintained by the Commission and to collect and submit data on these indicators.

There is a required list of indicators, which hospitals are required to participate in, as well as an additional list of indicators, of which hospitals are required to participate in a self-selected subset. The specific accreditation requirements depend on the nature of the healthcare organization. JCAHO offers accreditation programs for ambulatory care, behavioral healthcare, critical access hospital, home care providers, hospital, nursing care center, office-based surgery facilities, and pathology and clinical laboratory, each with different accreditation requirements. Hospital indicator requirements are further defined by the type of facility—freestanding psychiatric facility, small hospital, or hospital—and the number of live births per year, if any.

To receive accreditation, organizations must have a written plan that is systematic, pervasive, and involves the active support of medical staff, senior management, and the governing board. The Commission's international equivalent, the Joint Commission International (JCI), promotes quality standards that reflect practices outside of the United States.

2.2.2 *Centers for Medicare and Medicaid Services*

CMS requires hospitals seeking Medicare certification to have an organization-wide quality assurance program in place to evaluate the quality and cost of patient care and to monitor outcomes. According to CMS, an effective quality initiative is

- Planned, systematic, and ongoing. It is not a single, magic bullet approach to improving whatever ails the organization.
- Comprehensive. It applies to the organization's clinical, financial, managerial, and governance functions.
- Reliant on objective measures of quality. Specific, predetermined indicators and benchmarks form the basis of the indicators.
- Designed to link specific responses with results of indicator analysis.
- Integrated across department lines and among different quality functions.

- Designed to involve all staff and providers.
- Designed to improve both internal processes and patient outcomes.

CMS is particularly influential because of its relationship with the Meaningful Use Incentive program, which is covered in depth in Chapter 3.

2.2.3 Agency for Healthcare Research and Quality

The AHRQ is a treasure trove of information and practical tools that can be applied to any Performance Management Initiative. For example, among the many offerings of the AHRQ is a library of indicators that cover access, utilization, cost, effectiveness, safety, timeliness, and patient-centeredness. The AHRQ's annual National Healthcare Quality Report is also a must-read for anyone contemplating a Performance Management Initiative. In addition, the AHRQ has developed quality indicator modules for inpatients, prevention, and patient safety. For the list of quality indicators, including those endorsed by the National Quality Forum (NQF), see Appendix B. The NQF is an independent, voluntary, consensus-based member organization that endorses standardized quality measures.

The great advantage of the AHRQ quality program is the free access to quality indicators, tools, and case studies through the CMS web portal. The AHRQ also maintains a comprehensive library of quality measures, including those authored by other organizations, in its searchable online database. Perhaps the most valuable of the AHRQ's free offerings is the AHRQ QI toolkit. The toolkit is composed of a variety of resources, grouped in a logical progression from assessing readiness to change to determining ROI on the initiative:

- Assessing Readiness to Change
- Applying QIs to Your Hospital's Data
- Identifying Priorities for Quality Improvement
- Implementing Evidence-Based Strategies to Improve Clinical Care
- Monitoring Progress and Sustainability of Improvements
- Analyzing ROI

The AHRQ QI toolkit is one of many toolkits offered by the AHRQ that may have a bearing on your Performance Management Initiative. For example, there is a stand-alone pediatric version of the QU toolkit, as well as toolkits for assessing EMR design and usability and Health IT projects. See Appendix C for a complete list of AHRQ toolkits and Appendix D for a summary of the AHRQ QI toolkit components.

2.2.4 UK's National Health Service

The UK's NHS was established in 1948 to provide healthcare for all citizens based on need. Each of the four countries of the UK has its own, independent NHS. England's NHS, the largest and oldest single-payer healthcare system in the world, is organized into trusts, which are loosely public sector corporations. Trust types include hospital, mental health, ambulance service, and community health. The quality standards and indicators established for these trusts, from low-level statistical validation to descriptions intended for patient consumption, are freely available for public inspection on the web.

England's NHS quality indicators are discussed in more detail in Chapters 6 and 7, and a subset is listed in Appendix I. Because the NHS quality initiative is government-funded, it is the subject of numerous journal articles questioning the strategy and illuminating the shortcomings of a Performance Management approach in medicine. Readers are encouraged to review the current literature describing the successes and unmet challenges of the NHS in its efforts to improve healthcare quality in England. In addition, the Wikipedia entry for England's NHS provides a detailed political history of the system, including the effect of Brexit on staffing.

2.2.5 International Organization for Standardization

As noted earlier, the ISO standards are designed to be generic, in that they are equally applicable to any size product or service organization. However, there are also medical-specific standards that target specific niches. For example, ISO 13485:2016, which is based on ISO 9001, pertains specifically to medical devices. ISO 15189:2012 specifies requirements for quality and competence in medical laboratories. In addition, the International Classification for Standards (ICS) fields defined within ISO includes healthcare technology, ICS-11, among the 40 fields of activity. Healthcare technology is further subdivided into the following areas:

- 11.020 Medical sciences and healthcare facilities
- 11.040 Medical equipment
- 11.060 Dentistry
- 11.080 Sterilization and disinfection
- 11.100 Laboratory medicine
- 11.120 Pharmaceutics
- 11.140 Hospital equipment
- 11.160 First aid
- 11.180 Aids for disabled or handicapped persons
- 11.200 Birth control

Each of these areas is further subdivided into more specific areas. For example, the classification for standards applicable to healthcare facilities (ICS-11.020) includes healthcare management systems, IT applications in healthcare technology, quality and environmental management in healthcare technology, care homes, assisted living, aesthetic surgery, and regenerative medicine, among other areas. For a fully expanded listing of ICS-11, see *www.iso.org/ics/11.020/x/*.

2.2.6 Baldrige Healthcare Criteria for Performance Excellence

Healthcare organizations employing a Performance Management strategy are eligible to apply for the Baldrige Award. This quality award is administered by the National Institute of Standards and Technology (NIST), which promotes US economic growth by working with industry to develop and deliver high-quality measurement tools, data, and services. The award is valuable beyond the obvious marketing uses because it serves as a voluntary quality audit that can help the organization focus its performance efforts. The seven core criteria areas in the healthcare framework are as follows:

- Leadership—senior leadership and governance/societal responsibilities
- Strategy—development and implementation

- Customers—attention to the voice of the customer and customer engagement
- Measurement, Analysis, and Knowledge Management—organizational performance and information and KM
- Workforce—environment and engagement
- Operations—work processes and effectiveness
- Results—healthcare and process, customer focused, workforce focused, leadership and governance, and financial and market results

The core criteria establish de facto Performance Management standards. For more detailed information on the award, see the document, 2017–2018 Baldrige Performance Excellence Framework Health Care Criteria Commentary, downloadable at *www.nist.gov/sites/default/files/documents/2017/01/12/2017-2018-health-care-category-commentary.pdf*.

2.2.7 Truven Health Analytics

There are also standards established by academia and private industry. For example, Truven Health Analytics–IBM Watson Health identifies the top 100 hospitals in the United States every year based largely on key performance indicators. Awards are made in five categories: major teaching hospitals, teaching hospitals, large community hospitals, medium community hospitals, and small community hospitals. Based on the Truven Health 100 Top Hospitals Study, the following were the 11 indicators used to identify the 2017 top 100 hospitals in the United States:

- Risk-adjusted inpatient mortality index
- Risk-adjusted complications index
- Core measures mean percent
- Mean 30-day risk-adjusted mortality rate
- Mean 30-day risk-adjusted readmission rate
- Severity-adjusted average length of stay
- Mean emergency department throughput
- Case mix- and wage-adjusted inpatient expense per discharge
- Medicare spend per beneficiary index
- Adjusted operating profit margin
- Hospital consumer awareness of healthcare

Unlike the Baldwin award, there is no application process for the Truven Heath Analytics Top 100 Award. The top 100 hospitals in the United States are simply identified in the annual award.

2.3 Performance Management Tools

The tools available to support a Performance Management Initiative range from paper forms, statistical analysis software, data mart and data warehouse systems, and groupware to high-resolution wall displays, tablets, and smartphones, to radio-frequency identification (RFID)–based patient and equipment tracking systems. Because the IT infrastructure of a typical healthcare organization includes different software packages running on different, incompatible hardware and abiding by various protocols, the most valuable tools enable or enhance the sharing of clinical and business data. Whether these tools take the form of a common data store or interfaces between applications, they typically support unstructured data management.

The data warehouse is one method of streamlining the reporting operation. The ideal data warehouse is a central, homogenous repository of a carefully selected subset of data from disparate, often loosely integrated applications in the organization. The repository is optimized to support rapid data mining, report generation, and decision support. Software and hardware technologies are harnessed to integrate the unstructured data, according to location mapping of where key data can be found in each application. For example, although, from a logical perspective, the data warehouse is centralized, from a physical, implementation perspective, the repository may be distributed around the globe in the cloud. What matters is data management, regardless of the physical home for specific bits and bytes.

Many CIOs have a plan to transition from an unstructured data management approach to a structured KM approach once the business and clinical processes within their organization have stabilized. However, even if a hospital system is constructed from scorched earth, there are usually several legacy systems to deal with because of inevitable mergers and acquisitions. Moreover, even if the hospital enterprise is stable, there is the issue of importing patient data from external sources, such as insurers—each of which may use different data structures and different hardware platforms. From an IT perspective, enabling a Performance Management Initiative with the appropriate IT toolset is a challenge on several fronts:

Data Capture. Data from computers, manual transcription, automatic transcription with optical character recognition (OCR) and optical mark recognition (OMR) processing of paper forms, RFID sensors embedded in walls and doorways, bar code readers, and bedside terminals must be acquired in a way that is timely, accurate, and HIPAA (Health Insurance Portability and Accountability Act) compliant. Web and Bluetooth-enabled medical devices increasingly contribute to the pool of medical patient data and to the demands of data capture.

Data Transfer. Data must be transferred from barcode readers, RFID readers, tablets, and other acquisition devices to applications running on different hardware and from long-term storage on tape or optical media to local hard or flash drives. Decision makers may need to access clinical or administrative data on the wards, in the clinic, in the office, in the boardroom, at home, or while traveling. As such, many EMR systems are designed to support access through tablets and smartphones enabled with Wi-Fi, Bluetooth, and cellular connectivity.

Data Modification. Raw indicator values are typically of little use before they are processed, filtered, and formatted. For example, many of the standard financial indicators are defined as ratios of two or more variables.

Supporting Data Use. Data drives the software tools that enable decision makers to identify interventions that will provide the most significant results with the fewest resources. These applications must be selected, installed, and maintained. Decision makers may need significant training before they can fully utilize the power of the tools available to them.

Data Archiving. Raw and modified data must be stored in a form and format that will survive the elements and time. At one time, data archives were simply cost centers. Today, with interest in outcomes and in translational medicine, patient data archives are closely guarded, valuable assets.

Data Translation. Indicator data often require translation to application-specific forms and formats. This can be as simple as changing date formats from D/M/Y to M/D/Y or as complex as concept mapping, as in equating a diagnosis of "Myocardial Infarction (MI)" with "Heart Attack."

Controlling Data Access. Long before the advent of HIPAA regulations, maintaining secure electronic records was a major IT activity—and challenge. Access control technologies that supplement the usual username/password combination, such as biometric measures popularized by smartphones and other consumer electronics, are increasingly common.

Disposal of Data. Eventually, some clinical and financial data must be (or at least can be) disposed of in a manner that does not compromise patient or physician security or privacy. Digital shredder programs are becoming popular for this component of the KM process.

2.4 Further Thinking

Numerous IT vendors target each of these challenge areas. Some CIOs put their faith in these vendors, whereas others elect to develop at least some of the infrastructure and Performance Management tools in-house. For example, moving patient data to a cloud platform avoids local investment in server farms. Local tool development and hosting has the advantage of custom fitting to the organization. The downside of in-house development is the inevitable delay while the tools and infrastructure are designed, developed, and tested. There is also the loss of control when data are residing in the cloud—that is, a basement warehouse somewhere in the Midwest—instead of on a server in the hospital basement. Whatever the technological concerns, finances usually dictate how tool development is handled.

Sources and Further Reading

10 Patient Safety Tips for Hospitals: Evidence-based tips to prevent adverse hospital events. AHRQ Publication No. 10-M008, Dec 2009. Agency for Healthcare Research and Quality, Rockville, MD. *www.ahrq.gov/patients-consumers/diagnosis-treatment/hospitals-clinics/10-tips/index.html*

Bates, D., Frequency, consequences and prevention of adverse drug events. *J Qual Clin Pract* 1999, 19(1): 13–7.

Bates, D. et al. Incidence of adverse drug events and potential adverse drug events. Implications for prevention. ADE Prevention Study Group. *JAMA* 1995, 274(1): 29–34.

Bergeron, B. *Essentials of Knowledge Management*. 2003. New York: John Wiley & Sons.

Bergeron, B. and P. Chan, *Biotech Industry: A Global, Economic, and Financial Overview*. 2004. New York: J. Wiley & Sons.

Briere, R., ed. *Crossing the Quality Chasm: A New Health System for the 21st Century*. 2001. Washington, DC: National Academy Press.

Graban, M., *Lean Hospitals*. 2016. Milwaukee: ASQ.

Harry, M. et al. *Practitioner's Guide to Statistics and Lean Six Sigma for Process Improvements*. 2010. New York: John Wiley & Sons.

Implementation Guidance for ISO 9001:2015. 2015. Geneva: International Organization for Standardization.

Levett, J. and R. Burney, *Using ISO 9001 in Healthcare, 2nd Ed.* 2014. Milwaukee: ASQ Press.

Meaningful Use Regulations. *www.healthit.gov/policy-researchers-implementers/meaningful-use-regulations*. Accessed April 7, 2017.

Quality Indicator Empirical Methods (Revised by Truven Health Analytics, Stanford University (prime contractor), under Contract No. HHSA290201200003I). 2014. Rockville, MD: Agency for Healthcare Research and Quality.

van Doormaal, J.E. et al. The influence that electronic prescribing has on medication errors and preventable adverse drug events: An interrupted time-series study. *J Am Med Inform Assoc* 2009, 16: 816.

Wittich, C.M. et al. Medication errors: An overview for clinicians. *Mayo Clin Proc* 2014, 89: 1116.

Chapter 3

Meaningful Use

The Health Information Technology for Economic and Clinical Health (HITECH) Act, enacted as part of the American Recovery and Reinvestment Act of 2009, was designed to promote the adoption and Meaningful Use of health information technology. Meaningful Use, in this context, is the use of electronic medical record (EMR) technology to improve quality, safety, and efficiency and reduce health disparities; to engage patients and families; to improve care coordination; and to improve public health, all while maintaining privacy and security of patient health data. The stated goals also include better clinical and population health outcomes, increased transparency, empowered patients, and robust research data. Clearly, Meaningful Use serves as the basis for a government-directed Performance Management Initiative.

3.1 Carrot and Stick

As with any government program, there are numerous rules for what constitutes an eligible professional or hospital, how and when payments are made, deadlines for the start and end, penalties, and a host of other issues. For example, when first implemented, the program enabled eligible professionals to qualify for EMR incentives of up to $44,000 through Medicare or $63,750 over 6 years through Medicaid. Eligible hospitals could qualify for incentives up to $2M or more.

See Figure 3.1 for the initial Meaningful Use stages and timelines, which I refer to as the Carrot Period. During this promotional period, hospitals and physicians were incentivized to leverage EMR technology as part of a Performance Management Initiative or suffer the financial consequences (i.e., leave money on the table). In 2017, the government introduced the stick. Physicians who refused to participate in the Meaningful Use initiative had their reimbursements adjusted downward.

While economics will certainly alter behavior for some physicians and hospitals, for our purposes, what matters is the health information technology (IT) regulations established for hospitals and professionals, including physicians. The Office of the National Coordinator for Health Information Technology (ONC) authors these regulations. The ONC also provided funding for the Nationwide Health Information Network (NwHIN), which is a set of standards, services, and policies that enable the secure exchange of health information over the Internet.

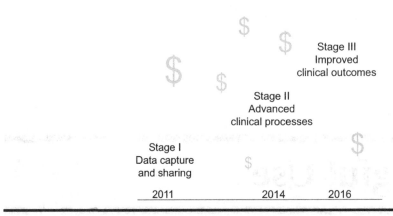

Figure 3.1 "Carrot" stages of Meaningful Use and timeline.

3.2 Meaningful Use Specifications for Hospitals

The EMR Incentive program established core and menu set objectives for hospitals and Critical Access Hospitals (CAHs). A summary of the set 13 core objectives for Stage 1, updated July 2014, is as follows:

- Use computerized provider order entry for medication orders.
- Implement drug–drug and drug–allergy interaction checks.
- Maintain an up-to-date problem list of current and active diagnoses.
- Maintain active medication list.
- Maintain active medication allergy list.
- Record preferred language, gender, race, ethnicity, date of birth, date, and preliminary cause of death in the event of mortality.
- Record and chart changes in height, weight, blood pressure, body mass index (BMI), and growth charts for children 2–20 years, including BMI.
- Record smoking for patients 13+.
- Report hospital clinical quality measures to CMS (Centers for Medicare and Medicaid Services).
- Implement one clinical decision support rule related to a high-priority hospital condition along with the ability to track compliance with that rule.
- Provide patients with an electronic copy of their health information (including diagnostic test results, problem list, medication lists, medication allergies, discharge summary, procedures) upon request.
- Provide patients with an electronic copy of their discharge instructions at time of discharge, upon request.
- Protect EMR health information.

A summary of the 10 items in the menu set objectives for hospitals/CAH, Stage 1, updated July 2014, is as follows:

- Implement drug formulary checks.
- Record advance directives for patient 65+.
- Incorporate clinical lab-test results into EMR as structured data.

- Generate lists of patients by specific conditions to use for quality improvement, reduction of disparities, research, or outreach.
- Use certified EMR technology to identify patient-specific education resources and provide those resources to the patient if appropriate.
- The eligible hospital or CAH that receives a patient from another setting of care or provider of care or believes an encounter is relevant should perform medication reconciliation.
- The eligible hospital or CAH that transitions their patient to another setting of care or provider of care or refers their patient to another provider of care should provide summary care record for each transition of care or referral.
- Capability to submit electronic data to immunization registries or immunization information systems and actual submission.
- Capability to submit electronic data on reportable lab results to public health agencies and actual submission.
- Capability to submit electronic syndromic surveillance data to public health agencies and actual submission.

3.3 Meaningful Use Specifications for Professionals

The EMR Incentive program established core and menu set objectives for eligible professionals. As you will see, there is overlap in the Meaningful Use specifications for hospitals and professionals. A summary of the set 14 core objectives for professionals, Stage 1, updated July 2014, is as follows:

- Use CPOE for medication orders directly entered by any licensed healthcare professional who can enter orders into the medical record.
- Implement drug–drug and drug–allergy interaction checks.
- Maintain an up-to-date problem list of current and active diagnoses.
- Generate and transmit permissible prescriptions electronically.
- Maintain active medication list.
- Maintain active medication allergy list.
- Record preferred language, gender, race, ethnicity, and date of birth.
- Record and chart changes in height, weight, blood pressure, BMI, and growth charts for children 2–20 years, including BMI.
- Record smoking status for patients 13+.
- Report ambulatory clinical quality measures to CMS, or in the case of Medicaid EPs, the States.
- Implement one clinical decision support rule relevant to specialty or high clinical priority along with the ability to track compliance with that rule.
- Provide patients with an electronic copy of their health information (including diagnostic test results, problem list, medication lists, and medication allergies) upon request.
- Provide clinical summaries for patients for each office visit.
- Protect electronic health information.

A summary of the 10 items in the menu set objectives for eligible professionals, Stage 1, updated July 2014, is as follows:

- Implement drug formulary checks.
- Incorporate clinical lab-test results into EMR as structured data.

- Generate lists of patients by specific conditions to use for quality improvement, reduction of disparities, research, or outreach.
- Send patient reminders per patient preference.
- Provide patients with timely electronic access to their health information within 4 business days of the information being available to the eligible professional.
- Use certified EMR technology to identify patient-specific education resources and provide those resources to the patient if appropriate.
- The eligible professional who receives a patient from another setting of care or provider of care or believes an encounter is relevant should perform medication reconciliation.
- The eligible professional who transitions their patient to another setting of care or provider of care or refers their patient to another provider of care should provide summary care record for each transition of care or referral.
- Capability to submit electronic data to immunization registries or immunization information systems and actual submission.
- Capability to submit electronic syndromic surveillance data to public health agencies and actual submission.

3.4 Meaningful Use Specifications Details

For each of the specifications listed above, for both hospitals/CAH and eligible professionals, the EMR Incentives Program specifies the following:

- Objective—the objective of the specification. For example, the objective of the core objective of using CPOE is to have healthcare professionals directly enter medication orders into the medical record.
- Measure—how fulfilling the specification requirement is measured. For example, the measure of the use of CPOE is that more than 30% of patients on medication have at least one medication order entered using CPOE.
- Definition of Terms—each significant term in the objective and measure is defined.
- Exclusion—exceptions to the specification. For example, patients above or below a certain age could be excluded.
- Attestation Requirements—exactly what the hospital or provider must attest to (i.e., legally state). For example, continuing with the CPOE specification example, attestation requirements include providing the numerator and denominator used to satisfy the 30% figure.
- Additional Information—added information about the specific specification, such as applicability to Stage 1 or Stage 2, method of transmission (e.g., electronic vs. physical), and what constitutes a healthcare professional.
- Related Meaningful Use FAQs (Frequently Asked Questions)—FAQs related to a given specification, such as what can or can't be considered as Meaningful Use.
- Certification and Standards Criteria—what measures and processes must be used. For example, the CPOE must support medications and laboratories.
- Related Certification FAQs—additional FAQs related to the specification.

Details of the actual indicators used for each of the core and menu set objectives are discussed in Chapters 6 (Nonclinical Indicators) and 7 (Clinical Indicators).

3.5 Meaningul Use in the Mix

Clearly, abiding by the Meaningful Use specifications constitutes a Performance Management effort. However, Performance Management has been practiced for decades, and isn't defined or limited by Meaningful Use. That is, demonstrating Meaningful Use for government financial enticements is but one example of a Performance Management Initiative. Moreover, the core and menu set objectives disclosed above may or may not have relevance to particular problem areas that need addressing, as illustrated in Figures 3.2 and 3.3.

A hospital highly reliant on Medicare and Medicaid reimbursements is likely to implement a Performance Management Initiative configured along the lines of Figure 3.2. In this example, Meaningful Use is fully incorporated into the initiative. In addition, there are indicators and

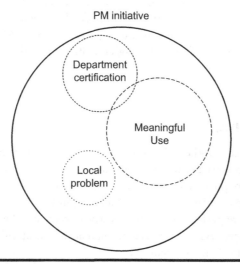

Figure 3.2   A Performance Management Initiative that incorporates Meaningful Use.

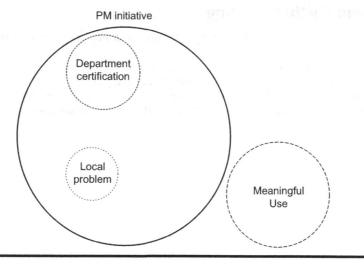

Figure 3.3   A Performance Management Initiative that does not incorporate Meaningful Use.

specifications specific to local problems in the hospital as well as the needs for departmental certification. As shown in the figure, there is overlap in the requirements for departmental certification, say, JCAHO (Joint Commission on Accreditation of Healthcare Organizations) certification of a lab, and Meaningful Use requirements. The local problem is attributed to a process not addressed by Meaningful Use or departmental certification. Of note is that Figure 3.2 is a snapshot in time of a Performance Management Initiative, in that the overlap and relative contribution of each element contributing to the Performance Management Initiative change with time.

In contrast with the previous figure, Figure 3.2 illustrates a Performance Management Initiative in which Meaningful Use does not play a role. This scenario might be typical of a hospital that doesn't accept Medicare or Medicaid, or simply isn't in a position to implement a Performance Management Initiative according to the Meaningful Use specifications. This isn't to say that some of the indicators used in Meaningful Use can't be used in the Performance Management Initiative, but that the indicators aren't used to fulfill Meaningful Use requirements. As with the previous example, Figure 3.2 is a snapshot in time during a Performance Management Initiative. The overlap and relative contribution of each element contributing to the Performance Management Initiative change with time.

3.6 Further Thinking

Meaningful Use, as defined by the HITECH Act, may be a significant motivator for many hospitals and physicians to start Performance Management Initiative. And that's a good thing. However, even with the core plus menu set objectives considered, Meaningful Use isn't a one-size-fits-all solution. Even complete compliance with Meaningful Use specifications doesn't guarantee that the hospital and staff are performing at top effectiveness or that their costs and other resource requirements aren't optimized. As such, it's the hospital administration's role to implement a low-risk, high-ROI (return on investment) solution.

Sources and Further Reading

EHR Incentives & Certification. *www.healthit.gov/providers-professionals/ehr-incentive-programs*. Accessed April 11, 2017.

Eligible Hospital and CAH Core Objectives. *www.cms.gov/Regulations-and-Guidance/Legislation/EHRIncentive Programs/downloads/Hosp_CAH_MU-TOC.pdf*. Updated July 2014.

Eligible Professional Meaningful Use Table of Contents Core and Menu Set Objectives. *www.cms.gov /Regulations-and-Guidance/Legislation/EHRIncentivePrograms/downloads/ep-mu-toc.pdf*. Updated July 2014.

Chapter 4

The Performance Management Cycle

Performance Management is a continuous process and one in which new performance indicators must be acquired, designed, or otherwise introduced to improve the process until the desired (or affordable) performance level in a particular area is achieved. Although every Performance Management Initiative is different, owing to differences in healthcare organizations' culture, patient demographics, and available resources, every successful initiative has clear ownership. Furthermore, rarely is this ownership confined to a single department or area of the organization. Rather, it is shared by a relatively small group representing the key stakeholders that stand to benefit most from the initiative.

This group, referred to here as the Performance Management Committee, minimally includes a senior-level executive from administration and representatives from finance, information technology (IT), nursing, physicians, and clinical services. A consultant experienced in Performance Management may be involved as well. The administrator provides resources, maintains the group's broad vision, removes barriers to progress, and helps publicize the committee's work throughout the organization. The finance representative will necessarily be involved in the numerous purchasing decisions related to the project. The physician, nurse, and clinician representatives can help assure buy-in from physicians, nurses, and clinical services by communicating their needs and concerns to the committee's other members.

The IT representative has the central role of assessing the infrastructure requirements for performance indicators, scorecards, and dashboards; selecting vendors; and evaluating the technical feasibility and cost of data collection and display. One of the Performance Management Committee's first tasks is to define exactly what it is trying to accomplish through a Performance Management Initiative, what organizational changes it is prepared to make, and how it will determine whether the initiative is successful.

Another characteristic of a successful Performance Management Initiative involves the nine key steps illustrated in Figure 4.1 and described below. Within the continuous cycle of measurement, analysis, and action, time is typically not proportional to the number of steps in each activity.

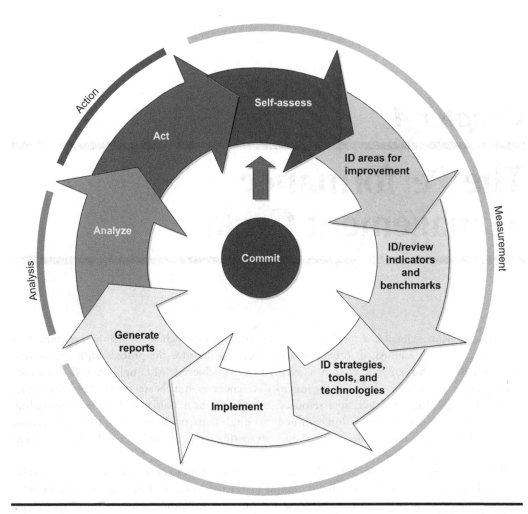

Figure 4.1 Performance Management as a continuous cycle of measurement, analysis, and action.

4.1 Commitment

The first step in a Performance Management Initiative, and one that comes before the Performance Management cycle proper, is to commit the organization's resources to a due diligence process focused on assessing the initiative's cost and likely return on investment (ROI). This commitment should be for a specified period of time—6 to 12 months is typical.

Commitment to a full-scale Performance Management Initiative should not be a blind, faith-based maneuver based on vendor promises, but should be based on solid research. The resources required for such an initiative can be substantial, and the minimum time required for realizing potential benefits can be significant—around 5 years in a large healthcare organization.

In today's healthcare environment, one does not have to look far to rationalize the need to invest in a methodology that improves the bottom line while maintaining or even improving quality. It is also true, however, that funds for major IT-enabled initiatives tend to be limited, and other IT resource-intensive projects will be displaced by a Performance Management Initiative.

The tools of due diligence can include everything from face-to-face interviews with staff and senior administrators, telephone and self-completed surveys, observations, and review of activity logs to medical chart audits, review of administrative records, and review of the literature. Some of the key questions the Performance Management Committee should answer during due diligence include the following:

- What is the expected outcome? If it involves increased quality, then what is the organization's definition of quality? Will an initiative enhance the organization's mission and vision?
- Where is the organization now and where should it be? A formal competitive assessment audit that examines what similar organizations are doing and includes a gap analysis can help answer these questions.
- How will the initiative support the organization's priorities today, over the next year, and 5 years? A strategy map can help in making this determination.
- How much will the initiative cost in terms of time, resources, and lost opportunities?
- How will the initiative change the organization's day-to-day operation and management?
- What are the major IT projects underway or planned for the near future that may have a bearing on implementation?
- Are there currently incentive programs in place for increased performance or compliance with the organization's other initiatives? If so, what is the baseline response to the incentives?
- Who are the stakeholders? Primary stakeholders typically include management, clinical staff, patients, and their families. Secondary stakeholders variably include the government, competing healthcare organizations, outside services, the public in general, shareholders, and regulators.
- Has the organization successfully engaged in an initiative that also involved behavior change? If so, what were the results? What were the initiative's problem areas?
- Does the organization use a shared services model for clinical services? If so, what provisions have been made for data sharing?
- Is senior management planning to acquire other hospitals and/or clinics? If so, is there an IT integration plan? How will infrastructure development in support of a Performance Management Initiative, such as the creation of a data mart or warehouse, make provision for this eventuality?
- How much could a successful initiative improve the efficiency and effectiveness of the current business process?
- Regarding frequency of reports, how often does executive management meet to discuss quality and performance? What about department heads or clinical departments?
- What are the risks to the organization if the initiative fails?
- What tools and technologies are required for implementation and ongoing maintenance?
- What is the in-house experience with data mining, statistical analysis, and use of decision support tools? If limited, are there plans to provide training?
- Which healthcare organizations of similar size and demographics have undertaken similar initiatives? Which have succeeded? Which have failed? What differentiates the two groups?
- What solutions are available from vendors, from consulting to hardware and software tools?
- What is the likely ROI associated with moving forward today versus waiting a year or two? In other words, is the timing right in light of the organization's other activities and outside factors?
- What, if anything, is lacking in the organization's IT infrastructure?

■ Has the committee or senior management established a separate advisory panel for this project? If so, are all key stakeholders represented?

■ What are the success metrics? After the organization adopts a Performance Management strategy, how will executive management know if the investment was worthwhile and whether to continue?

Because IT will be critical in maintaining data integrity, data collection, and data management, as well as supporting analysis and reporting software, the decision of whether to commit to an initiative should involve consultation with the chief information officer (CIO). Similarly, the head of Human Resources should be consulted to gauge employee readiness to change. Department chairs and representatives from the clinical services should have a voice in whether to commit to the initiative, especially since they may be directly involved in data collection. A committee composed of a well thought-out cross-departmental team that includes a senior executive sponsor can go a long way toward ensuring a fruitful due diligence exercise.

Assuming the results of the committee's fact-finding activities are positive and senior administration buy-in is achieved, the next hurdles are finalizing a budget and timeline for a full initiative. Commitment to a Performance Management Initiative should be marked by a limited kickoff that sets user expectations and acquires organizational commitment to assist in the project's various phases.

4.2 Self-Assessment

The first step in the Performance Management cycle proper, self-assessment is virtually identical to the commitment phase. The major difference is that deciding whether to commit to an initiative is a one-time decision; self-assessment is revisited repeatedly. In addition, instead of determining whether to start an initiative, the goal of self-assessment is to examine the organization's current process, workflow, and outcomes and determine if change is necessary.

Additional questions to answer during the self-assessment stage, which primarily involves measurement, are focused on quality and performance. For example, how does the organization define quality? Is there a need for a redefinition, based on previous organizational activities? Do the organization's vision, mission statement, and strategic plan incorporate a commitment to quality and enhanced performance? Besides patient demographics, how does the organization identify its customer base? What aspects of quality are important to patients? These and similar questions can be answered with data gathered through patient satisfaction surveys, patient and staff complaints, and clinical services outcomes. Interviews, surveys, and focus groups with clinical staff and employees; reports from business coalitions or other purchasers of services; and the analysis of legal, regulatory, and accreditation requirements are additional sources of data.

The Knowledge Management techniques of knowledge audits, structured collaboration, development of communities of practice, knowledge mapping, and social network analysis are directly applicable in this stage of the cycle. Knowledge audits, in the form of informal interviews, self-reporting through formal paper-based surveys, or group meetings can be used to determine exactly what intellectual capital exists in the organization. These snapshots of intellectual capital can provide benchmarks for objective comparisons on subsequent cycles.

Structured collaboration involves forming task- and project-oriented groups to facilitate information sharing. Formal collaboration normally involves the participation of management, clinical staff, and employees who would not normally interact in the course of their regular work.

Communities of practice and groups of staff and other employees who share tasks, projects, interests, and goals—normally within a specific work area—are another major data source. For example, a hospital's cardiac anesthesiologists can be considered a community of practice. Although communities of practice are generally self-forming, dynamic entities, they can be facilitated by management.

Knowledge mapping is a formal process of identifying who knows what, how, and where the organization stores information, and how the stores of information are organized and interconnected. A closely related technique is social network analysis, which aims to identify who interacts with whom and how information is communicated among individuals or groups. Techniques developed by the KM community and software applications are available to facilitate the knowledge mapping and social network analysis processes.

4.3 Identify Areas for Improvement

The next stage is to identify areas for improvement and establish the requirements that will drive Key Performance Indicator (KPI) and benchmark definitions. Building on the data collected during the self-assessment phase of the cycle, the organization's problem areas that need to be addressed should be evident. For example, a mortality rate that is higher than expected and more postoperative infections than reported by similar institutions all point to problem areas needing improvement. A document describing the areas marked for improvement, along with a list of improvement goals, should be circulated among the key stakeholders for their approval. With problem areas and the potential means of resolution defined, the next step is to identify KPIs and benchmarks.

4.4 Identify and Review Key Performance Indicators and Benchmarks

This stage of the cycle involves identifying sources of KPIs and benchmarks, assessing KPI and benchmark applicability to the organization, and assigning KPI ownership. A decision may be made at this time regarding whether to acquire or build KPIs. Developing local indicators can be a challenging exercise. Before embarking on a development process, readers should assess their organization's access to the necessary information and statistical analysis expertise to develop indicators.

External benchmarks are useful because they represent independent *minimum* improvement targets. These benchmarks should be from similar healthcare organizations with similar patient demographics. For example, the specifications for the indicators of Meaningful Use are established by the US Government.

Internal benchmarks can be as useful as those developed externally, especially if the available external benchmarks do not map well to the organization's needs. Once KPIs have been identified, the parameters they are intended to track should be measured before implementation of the initiative to establish a baseline or internal benchmark. After implementation of the Performance Management Initiative, the internal benchmark can be used to assess improvement, independent of the external benchmark, each time through this phase of the cycle. So-called "high-performance organizations" use this approach to establish themselves as external benchmarks for other institutions.

4.5 Identify Strategies, Tools, and Technologies

With KPIs and benchmarks clearly defined (or redefined in subsequent passes), the next step in the cycle is to identify the strategies, tools, and technologies needed to support the initiative. As part of the data gathering exercise, members of the Performance Management Committee may attend a national conference where vendors exhibit relevant products or services. After this group excursion, perhaps supplemented with site visits to healthcare organizations of similar size and patient demographics using a promising technology, the most impressive vendors may be invited to give a detailed presentation to the committee. Through these presentations, the committee can formulate an idea of what is possible, identify the likely costs, and derive a plausible implementation timeline. With this information, the committee should create a requirements specification document that can be incorporated into a request for proposal (RFP), a device useful for both information gathering and internal communications (see Section 4.10).

By the end of this phase, the Performance Management Committee should have a clearly defined strategy and explicit tool requirements that address any technology gap. After developing and issuing an RFP and assessing vendor proposals, the committee, together with the legal department and other members of the organization identified by senior management, negotiates a contract for the appropriate technology and work required for implementation.

Of course, another option is to develop the required technologies in-house. Industry standard tools, such as off-the-shelf business intelligence software, servers, and database management systems, can be assembled by the organization's IT department. A few organizations may even have the depth of IT experience and the budget to develop the business intelligence and related software in-house. For example, Partner's HealthCare in Boston, which developed most of its software in-house using a variant of MUMPS, had a $14 million annual IT budget during build-out of the system—the healthcare system's fastest-growing area. Partners HealthCare System, the umbrella organization for Brigham and Women's Hospital and Massachusetts General Hospital, has annual revenue in excess of $4.5 billion. Affiliated institutions include the Harvard Medical School, Dana-Farber/Partners CancerCare, and Partners Community HealthCare, a physician network encompassing more than 1000 practitioners.

4.6 Implement

The time and resources required for the IT components of the implementation depend on the state of the IT infrastructure and the scope of the initiative. Major infrastructure development, such as the creation of a data warehouse to source the performance indicators, can be a proposition that requires months of effort at considerable expense.

Note that implementation at this point in the cycle refers to measurement capabilities, not to the later action phase, based on the analysis of KPI values. This implementation phase involves the usual design reports, functional and technical assessment, and signoff common to most IT development projects. There are necessary infrastructure and timeline constraints that must be worked through, which will eventually lead to testing and training the decision makers and staff tasked with data collection. Implementation culminates in system go-live.

4.7 Generate Reports

Reports are the end product of intricate and often complex processes that center on creating, capturing, transporting, and managing data. Charts, tables, and dashboards ideally present data from disparate sources in a form that can be easily identified and processed by decision makers.

In addition to providing data where they are easily processed, by their very nature, reports apply filters or selection criteria to indicator data. The KPI values presented to decision makers should be in a readily assimilated form. Depending on the data and the viewer, the ideal reports range from logically designed spreadsheets and individual charts to integrated, graphical dashboards that combine multiple graphic elements in a single display. See Chapter 9 (Reporting) for more information on establishing reporting requirements and fitting data to reports and decision makers' needs.

4.8 Analyze

The analysis of report data should highlight problems in work flow, information breakdowns, inefficient work processes, inadequate resources, and problem individuals. Although analysis can be automated with alarms and flags for out-of-bounds indicator values and facilitated with analysis guidelines, the quality of the analysis ultimately depends on decision makers' expertise. Training on how to interpret statistical graphs and other indicators can assist decision makers with limited experience in this domain. For example, as detailed in Chapter 8, there are established rules for how certain charts should be interpreted.

4.9 ACT

Taking corrective action based on the analysis of indicator data represents one complete cycle and the basis for investing in a Performance Management Initiative. Management and other decision makers should establish change criteria and formulate an action plan with a budget and timeline. This action may take the form of communicating findings to appropriate individuals and groups to alter their behavior (and established but faulty processes), changing the compensation and reward system, formulating new work policies, or investing in new information technologies and processes.

In the end, meaningful action, whether directed at new information systems or new guidelines, results in organizational and individual behavior change. The goal should not be to correct KPI values that are below benchmark or expectation, but to change organizational behavior so that it supports the processes resulting in KPI values that reflect quality healthcare. Depending on the indicator, this behavior change may take weeks, months, or even years.

After the change has been made and the organization has been stabilized, the cycle begins again, assuming that the key stakeholders have shown their unwavering commitment to continuing the effort. The pace of the initiative may have to be adjusted to suit the organization's budget, timeline, and ability to change. Performance Management is not a sprint—it is an ultra-marathon.

4.10 Further Thinking

The RFP can be invaluable during the fact-finding period before committing to a Performance Management Initiative and when identifying appropriate strategies, tools, and technologies during the initiative's measurement phase. Not only is the RFP a means of gathering data on commercially available products and services, but it is also useful as an internal change agent that IT can use to galvanize the vision of the organization's key decision makers.

In authoring the RFP, the Performance Management Committee's clinical representatives have an opportunity to specify their clinical information handling and delivery requirements. Financial members can focus on ROI projections. The CIO or other IT representative can document his or her concerns and questions about a vendor's information handling, hardware, and software. Legal representatives can define their intellectual property concerns, such as the need to establish a software escrow account.

Often, time pressures may suggest that there is not time to develop and release an RFP, but avoiding the process can be short-sighted. In addition to providing an interactive forum where the organization's key stakeholders can contribute to the Performance Management Initiative's collective vision, the RFP addresses several core issues regarding technology and vendor selection. At a minimum, the RFP should address vendor assessment, pricing, requirement specifications, functional specifications, development and deployment timelines, licensing, and contractual issues. The document also codifies the organization's response schedule and criteria for evaluating each proposal. That is, it galvanizes the criteria for internal decision makers in a way that is open to vendors and, equally important, to the organization's key stakeholders.

In selecting vendors, the most important predictors of the long-term success of any collaboration are the vendor's market and financial status. Core metrics in this determination are vendor experience, defined by the size of the installed user base of the vendor's product or service, backed up with verifiable references. The gross revenue percentage derived from the vendor's top three clients provides a measure of the vendor's financial stability; this stability can also be determined by analyzing a certified copy of the vendor's bank account and credit references. The Chief Executive Officer's (CEO's) track record of achievements should be requested, as well as the vendor's composition—especially the percentage of work assigned to subcontractors and the relative numbers of permanent, temporary, contract, and overseas employees.

Pricing should be described in terms of up-front and long-term costs, such as annual maintenance contracts. In particular, the vendor should specify incidental costs that could otherwise swing wildly in the future. For example, if the purchase price or maintenance contract includes periodic software upgrades, the vendor should specify the number of manuals included with each upgrade and the cost of additional manuals. Additional pricing questions include the following:

■ What are the provisions for additional training and support?
■ If there is a new operating system introduced to the market, what are the installation, training, and upgrade costs?
■ Who pays for project overruns? If it is the vendor's responsibility, how and when is payment made?

The requirements specification component of the RFP should describe, in operational terms, what the Performance Management Committee expects the service or product to do for the organization. Exactly how this functionality is established is addressed in the RFP's functional specifications component.

The functional specifications can help pull together the committee's understanding of the requirements specifications, the organization's existing and optimal processes and data flow, current industry standards, and the shared vision of where the organization is headed. Typical functional specifications issues include functional capability, system software and hardware requirements, backup facilities and database software, system capacity, expansion capabilities, documentation, installation, and training. The RFP should also clarify project management responsibilities, the nature of support, and assurances of stability and security, backed up by a warranty against data loss due to system instability or security failure.

Related to project management is the development and deployment of timelines. The vendor should specify the time required, in exacting detail, for every step—from contract acceptance to sign-off. Timelines should be included for training, testing, editing, deployment, training, and conflict resolution. Ideally, this timeline should be keyed to a process flowchart that depicts the milestones along the way, alternative routes for completing the project, and final contract resolution. For a significant project, the vendor's commitment to the proposed timeline should be formalized in writing, with specific penalties for failure to meet goals.

Licensing and contractual details should include a copy of a vendor's standard business contract. The vendor should also answer the following questions:

- What is the procedure for sign-off and acceptance?
- What is the acceptance test procedure and schedule?
- Will the vendor supply a primary contact for all contract issues and disputes?
- What is the warranty period? When does it start, and how long will it last?
- What remedies will the vendor offer if the system cannot meet performance specifications during the warranty period? What about after warranty period?
- Will the vendor agree to a finite period to correct deficiencies following a reevaluation of nonperformance?

An organization's evaluation criteria are information that the organization may choose to share or not to share with vendors. However, even if it is not shared with vendors, it should be discussed within the committee. Evaluation criteria, established before receiving proposals, are helpful in overcoming personal biases and emotional attachments to a particular vendor. Together with other internally developed criteria, evaluation criteria integrate individual concerns and help solidify a singular vision for how the Performance Management Initiative will improve the organization.

Sources and Further Reading

100 Top Hospitals Study, 2017. Truven Health Analytics. 24th ed. 2017. Ann Arbor, MI.

Blander, J. and B. Bergeron. *Clinical Management Systems: A Guide for Deployment.* 2004. Chicago: HIMSS.

Evans, J.R. and W.M. Lindsay. *Managing for Quality and Performance Excellence.* 2016. South-Western College.

Hale, J. *The Performance Consultant's Fieldbook.* 2006. San Francisco: Jossey-Bass.

Marshall, M. et al. *Quality Indicators for General Practice: A Practical Guide for Primary Health Care Professionals and Managers.* 2002. London: Royal Society of Medicine Press.

Mays, G.P. and P. Halverson. Conceptual and methodological issues in public health performance measurement: Results from a computer-assisted expert panel process. *Journal of Public Health Management and Practice* 2000, 6(5): 59–65.

ORYX® Risk Adjustment Guide Version 2013, November 2012, is the work of The Joint Commission. The manual is periodically updated by The Joint Commission. Users of the ORYX® Risk Adjustment Guide must update their software and associated documentation whenever The Joint Commission releases a new version of this manual.

Porter-Roth, B. *Request for Proposal: A Guide to Effective RFP Development.* 2001. New York: Addison-Wesley Professional.

Spath, P.L. and D. Kelly. *Applying Quality Management in Healthcare: A Systems Approach, 4th Edition.* 2017. Chicago: Health Administration Press.

Chapter 5

Key Performance Indicators

Key Performance Indicators (KPIs) are a means, not an end. Core measures that gauge the organization's past or current performance in particular areas, KPIs reflect how closely the organization's underlying processes are aligned with best practices. KPI application areas range from financial administration, patient records management, personnel administration, economic analysis, facilities and equipment utilization, practice activities, and operating methods to organizational behavior, patient safety, and myriad clinical areas.

As indicators of process effectiveness and efficiency, KPIs can quantify otherwise abstract notions of quality, establish benchmarks for comparison, and serve as evidence that structure or processes have undergone positive change. Well-crafted KPIs can also facilitate accountability and provide the basis for behavior change and policy initiatives. In fulfilling these roles, KPIs—exhaustively defined variables that can provide decision makers with insight into an organization's processes—can be as varied as the processes and outcomes they are intended to monitor.

Rarely considered alone, indicators are arranged in a logical collection referred to as a scorecard. These logical groupings can be user, department, service, or organization focused, with one scorecard feeding another. For example, Brigham and Women's Hospital, Boston, started with nursing service and surgical scorecards and rolled these into an executive level scorecard that contains indicators applicable across the organization. Deeper-level scorecards featuring lower-level indicators that roll up to the surgical and nursing scorecards were then developed.

Whether considered alone or arranged within a scorecard, a KPI is just that: an indicator. As an analogy, simply having the instruments used in a race car—tachometer, speedometer, and so on—will not make a commuter driving to work a more capable driver. However, in the hands of a driver focused on honing his or her skills to mimic those of a race car driver, the instruments can be invaluable.

5.1 KPI Taxonomy

What gets measured gets noticed, and KPIs are the focal point for that measurement. The KPI perspective can be clinical, financial, or patient focused. KPIs may also be quantitative or qualitative—or a hybrid of the two—and expressed as a fixed value, percentage, ratio, average, or rate, depending on the measure (see Table 5.1).

Table 5.1   KPI Perspectives

Clinical
Financial
Patient-focused
Insurer-focused
Quantitative
Qualitative
Hybrid
Process
Output
Outcome
Community-wide
US-wide
Hospital-wide
Department-wide

Some healthcare quality organizations categorize KPIs according to their functionality. For example, the AHRQ categorizes its KPIs as process, output, or outcome. Process KPIs are used to assess whether protocols are being followed. Output KPIs are used to quantify volume and utilization. Outcome KPIs, such as mortality and infection rates, follow patient status after care. There is nothing sacred about KPI categories; they serve as a means of locating indicators that may be of use to an area within the organization.

Performance indicators can be categorized by scope and intended audience. Hospital-wide indicators are intended for review by senior management and the board. Examples include measures such as infection control, safety and security, utilization and volume, patient and employee satisfaction, and clinical risk management, including a summary of incidents and claims. Department-wide indicators are intended for review by department administrators, such as the number of vaginal deliveries for the department of OB/GYN. Blood and medication use, medical record review, and credentialing are additional examples of department-wide KPIs.

In this book, KPIs are discussed in terms of clinical and nonclinical indicators. Nonclinical indicators are used primarily to monitor parameters such as capacity and utilization, revenues, and profitability. For example, capacity and utilization KPIs are analyzed to determine whether the organization has the staff, equipment, and other resources to reach the financial goals established by the board of directors. Clinical indicators, such as postoperative infection rate and mortality, are used to assess the organization's clinical side.

5.2 Selecting Indicators

There are hundreds of KPIs discussed in the following chapters and appendices, and many more are freely available online and for sale by quality organizations. Those included in this book have been compiled over nearly two decades from a variety of sources. Indicators don't age per se, but different groups of indicators are promoted for a particular cause, by a particular organization, or from specific perspectives. For example, the National Committee for Quality Assurance (NCQA) produces a range of indicators, such as the Healthcare Effectiveness Data and Information Set (HEDIS). Similarly, the Centers for Disease Control and Prevention (CDC) (*www.cdc.gov*) maintains medical outcomes indicators, clinical disease indicators, and clinical and laboratory performance indicators, and the American Hospital Association (AHA) (*www.aha.org*) is considered one of the major standards organizations for indicator definitions in the industry. The AHA publication *American Hospital Association Hospital Statistics* contains definitions of industry standard indicators as well as the values for many US hospitals.

In addition to relying on nationally recognized quality groups and standards organizations, it is also common practice to develop custom KPIs to address unique problem areas of a particular healthcare organization. Regardless of whether the decision is to buy, build, or borrow, the KPIs should reflect the challenges facing the organization, the need to compare performance with external benchmarks for accreditation, and executive management's experience with Performance Management. At a minimum, every KPI's name, application in decision making, formula, source of data, adjustments, and exceptions should be documented.

Although it may be tempting to simply page through a list of KPIs and select one or two "promising" indicators for each clinical department and a dozen or more for administration, doing so would be like selecting surgical instruments based on the elegance of their design and without thought to the surgical procedure. A better approach to indicator selection is to identify the high-risk, high-volume, problem-prone areas. High-risk patients, such as those admitted for acute myocardial infarctions, are typically vulnerable, fragile, and unstable. High-volume services, such as delivery in a women's hospital, are provided to large numbers of patients. Problem-prone areas, such as lengthy emergency room (ER) wait times, vary from one hospital to the next. The downside to selecting KPIs based on risk, volume, and problem areas is that the indicators may suffer from superficiality. It can be a hit-or-miss proposition unless the problems, risks, and volumes are explicitly linked to the organization's underlying goals and culture.

Selecting one KPI or a scorecard filled with KPIs requires foremost a shared understanding of the organization's mission, vision, and priorities. There should also be a shared understanding of the current and future expectations of the patients who receive services from the organization. In addition, it is critical from an IT perspective to determine whether the organization has the management expertise needed to act on the data represented by a KPI once the IT infrastructure needed to capture, translate, and properly report the indicator values has been developed.

Defining a shared vision and expectations need not involve multiple management retreats to a quiet cabin in the woods or white water rafting. Simply put: senior management and key stakeholders should be able to answer the following questions for every KPI considered:

■ **Why is it important to the organization?** There should be a compelling reason why the organization should invest tens of thousands of dollars over the course of several years to monitor a particular indicator.

- **How does the parameter measured by the indicator affect the organization's mission and vision?** The relationship between the indicator and the organization's mission and vision should be transparent and explicitly defined.
- **Is there an alternative, next-best indicator?** Acquiring the data for the optimal indicator may be too expensive and take too long.
- **How is the indicator calculated?** Even the simplest indicators must be precisely defined, especially when used against benchmarks or for accreditation.
- **What data are required, where do data reside, and how will they be acquired?** The data for a single KPI may reside on a half-dozen different computer systems connected by a network or on a simple paper questionnaire completed by patients.
- **Is the current IT infrastructure adequate? If not, what additional technologies are required?** Creating interfaces between clinical and administrative computers and building a hospital-wide data warehouse are significant IT projects. If a new IT infrastructure must be created, the actual use of KPIs could be years away.
- **How often will the indicator be reported?** Some indicators only make sense when trended over years (i.e., the percentage change in indicator value from a reference or base year is calculated), while others are of value when reported daily or weekly. More frequent reporting may place unreasonable demands on a heavily loaded IT infrastructure.
- **How will the indicator be analyzed?** Management and staff may need training on how to interpret process charts and other statistical reports.
- **What are the resource requirements in terms of time and money?** Supporting a Performance Initiative with 40 or 50 KPIs can cost millions of dollars and require years to implement.
- **Can the organization control the variability measured by the indicator? If not, what is the value in knowing the indicator value?**
- **What will be the demands on the staff?** If capturing the indicator is too arduous, such as requiring staff to fill out new forms for each patient encounter, staff compliance may be low.
- **What are the expectations of management and staff?** Simply putting the KPI in place will not solve the underlying problem the indicator is designed to monitor. Furthermore, positive process outcomes do not necessarily translate to clinical benefits.
- **Is the parameter measured amenable to intervention?** As in clinical medicine, there is no point in wasting resources to perform a test when there is no known recourse.

At first glance, KPIs may seem deceptively simple. Take the Mortality Index, for example, which is defined as

$$\text{Mortality} = \text{Actual Deaths/Expected Deaths}$$

This clinical KPI shows patient survival compared with what is expected, and a ratio of less than 1.0 is preferable. However, the Mortality Index is normally risk-adjusted for patient age, sex, and diagnosis, as well as the hospital type and size. Sicker, elderly patients have a greater likelihood of expiring during their hospital stay than, say, college athletes. Furthermore, survivability is generally better in large urban teaching hospitals than small rural hospitals.

In analyzing the indicator, exactly what constitutes a death? Does the measure include patients brought into the ER who die within five minutes? What about patients who live five hours? Five days? What about patients on mechanical ventilators and life support who are transported to other facilities? As described below, indicators should be defined in exquisite detail, including the intended use.

5.3 Top-Down Versus Bottom-Up

Regardless of the selection criteria, KPIs can filter throughout the organization from the department level or up from the boardroom. One of the challenges of defining indicators at the department level and then propagating them through the healthcare organization is the potential lack of congruence. What is best for a specific department may not be best for another department or the organization as a whole. For example, when multiple departments share assets, it is difficult to determine return on investment (ROI). Moreover, one department may aim to minimize use of a resource that has an expensive variable ownership cost, while another department simultaneously seeks to maximize use.

When defining performance indicators from the confines of the boardroom, the challenge lies in the potential for a poor fit at the department level. A workaround is to encourage communications and planning at the administrative level. In practice, performance indicator selection is often a hybrid approach in which top-level decisions are modified by department-level administrators with detailed knowledge of day-to-day operations.

While on the topic of indicator selection, it is important to note that indicators need not be limited to the traditional areas of finance, utilization, administration, and clinical medicine; they can serve the needs of IT as well. When Berger Clinic, part of the PeachHealth integrated delivery system in Eugene, Oregon, decided to adopt an EMR, an effective Performance Management system to gauge the system's performance was crucial to gaining senior management support. The IT group at Berger Clinic defined KPIs related to the speed and efficiency of patient visits, reduced volumes of paper documents, reduced potential adverse drug events, and reduced costs through better utilization of clinicians and staff. The group then established a baseline measurement for each KPI and compared them with industry benchmarks and best practices. The KPIs were assessed again at 45 and 90 days after EMR go-live to assess improvement. Within 2 years of go-live, IT could demonstrate with KPI metrics the ROI provided by the EMR, in terms of financial savings and increased clinical value for patients.

5.4 Data Driven Versus Needs Driven

A dilemma faced by every chief information officer (CIO) involved in a Performance Management Initiative is how to balance indicator need versus data availability. One solution is to simply provide indicators based on what data are easily extracted from hospital applications. However, a better approach is to design a decision matrix in Excel in which each indicator is weighted based on organization need, technical feasibility, data availability, and cost. The matrix should be made available to the Performance Management Committee, which may choose to share it with department heads and other decision makers to counter any calls of favoritism or bias toward indicators that may benefit one department or service over another.

Although any number of decision matrices can be constructed based on local issues, a general formula that is applicable to most circumstances is

$$\text{Indicator Score} = [(\text{Need} \times W_{\text{need}}) + (\text{Technical Feasibility} \times W_{\text{tech}})$$
$$+ (\text{Data Availability} \times W_{\text{data}})]/(\text{Cost} \times W_{\text{cost}}).$$

Need, Technical Feasibility, Data Availability, and *Cost* are assigned values of 1, 2, or 3, corresponding to low, medium, or high. For example, an indicator with high cost has a *Cost* value of 3.

Need is an assessment of the indicator's need, based on the Performance Management cycle defined in Chapter 3. The score assigned to *Need* may be increased because a decision maker expresses need for the indicator, because the indicator is a national benchmark that has been identified as important to the organization's accreditation purposes, or because the indicator has been earmarked by the organization's executive board as critical to the organization's long-term management. *Need* should generally have the highest weighting.

Technical feasibility is an assessment, from an IT perspective, of the feasibility of providing the indicator value to decision makers. Feasibility may reflect the difficulty in extracting the data from a closed, stand-alone application or of the performance hit on a system operating near capacity that may not be able to tolerate the daily load of data extraction.

Data availability is an operational issue that relates to data's accuracy and completeness. Data will not be available if the clinicians systematically avoid entering the ICD-9 or ICD-10 (International Classification of Diseases, 9th Revision and 10th Revision, respectively) codes in the diagnosis in the EMR, for example. *Cost* reflects the relative cost of acquiring, manipulating, and otherwise making the data available to decision makers. A new data warehouse, data mart, data extraction, and loading software package; ongoing system maintenance; and end user training all affect *Cost*.

The weights associated with each measure represent the relative importance given to each measure. For example, the weighted assigned need can be double that of the other measures (e.g., $W_{need} = 2$, $W_{tech} = 1$, $W_{data} = 1$, and $W_{cost} = 1$). In a spreadsheet, weights can be easily changed, and the relative indicator scores for the working set of indicators can be assessed.

To illustrate the utility of a decision matrix, consider that the Performance Management Committee has assembled a list of some 60 indicator candidates. Included in the list are two indicators of inpatient procedure mortality—esophageal resection mortality (ERM) and pancreatic resection mortality (PRM). The chairman of the department of surgery states that both are equally critical to assessing his department's performance, but ERM is the higher volume indicator. For this reason, he rates ERM need as high (need = 3) and PRM need as medium (need = 2). Now, assume that providing ERM is technically challenging because the data reside in a closed, undocumented database (technical feasibility = 1) and that the surgeons have been amiss about entering the relevant ICD-9 codes in the EMR (data availability = 2). Furthermore, the cost of tracking ERM is high (cost = 3).

In comparison, providing PRM data is only modestly technically challenging (technical feasibility = 2). Data are easily available (data availability = 3), and the associated cost is modest (cost = 2). Assume further that the Performance Management Committee has assigned each measure the following weights: $W_{need} = 2$, $W_{tech} = 1$, $W_{data} = 1$, and $W_{cost} = 2$.

The indicator scores for PRM and ERM are calculated as

$$\text{Indicator Score}_{ERM} = [(\text{Need} \times W_{need}) + (\text{Technical Feasibility} \times W_{tech})$$
$$+ (\text{Data Availability} \times W_{data})]/(\text{Cost} \times W_{cost})$$
$$\text{Indicator Score}_{PRM} = [(3 \times 2) + (1 \times 1) + (2 \times 1)]/(3 \times 2) = 9/6 = 1.5$$

$$\text{Indicator Score}_{PRM} = [(\text{Need} \times W_{need}) + (\text{Technical Feasibility} \times W_{tech})$$
$$+ (\text{Data Availability} \times W_{data})]/(\text{Cost} \times W_{cost})$$
$$\text{Indicator Score}_{PRM} = [(2 \times 2) + (2 \times 1) + (3 \times 1)]/(2 \times 2) = 9/4 = 2.25$$

According to the decision matrix calculation, PRM is ranked higher than ERM. Whether ERM appears in the final list of KPIs depends on the total number of indicators and the relative ranking of other indicators. When the matrix is defined in a spreadsheet, the Performance Management Committee members can quickly perform "what-if" scenarios by changing relative weighting.

A less technical means of deciding between needs- and data-driven KPIs is to use a phased approach that incorporates both perspectives. For example, when the Mid Western Area Health Service in New South Wales set out to establish a library of KPIs, it used a three-phased approach. Phase 1 was limited to indicators developed from data that were in the New South Wales database. Phase 2 involved refining information available in the database that was not yet in a form suitable for indicators. In Phase 3, new indicators and new data collection processes were developed.

5.5 Data Collection

The previous spreadsheet model of the relative merit of various measures highlights the need for high-quality, accurate data. As in any scientific experiment, the quality of the data limits the quality of the analysis. Furthermore, quality data do not appear by accident, but require a carefully designed and executed data collection plan. Such a plan should completely specify how data are observed, captured, and recorded; who is involved; where the data are collected; and how the data will be used to calculate a performance indicator.

Just as the organization's mission drives the performance indicator, the indicator choice drives the data collection requirements. For example, in tracking medication errors, the purpose of the indicator determines whether the data collected should measure presence or absence of a drug reaction or measure the severity of a reaction. If only presence or absence is measured, then analysis will be limited to simple classification. If degree of drug reaction severity is measured, then more advanced statistical analysis is possible. Of course, collecting four or five times the data may be more labor-intensive, costly, and error-prone, compared with capturing presence or absence measures. See Chapter 11 for a more detailed discussion of data types, statistical methods, and key data collection issues, such as how to deal with missing data.

5.6 How Many Indicators?

What constitutes a reasonable number of indicators depends on the scope and purpose of the indicators, as summarized in Figure 5.1. If the goal is to demonstrate Meaningful Use, then there's a mandatory minimum of a dozen core indicators and at least half-dozen menu set indicators. Free of external requirements, 10 to 20 indicators per department and perhaps a dozen global indicators for executive management is a reasonable long-term goal. In larger institutions, because of the complexity of each department, department heads may require more indicators than executive management. Assuming a healthcare organization has 40 major departments and a dozen indicators per department, for upper management, the total number of unique indicators that need to be defined can easily approach 200 or even 300 (there is typically overlap in indicators appropriate for each department, which decreases the total indicator count). Even a total count of only 100 indicators constitutes a major investment of time and institutional resources.

The most appropriate number and type of indicators for a given area depends on the needs and perspectives of the decision makers. As a benchmark of the most appropriate number of indicators for executive management, consider that when Mayo Clinic started on its scorecard project,

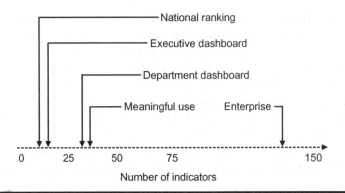

Figure 5.1 Typical indicator count by purposes and area.

it created an unwieldy KPI wish list. After assessing the needs of the organization and availability data, 14 indicators were chosen for the clinic's initial executive-level scorecard. This number of indicators is more in line with what top management in a healthcare organization can use initially. Although seven or eight indicators may be sufficient for ranking purposes, it is not likely that the same indicators can address any unique problem areas in the organization or leave room for innovation.

The process of honing down the number of service- and department-level KPIs to a number appropriate for high-level management was also followed by Brigham and Women's Hospital. The Boston-based hospital initially condensed about 80 indicators in its surgical and nursing scorecards into a more manageable list of 35 indicators for surgery and 30 indicators for nursing. It then created a 30-indicator executive-level scorecard composed primarily of indicators from the surgical and nursing scorecards. Similarly, when the Ontario Hospital Association (OHA) created a balanced scorecard for upper management, it identified and collected data on 38 enterprise-wide indicators.

In presenting upper management or department heads with a scorecard composed of a large number of KPIs, the danger is that the indicators may be too diverse *relative to decision makers' needs*. If so, then the resulting scorecards will serve merely as distractions. Even when data are available for hundreds of indicators, it is a good idea to roll out the indicators slowly to assess the effect on decision maker behavior and to allow time for change. Another advantage of implementing a Performance Management Initiative by introducing at most two dozen KPIs at a time is the reduced burden on the training staff; this is directed at a single department or to senior management. Decision makers have to be trained on how to interpret indicator values and graphical charts and then given time to adjust their decision-making processes to accommodate the new information.

The number of KPIs actually deployed in a department or institution should not be confused with the total number of indicators that need to be developed. It is in the organization's best interest to have a library of KPIs on hand in areas parallel to the organization's needs. With some forethought, it is possible to plan for KPI needs and to have a pipeline of KPIs under development to service future needs. As demonstrated in Chapter 1, medication errors are a common problem in healthcare organizations. If reducing medication errors is an organizational priority, then KPIs addressing various aspects of medication ordering can be developed and included in the active list of KPIs or scorecards. Furthermore, benchmarks are frequently announced by quality organizations and healthcare organizations. If the local organization wants to compare its processes with those of the benchmark institutions, it will have to develop and deploy the relevant KPIs.

5.7 Defining Indicators

Indicators must be completely defined so that there is no room for misinterpretation. Most of the quality groups, including the Joint Commission on Accreditation of Healthcare Organizations (JCAHO), define what should be included in indicator definitions for accreditation. However, there is no universal indicator definition template, and technical circumstances often dictate template contents. For example, data flow diagrams should be included with complex indicators involving data from several databases. At a minimum, the definition of a KPI should include the following elements:

- **Name:** Name of KPI, using a standard naming system. The name should be self-explanatory, such as "average length of stay or ALOS."
- **Internal ID Number:** An internal ID number for tracking purposes. This number ID should be fixed and unique, for use in searching a database of KPIs.
- **External ID Number:** If applicable, an external ID number associated with a particular source, such as CMS, should be associated with the KPI. External IDs can change, based on the source. As such, it should not be the primary lookup key when storing information on the KPI.
- **Short Definition:** A one-line definition of the KPI, akin to a descriptive name, for example, "Number of days an inpatient stays in the hospital, on average, unadjusted."
- **Long Definition:** An extensive textual definition of KPI, including sources, formulas, limitations, and applicability to the organization. The long definition should include a rationale for the organization's use of the indicator. The rationale is especially critical in describing adjusted indicators, or indicators that make use of adjusted metrics because adjustments tend to be context specific.
- **Formula:** Mathematical equation of the KPI, less details of any adjustments. Continuing with the ALOS example:

$$\text{ALOS} = [\text{Discharge Days/Total Discharges}]$$

- **Numerator:** Description of the numerator, including the data elements as well as populations included and excluded from the data. For example, *Discharge Days* often include all patients except newborns.
- **Denominator:** Description of the denominator, including the data elements as well as populations included and excluded from the data. For example, *Total Discharges*, like *Discharge Days*, often excludes newborns.
- **KPI Format:** Format of KPI output, such as days, months, or percentage. For example, ALOS = 2.3 days.
- **Data Source(s):** The sources of data used in the numerator and denominator. Sources may include a computer system, application, survey, or other data source needed to compute the KPI.
- **Collection Approach(es):** The approach(es) to collecting data for the numerator and denominator. For example, JCAHO categorizes the approaches to data collection in terms of timing, which may be retrospective, concurrent, or prospective. A retrospective approach involves the capture of events that have already occurred. A concurrent approach involves data collection on a working process, while a prospective approach involves data collected in

anticipation of an event or occurrence. Following the ALOS example, Discharge Days and Total Discharges are typically collected using a retrospective approach.

■ **Statistical Adjustment:** The statistical manipulations that can reduce the contribution of confounding factors, such as outliers, to the indicator value. Statistical adjustment also includes recommendations for minimizing errors introduced by the data collection process.

■ **Benchmark Value(s):** External benchmark KPI values from similar organizations that are indicative of recognized best practices and internal benchmarks that provide a relative basis for process improvement.

■ **Target Value:** Current target value of KPI. For example, the target value for ALOS in a given hospital may be 5.3 days. The target value can also include a qualitative improvement measure, such as an increase or decrease in the indicator value. A decrease in the length of stay is normally considered an improvement.

■ **Trigger Value(s):** The out-of-bounds values, both high and low, that can be used to notify the appropriate decision makers through trigger alerts and e-mails, for example. An ALOS of less than one is and greater than six may be an appropriate trigger range, for example, depending on the patient population.

■ **Adjustments:** The adjustments to the core KPI, including the rationale. In general, no legacy formula should be used as is for benchmark purposes.

■ **Adjustment Formula:** Mathematical equation detailing adjustment calculation. For example, ALOS might be increased upward or downward by 10%, depending on the value of ALOS.

■ **Recommended Analysis:** Analysis related to the KPI, such as descriptive statistics, trend analysis, horizontal analysis, and predictive modeling, for optimum interpretation of indicator data. When predictive analysis is used, a detailed definition of the curve fitting algorithm and other parameters related to the analysis must be provided. If a specific analysis software tool is used, it should be listed, with the version noted.

■ **Department/Service Affected:** A list of the hospital departments and/or services affected by the KPI. For example, the ALOS KPI may be used by several clinical departments, medical records, and the finance department.

■ **Process Affected:** A description of the particular processes targeted by the KPI, including a summary of any problem area(s) addressed.

■ **KPIs Affected:** Other KPIs that use this KPI as a data element, which would be affected by changing this KPI's definition.

■ **Charting:** Optimal type of chart(s) used to display the KPI, for example, a boxplot or pie chart, as defined by the type of data and decisions that must be supported by the chart. The chart may be defined by the number of data elements. For example, a simple line chart may be used until 12 data points are available, at which point a process control chart may be used. The optimal charting for particular data may be specified by an accrediting institution. JCAHO's ORYX requires the organization to evaluate its performance against both its own history, using control charts, and the other organizations' performance, using comparison charts.

■ **References:** A list of published articles, reports, specific URLs of quality organizations, and other sources in the following areas:
  - **KPI:** The source of the KPI, for example, American Hospital Association, and its application.
  - **Benchmark:** Sources of benchmark values. Reference should validate the applicability of the benchmark to the organization.

- **Target:** Source for target value.
- **Triggers:** A list of publications, internal benchmarks, or other sources that provide the basis for trigger values.
- **Adjustments:** The basis for case mix, wage, and other adjustments.
- **Related Analysis:** The basis for analysis.
- **Charting:** The basis for chart selection. For more information, see Chapter 9 (Reporting) and the publication *Tools for Performance Measurement in Healthcare: A Quick Reference Guide.* 2008, Oakbrook Terrace, Illinois: Joint Commission Resources.

■ **Security/Privacy:** A description of the security and privacy issues related to the KPI, to address local and HIPAA (Health Insurance Portability and Accountability Act) requirements. For example, a mortality indicator may be limited to distribution within the organization's intranet, whereas other indicators may be available for public scrutiny. Financial indicators may be limited to the finance department or only high-level financial indicators may be available to department heads or physicians.

■ **Access Level:** Related to security and privacy, the level of access to the KPI that is available to the organization's employees and decision makers. KPIs may be viewable by physicians but not nurses, for example.

■ **Author:** Local author(s) of the KPI.

■ **Acronyms and Definitions:** Acronyms and definitions of processes and data elements that may not be known to readers outside of the KPI's domain, and may vary from department to department. For example, the surgical department may use one formula for ALOS and the medicine department may use another.

■ **Owner:** The person(s) assigned to monitor the KPI on a periodic basis; who may not be the KPI's author or end user.

■ **Creation Date:** Date of creation.

■ **Frequency of Validation:** Recommended frequency of validation by the KPI owner, typically done quarterly or semiannually. Validation includes updating the latest benchmark figures, determining if the definition provided by the source organization has changed (and, if so, notifying the appropriate decision maker to assess whether a new version of the KPI definition should be constructed to reflect the change), and updating target and trigger values, if appropriate. For example:
  - Definition—Annually
  - Benchmark—Quarterly
  - Trigger—Quarterly
  - Target—Annually
  - Adjustments—Annually
  - References—Annually

■ **Revision History:** A listing of dates and the nature of revisions made to the above elements.

■ **Status:** The current status of the KPI, such as "in use," "inactive," or "in review."

When reviewing the clinical and nonclinical indicator descriptions in the following chapters, readers should not consider the brief descriptions as complete definitions. Consider the short CMS/JCAHO definition of Aspirin at Arrival: "Acute myocardial infarction (AMI) patients without aspirin contraindications who received aspirin within 24 hours before or after hospital arrival." The definition seems complete enough until the exact definition of AMI is considered. CMS/JCAHO define AMI completely by referencing a list of acceptable ICD-9 or ICD-10 codes for AMI. In addition, the complete definition identifies the excluded population as patients less than

18 years of age who transferred to another acute care hospital or federal hospital on the day of arrival; were received in transfer from another acute care hospital, including another emergency department; were discharged on the day of arrival; expired on the day of arrival; left against medical advice on the day of arrival; and had one or more aspirin contraindications/reasons for not prescribing aspirin documented in their medical record.

Even a completely defined indicator can be misused. Consider the indicators Patient Days and Patient Days (Adjusted). A Patient Day is a period of service between the census-taking hours on two successive calendar days, with the day of discharge being counted only when a patient is admitted the same day. That is, assuming a census taking hour of midnight, a patient admitted at 10 a.m. on Friday and discharged at noon on the following Saturday constitutes one Patient Day of service. As an indicator, Patient Days is useful as a utilization measure of the clinical staff's workload and the organization's acute fiscal status. To provide a closer approximation of these measures, Patient Days can be adjusted for inpatient revenue, contribution of outpatient services to clinical staff workload, or acuity of illness. In each case, the indicator is referred to as "Adjusted Patient Days" or "Patient Days (Adjusted)."

The most appropriate version of Patient Days depends on the purpose of the indicator. For example, unadjusted Patient Days is often used in calculating ALOS, according to the following formula:

$$ALOS = Patient\ Days/Number\ of\ Admissions$$

Note that this is a valid formula for ALOS, but very different from the formula for ALOS used above—hence the need to clearly indicate how this KPI is calculated. Now, in the context of comparing a hospital's ALOS with published global benchmarks from similar institutions, unadjusted Patients Days may be a valid version of the metric. Adjusting Patient Days for revenue may be used for a comparison with other institution's revenue-adjusted Patient Days, but should not be used to compute ALOS. Similarly, the relative contribution of outpatient services—an indicator of workload for nursing and other services—should not be used to compute ALOS.

The ALOS figure will be abnormally low because outpatient volume contributes to the denominator in the formula. Acuity-adjusted Patient Days, which indicates the presence or absence of a major or minor morbidity, can be used to compute an Adjusted ALOS. Comparing Acuity-Adjusted ALOS figures enables management to make a more valid comparison of healthcare organizations serving significantly different patient demographics. Readers are cautioned not only to understand the high-level definition of an indicator but also to critically examine the underlying assumptions of applicability and to understand that the metrics are used to compute the indicator.

Precisely defined indicators provide a common language for communications on the structure and flow of business processes. Because the financial and operations processes in a healthcare organization are highly structured and standardized, the corresponding KPIs are much less open to misinterpretation compared with clinical indicators. Clinical KPIs often quantify processes that are more discretionary and free form and often never repeat in exactly the same way. For example, everyone in the boardroom understands the concept of profit margin. However, exactly what is a medication error, and what is the root cause? Patient satisfaction metrics are even more open to misinterpretation. Even so, the more tightly defined the metrics describing the indicators are, the more decision makers with different perspectives can communicate. Because intra-organization communications are critical for a successful Performance Management Initiative, the indicators selected in the nonfinancial areas should represent the more structured and repeatable elements of the clinical process, and the results should be shared and reported in a consistent manner.

5.8 Further Thinking

KPIs should not be defined once and then left to filter through the organization. Each indicator requires an owner who is involved from the start. Owners, who might be clinicians or administrative staff tapped by the Performance Management Committee, should be involved in the operational definition of their indicator, including its derivation, scope, and application. The owner should also take responsibility for monitoring any adjustment variables, such as shifts in patient demographics, and for monitoring external definitions of optimal indicator values that reflect new information from regulatory agencies, quality organizations, or other healthcare organizations. Finally, it is the duty of the KPI owner to periodically review the indicator for statistically significant anomalies.

The owner should not be confused with the KPI's source or ultimate user. A KPI may be used by dozens of decision makers in the organization, none of whom are owners. Similarly, the medical records department may be the source of several KPIs, but the owners may be part of a clinical department. In addition, a single KPI may have several components that span several sources. For example, a utilization KPI, such as surgical cases per FTE, may incorporate data from human resources and the surgery department.

Having a KPI owner assigned to each indicator does not obviate the need for a "super owner" who periodically examines classes of indicators. A super owner for clinical indicators would look after the clinical indicators as a whole. One of the most important factors to monitor at the indicator class level is the correlation of predictive value. Examined individually, two indicators may be up to date, accurate, and reflect the latest standards. However, taken together, the indicators may overlap in the predictive value they offer decision makers. For example, if two different measures of OR utilization consistently increase and decrease together, as though they are coupled, then monitoring both may be unnecessary. Perhaps one of the indicators could be dropped without diminishing the end user's decision-making capabilities. The statistics behind this determination are discussed in Chapter 11.

Sources and Further Reading

AHA Hospital Statistics 2016. 2016. Chicago, Illinois: American Hospital Association.

CAHPS Ambulatory Care Improvement Guide: Practical Strategies for Improving Patient Experience. Content last reviewed October 2016. Rockville, MD: Agency for Healthcare Research and Quality. *http://www.ahrq.gov/cahps/quality-improvement/improvement-guide/improvement-guide.html.*

Guidance on Mode Selection in Patient Experience Surveying. 2016. Ontario Hospital Association. Download from: *www.oha.com.*

hfm Magazine. Healthcare Financial Management Association. *www.hfma.org.*

Hospital Report Series. Canadian Institute of Health Information. *https://secure.cihi.ca/estore/productSeries .htm?pc=PCC219.*

Journal for Healthcare Quality. National Association of Healthcare Quality. *www.nahq.org/education/journal -healthcare-quality.*

Journal of Healthcare Management. American College of Healthcare Executives. *www.ache.org/Publications /SubscriptionPurchase.aspx#jhm.*

Kohn, L., J. Corrigan, and M. Donaldson, eds. *To Err Is Human: Building a Safer Health System.* 2000, National Academy Press: Washington, DC.

Kottke, T.E. and G.J. Isham. Measuring health care access and quality to improve health in populations. *Prev Chronic Dis* 2010, 7(4): A73. *www.cdc.gov/pcd/issues/2010/jul/09_0243.htm.* Accessed April 13, 2017.

National Forum for Health Care Quality Measurement and Reporting (NQF). *www.qualityforum.org*.

Paton, J. Clinical performance indicators–good, bad, or ugly duckling? *Br J Healthcare Comput Info Manage* 2002, 19(5): 26–8.

Performance Measurement for Hospitals. Joint Commission. *http://www.jointcomission.org*. Accessed April 26, 2017.

Rodak, S. 16 Potential Key Performance Indicators for Hospitals. 2013. Becker's Hospital Review. *www.beckershospitalreview.com/strategic-planning/16-potential-key-performance-indicators-for-hospitals.html*. Accessed April 25, 2017.

Schilp, J. and R. Gilbreath. *Health Data Quest: How to Find and Use Data for Performance Improvement*. 2000, San Francisco: Jossey-Bass.

Starr, G., T. Rogers, M. Schooley, S. Porter, E. Wiesen, and N. Jamison. *Key Outcome Indicators for Evaluating Comprehensive Tobacco Control Programs*. 2005. Atlanta, GA: Centers for Disease Control and Prevention.

Vancil, R. Uncommon denominators: Metrics that matter. *CMO Magazine* 2004, 1(3): 54–5.

Chapter 6

Nonclinical Indicators

Performance Management is skillful business accomplishment through effective use of resources. The fate of these resources—from personnel to working capital and IT—hinges on the healthcare organization's financial well-being. According to the American Hospital Association, the number of US hospitals has declined for the past several years. This development illustrates how even the brightest and most caring clinicians cannot care for patients if their healthcare organization is moribund. This chapter introduces the key financial, operational, and utilization performance indicators that administrators can use to monitor the health of their organization. These nonclinical indicators are grouped as in Figure 6.1.

6.1 Accounting

The healthcare organization's financial profile is reported externally in two documents: the balance sheet and the income statement. A statement of the organization's financial position at a particular time, the balance sheet shows assets, liabilities, and shareholders' equity. Assets are divided into current and fixed assets, and liabilities are categorized as current or long term. Shareholders' equity is the difference between assets and liabilities.

The income statement, an accounting of sales (revenue), expenses, and net profit for a given period, reflects profitability. While the financial data in a balance sheet have value alone, when combined with utilization and operational data, skilled managers can gain deeper insight into the organization's health.

Most utilization indicators are volume measures, while the key financial and operational indicators tend to be ratios. Regardless of their mathematical formulation, whenever performance indicators are compared against benchmarks or other organizations, it is critical for management to verify that the same formulas were used to compute the indicators, including any adjustments made for case mix, wages, and other factors. Consider, for example, how ranking athletes by their strength-to-weight ratios is a valid comparison between athletes of the same age and sex. A 65-year-old female may be considered an athlete when compared with someone in her peer group, but not when compared with a 24-year-old male college football player. Similarly, the inter-organization comparison of indicators is most useful when the healthcare organizations have similar operating characteristics, size, and, patient demographics.

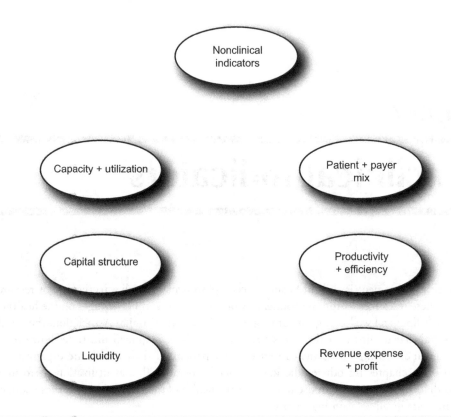

Figure 6.1   Nonclinical performance indicators.

Whether used against external benchmarks or within the organization, performance indicators are at best estimates—incomplete, lacking in detail, not completely accurate, and limited in their decision support capabilities. For example, many financial ratios are sensitive to the mix of debt and equity (financial leverage) and are easily misinterpreted. Similarly, some performance indicators are valuable only in the short term (less than a year), while others are of primary value when used to track trends over several years. With these limitations in mind, let us discuss the performance indicators.

Most nonclinical performance indicators fall into one of seven categories:

- **Capacity and Utilization**—provide a global view of how efficiently and effectively the organization's resources are being used, and can be used by management to predict financial performance.
- **Capital Structure**—assess the debt-carrying capacity of the organization.
- **Liquidity**—assess the organization's ability to cover short-term debt.
- **Patient and Payer Mix**—reflect the source and nature of third-party reimbursements, the lifeblood of US hospitals.
- **Pricing Strategies**—help management assess relative competitiveness in the marketplace.
- **Productivity and Efficiency**—highlight underlying causes of financial performance.
- **Revenues, Expenses, and Profitability**—assess the potential of the organization to generate revenues in excess of expenses, whether in a for-profit or not-for-profit structure.

In the following discussion, note that the time and other variables associated with each indicator must be defined exactly. For example, in many locations, 40 hours per week is considered one full-time equivalent (FTE), but in other locations, an FTE is considered 9 hours per day. When does the day start and end? Are ratio values rounded up or down? Also note that there are frequently several formulas that can be used to derive the same indicator. Often, the alternative formulas reflect differences between profit and not-for-profit organizations.

6.2 Capacity and Utilization

Most capacity and utilization performance indicators are volume measures per reporting period (see Table 6.1). Many of these indicators can be referenced to a base year (i.e., trended).

6.2.1 Adjusted Patient Days

Patient days—the number of days of care rendered to adult and pediatric patients (newborns excluded) during the entire reporting period—adjusted for inpatient revenue (most common), outpatient services, or acuity of illness. Acuity-adjusted patient days of care, in addition to accounting for outpatient care, adjust for each patient's illness by assigning it a severity score, which indicates the presence or absence of a major or minor morbidity.

Formula 1: (Total revenue × Inpatient days)/Inpatient revenue

Formula 2: Inpatient days + (Outpatient days/5)

Note: The most appropriate denominator in Formula 2 depends on the relative contribution of outpatient services to staff demand.

6.2.2 Adjusted Discharges

Patient discharges, adjusted for inpatient revenue.

Formula: (Total revenue × Inpatient discharges)/Inpatient revenue

6.2.3 Available Bed Days

The total number of available beds multiplied by the number of days.

Formula: (Available beds × Days)

6.2.4 Average Length of Stay

Average number of days that patients were inpatients (patient days), a productivity measure often trended and compared with benchmarks. Because the majority of hospital expenses are related to

Table 6.1 Capacity and Utilization Performance Indicators

Capacity and Utilization
Adjusted discharges
Adjusted patient days
Admissions
Ancillary outpatient service visits/procedures
Average length of stay
Beds
Births
Capitated member visits
Discharges by service
Discharges to other acute care hospitals
Discharges to skilled nursing facilities
Emergency department visits
Fee-for-service visits
Home health service visits
Inpatient surgical operations
Nursing home admissions
Observation days
Occupancy rate
Outpatient surgical operations
Outpatient visits
Patient days
Proportion of outpatient revenue
Rehabilitation discharges
Routine discharges to home
Same-day surgery procedures
Total discharges

inpatient care, the current practice is to minimize average length of stay (ALOS) in favor of more lucrative outpatient services. ALOS naturally varies with severity of illness and patient health. As such, this indicator can be adjusted with a severity measure, such as the Case Mix Index (CMI), refined diagnosis-related group (RDRG), or commercially available severity score. As with Adjusted Patient Days, however, the adjustment is most often by inpatient revenue.

Formula 1: Patient Days/Total inpatient discharges

Formula 2: Patient Days/Number of admissions

Note: ALOS can be adjusted to ignore outlier, such as patients with stays beyond the 97th percentile.

6.2.5 Admissions

Number of inpatient admissions. Note that what constitutes an admission and over what time period should be defined exactly.

6.2.6 Ancillary Outpatient Service Visits/Procedures

Number of ancillary services, such as laboratory, radiology, physical therapy, speech therapy, and pharmacy, performed. This indicator is difficult to define because of the variability in how services are defined.

6.2.7 Beds

Total number of available hospital beds, also referred to as **Available Beds** or **Bed Count**. Beds should be precisely defined to include or exclude bassinets, warming beds, and beds out of service for some time during the reporting period. For example, the AHA defines beds as the number of beds, cribs, and pediatric bassinets that are set up and staffed for use by inpatients on the last day of the reporting period—that is, **Operational Beds**. Some hospitals report **Licensed Beds**, which reflects the number of beds the hospital can offer to patients by law, not the number of beds actually available.

6.2.8 Bed Turnover Rate

The average length of time, in days, that elapses between the discharge of one patient and the admission of the next inpatient to the same bed over any period of time. Occupied Bed Days is the sum of the occupied beds for each day.

Formula: (Available Bed Days − Occupied Bed Days)/Inpatient Discharges

6.2.9 Births

Total number of live births. Stillborns are not counted toward births.

6.2.10 Capitated Member Visits

Number of visits by capitated members to a physician's office. In a capitated system, the caregiver is paid a set amount per patient in advance, regardless of how many procedures are performed.

6.2.11 Discharges to Other Acute Care Hospitals

Number of inpatients discharged to other acute care hospitals, excluding discharges to long-term and rehabilitation hospitals. Normally trended.

6.2.12 Discharges to Skilled Nursing Facilities

Number of inpatients discharged to skilled nursing facilities (SNFs), which are institutions primarily engaged in providing skilled nursing care and rehabilitation services, not the care and treatment of mental diseases. Normally trended.

6.2.13 Discharges by Service

Number of inpatients discharged by medical services, that is, medicine, surgery, psychiatry, and neurology. Trended.

6.2.14 Emergency Department Visits

Number of emergency department outpatient visits.

6.2.15 Fee-for-Service Visits

Number of fee-for-service physician office visits. Fee for service is a traditional method of paying for medical services in which a physician charges a fee for each service provided, and the insurer or patient pays all or part of that fee.

6.2.16 Home Health Service Visits

Number of outpatient at-home visits.

6.2.17 Inpatient Surgical Operations

Number of inpatient surgical operations.

6.2.18 Nursing Home Admissions

Total number of inpatient admissions from nursing homes, which are facilities including intermediate care facilities and SNFs that provide daily nursing supervision and limited medical care to persons who do not require hospitalization.

6.2.19 Observation Days

Number of outpatient observation days. Observation is a level of care comprising short stay encounters for patients who require close nursing observation or medical management after surgery or during treatment.

6.2.20 Occupancy Rate

The percentage of all hospital beds occupied at a given time. Alternatively, occupancy rate is the average daily census divided by the number of hospital beds, cribs, and pediatric bassinets set up and staffed on the last day of the reporting period, expressed as a percentage. Average daily census is calculated by dividing the total annual number of inpatients, excluding newborns, by 365 days to derive the number of inpatients receiving care on an average day during the annual reporting period. Occupancy Rate indicates success at attracting patients.

Formula 1: (Beds occupied/Beds available) × 100

Formula 2: [(Total annual number of inpatients/365)/
Number of hospital beds, cribs, and pediatric bassinets set up
and staffed on the last day of the reporting period] × 100

6.2.21 Outpatient Surgical Operations

Total number of outpatient surgical procedures performed.

6.2.22 Outpatient Visits

Total number of ancillary outpatient service visits.

6.2.23 Patient Days

The number of adult and pediatric days of care rendered during the entire reporting period. Days of care for newborns are excluded. A patient day, also referred to as an "inpatient day" or "day of care" is a period of service between the census-taking hours on two successive calendar days. The day of discharge is counted only when the patient was admitted on the same day.

6.2.24 Proportion of Outpatient Revenue

Proportion of outpatient revenue to total patient revenue derived from outpatient sources. The ideal proportion is dependent on payer mix.

Formula: (Outpatient revenue/Total patient revenue)

6.2.25 Rehabilitation Discharges

Number of rehabilitation inpatients discharged. Trended. Rehabilitation patients are those admitted for treatment of mental illnesses, drug or alcohol addictions, or physical disabilities.

6.2.26 Routine Discharges to Home

Number of routine inpatient discharges to the patient's home. Trended.

6.2.27 Same-Day Surgery Procedures

Number of same-day outpatient surgical procedures.

6.2.28 Total Discharges

Total number of discharges during the reporting period, also called **Inpatient Discharges**. A discharge is a completed inpatient hospitalization. A hospitalization may be completed by death or by releasing the patient to the customary place of residence, a nursing home, another hospital, or other locations. Trended.

6.3 Capital Structure

Most Capital Structure performance indicators are simple ratios, expressed either as a proportion or as a percentage (see Table 6.2).

Table 6.2 Capital Structure Performance Indicators

Capital Structure
Average age of plant (years)
Capital expense as a percentage of total expenses
Cash flow to total debt
Debt-to-net worth ratio
Debt to capital (long term)
Debt to capitalization
Debt to equity (long term)
Debt to net assets (long term)
Debt to net assets (total)
Debt-to-service ratio
Financial leverage
Net worth
Point-of-service collections as a fraction of goal

6.3.1 Average Age of Plant (Years)

The average age of a healthcare organization's plant and equipment, computed by dividing the balance of accumulated depreciation by annual depreciation expense. The indicator describes the weighted average age of plant and equipment, taking into account assets ranging in financial life expectancy from less than 3 years to more than 30 years. A low value is desirable.

Formula: Accumulated depreciation/Depreciation expense

6.3.2 Capital Expense as a Percentage of Total Expenses

Interest expenses, combined with depreciation and amortization expenses as a percentage of total operating expenses. Capital Expense as a Percentage of Total Expenses is linked to Average Age of Plant because capital expenditures affect both ratios.

Formula: [(Interest expense + Depreciation and amortization expenses)/

Total operating expenses] × 100

6.3.3 Cash Flow to Total Debt

The proportion of cash flow to total liabilities, useful in determining financial viability and ability to repay principal and interest on an outstanding bond issue. A low ratio suggests future financial problems.

Formula: (Revenues and gains in excess of expenses and losses + Depreciation)/

(Current liabilities + Long-term debt)

6.3.4 Debt-to-Net Worth Ratio

An indicator or total debt coverage, in terms of the relationship between capital contributed by creditors and that contributed by shareholders. A low Debt-to-Net Worth Ratio suggests that either the organization could borrow money more easily or the organization is too conservative. A high ratio indicates that most of the risk in the organization is assumed by creditors, and obtaining additional money from outside sources may be difficult.

Formula: (Total debt/Net worth)

6.3.5 Debt to Capital (Long Term)

A measure of financial performance equal to long-term fixed obligations divided by liabilities and equity. Long-Term Debt to Capital over 50% is considered a risky level of debt.

Formula: [Long-term debt/(Liabilities + Owner's equity)] × 100

6.3.6 Debt to Capitalization

The proportion of long-term debt divided by the sum of long-term debt plus unrestricted net assets or equity. A high value implies reliance on debt financing and reduced ability to carry additional debt.

Formula 1: (Long-term debt + Capital leases − Current maturities)/
(Long-term debt + Capital leases −
Current maturities + Unrestricted net assets)

Formula 2: (Long-term debt + Short-term debt)/
(Long-term debt + Short-term debt +
Unrestricted fund balance)

Formula 3: (Long-term liabilities)/(Long-term liabilities + Unrestricted net assets)

6.3.7 Debt to Equity (Long Term)

A measure of the proportion of assets that are financed through long-term debt relative to those that are not. Used in for-profit organizations.

Formula: Total long-term debt/Owner's equity

6.3.8 Debt to Net Assets (Long Term)

A measure of the proportion of assets that are financed through long-term debt relative to those that are not. If the ratio is greater than 1, the organization is highly leveraged and could be in danger if creditors demand repayment of debt. Debt to Net Assets (Long Term), which applies to not-for-profit organizations, is equivalent to Debt to Equity (Long Term) in a for-profit organization.

Formula: Total long term liabilities/(Total assets − Total liabilities)

6.3.9 Debt to Net Assets (Total)

A measure of the proportion of assets that are financed through debt through long- and short-term liabilities. If the ratio is greater than 1, most of the assets are financed through debt. More conservative than Debt to Net Assets (Long Term).

Formula: Total liabilities/(Total assets − Total liabilities)

6.3.10 Debt-to-Service Ratio

A measure of total debt–service coverage from the organization's cash flow. Indicates how effectively the organization is meeting its annual principal and interest charges on its outstanding debt. A high ratio suggests good ability to repay debt.

Formula 1: (Net income + Provisions for income taxes + Interest expense +

Depreciation)/(Interest expenses + Current loans + Notes payable)

Formula 2: (Total margin + Depreciation expense + Interest expense)/

(Principal payment + Interest expense)

6.3.11 Financial Leverage

The degree to which the organization assumes a larger proportion of debt than the amount invested by its owners. An organization with a ratio greater than 2.0 is considered highly leveraged and may be at risk for bankruptcy if it is unable to make payments on its debt. A highly leveraged organization may also be unable to find new lenders in the future. Financial leverage is not always bad, however, because it can increase the shareholders' return on their investment, and there may be tax advantages associated with borrowing.

Formula: (Total liabilities + Owner's equity)/Owner's equity

6.3.12 Net Worth

Total assets minus total liabilities for the organization, also called **Net Assets**. Indicates the organization's excess of assets over liabilities and the organization's value with respect to equity.

Formula: Total assets − Total liabilities

6.3.13 Point-of-Service Collections as a Fraction of Goal

Percentage of target monies collected at the time of service. A higher percentage is associated with improved cash flow, reduced billing costs, and reduced turnover to collection agencies.

Formula: (Collection/Goal) × 100

6.4 Liquidity

Liquidity indicators, which provide a measure of how easily the organization can get to cash to pay for debt, are often computed as ratios. Moreover, there tend to be multiple formulas for a given indicator—a point to consider when comparing other organizations' liquidity figures. Table 6.3 lists common liquidity indicators.

Table 6.3 Liquidity Performance Indicators

Liquidity
Acid test ratio
Average collection period (days)
Average payment period (days)
Cash on hand (days)
Cash-to-claims payable ratio
Current ratio
Cushion ratio
Days in net patient accounts receivable
Days in net total receivable
Days in unpaid claims
Fixed assets-to-net worth ratio
Maximum annual debt service coverage
Maximum annual debt service coverage ratio (DSCR)
Quick ratio
Turnover of cash ratio

6.4.1 Acid Test Ratio

The most stringent test of liquidity, based on how much cash is readily available relative to current liabilities.

Formula: (Cash + Marketable securities)/(Current liabilities)

6.4.2 Average Collection Period (Days)

Accounts receivable over net revenue. A measure of the number of days required to collect outstanding debts, also called **Days in Accounts Receivable**. A shorter period is preferable.

Formula 1: (Accounts receivables)/(Revenue/day)

Formula 2: (Accounts receivables)/(Total revenue/365)

Formula 3: (Net patient accounts receivables × 365)/Net patient revenue

6.4.3 *Average Payment Period (Days)*

A measure of the average length of credit given to the organization by its suppliers. The trend is often more important than the actual value.

Formula 1: Total current liabilities/[(Total operating expenses +

Total other expenses − depreciation expense)/365]

Formula 2: (Total current liabilities × 365)/Total operating expenses −

Depreciation and amortization expenses)

6.4.4 *Cash on Hand (Days)*

The number of days the organization is able to cover operating expenses with its current cash on hand. Days Cash on Hand indicates the organization's ability to meet its obligations as they come due without needing to liquidate any investments. A rising ratio signifies increasing liquidity. A high ratio compared to benchmarks is preferable.

Formula 1: (Cash on hand + Market securities)/

[(Total operating expenses − Depreciation)/365]

Formula 2: (Unrestricted cash and investments × 365)/

(Total operating expenses − Depreciation and amortization expenses)

Formula 3: (Cash on hand + Market securities + Investments)/

[(Total operating expenses − Depreciation expense)/365]

Formula 4: [(Cash + Cash equivalents + Board-designated funds for capital) × 365]/

(Total operating expenses − Depreciation and amortization expenses)

Formula 5: Unrestricted cash and investments/Daily cash operating expenses

Formula 6: (Cash + Cash equivalents + Short-term investments)/

[(Total medical and hospital Expenses + Administrative expenses)/365]

Note: Market securities include other temporary investments.

6.4.5 Cash-to-Claims Payable Ratio

The organization's ability to pay off health, medical, and accounts payable with available cash and cash equivalents.

Formula: (Cash and equivalents)/Claims payable

6.4.6 Current Ratio

Current assets divided by current liabilities. An indication of the organization's ability to meet short-term debt obligations with its current base of short-term assets. A ratio greater than 1 signifies liquidity. While a ratio of 2 is considered good, a higher ratio could mean cash is not being put to best use. Current Ratio ignores timing of cash received and paid out.

Formula 1: (Total current assets/Total current liabilities)

Formula 2: (Current assets − Inventory − Accounts receivable)/Current liabilities

Note: Formula 2 is considered more conservative than Formula 1.

6.4.7 Cushion Ratio

The amount of cash and cash equivalents available to pay off future peak debt service. A higher ratio is preferable.

Formula 1: Unrestricted cash and investments/Estimated future peak debt service

Formula 2: Unrestricted cash and investments/Maximum annual debt service

Formula 3: (Cash and cash equivalents + Board-designated funds for capital)/
Estimated future peak debt service

6.4.8 Days in Net Patient Accounts Receivable

Number of days worth of net patient revenue, which is uncollected and tied up in net receivables (total receivables less uncollectible receivables).

Formula: (Accounts receivable − Allowances for uncollectible)/
(Total operating revenue/365)

Note: Total operating revenue = Net patient revenue.

6.4.9 Days in Net Total Receivable

A measure of the time it takes to collect account receivables. Most useful for trend analysis and comparison with benchmarks.

Formula: (Accounts receivable + Notes receivable + Other receivables −
Allowance for uncollectible)/(Total operating revenue/365)

Note: Total operating revenue = Net patient revenue.

6.4.10 Days in Unpaid Claims

The number of days of claims the organization owes its members. This ratio is useful for determining whether an organization is meeting its health and medical liabilities effectively, efficiently, and in a timely manner. An upward trend suggests that the organization is becoming less able to meet its obligations as they come due.

Formula: Claims payable/[(Total medical + Hospital expenses)/365]

6.4.11 Fixed Assets-to-Net Worth Ratio

Indicates the portion of net worth composed of fixed assets. A low ratio suggests net worth may be more liquid. High ratio suggests the organization may be hurting for working capital (monies tied up in buildings and equipment).

Formula: (Fixed assets/Net worth)

6.4.12 Maximum Annual Debt Service Coverage

The ratio of revenue to cover debt to the estimated peak in debt payments.

Formula: Net revenue available for debt service/
Estimated future peak principal payments and interest expense.

6.4.13 Maximum Annual Debt Service Coverage Ratio

The ratio of net operating income to maximum annual debt service. The higher the debt service coverage ratio (DSCR), the more net operating income is available to service the debt.

Formula: Revenue − (Excess income + Interest, depreciation, and amortization expenses −
Amortization of advances fees)/Maximum annual debt services

6.4.14 Quick Ratio

The ratio of all assets quickly convertible into cash to all current liabilities, excluding inventory. A measure of liquidity without relying on the sale of inventory, used to evaluate creditworthiness. The ratio ignores timing of receipts and payments.

Formula: (Total current assets – Inventory)/Total current liabilities

6.4.15 Turnover of Cash Ratio

Net revenue divided by working capital. Indicates adequacy of organization's working capital. A low Turnover of Cash Ratio suggests that funds are tied up in short-term, low-yield assets. A high ratio suggests an inability to pay bills.

Formula: (Net revenue – Working capital)

6.5 Patient and Payer Mix

Patient and payer (payor) mix indicators reflect the influence of third-party payers on the well-being of the organization. Most of the key performance indicators are volume measures associated with patient and payer groups (see Table 6.4).

The Patient and Payer Mix indicators described here are referenced to Zip code, the CMI, the Outpatient Prospective Payment System (OPPS) and Ambulatory Payment Classification (APC), medical diagnosis (International Classification of Diseases, 9th Revision, with Clinical Modifications/International Classification of Diseases, 10th Revision [ICD-9-CM/ICD-10]), Diagnostic Related Group (DRG), and medical procedure (Healthcare Common Procedure Coding System/Current Procedural Terminology [HCPCS/CPT] code).

Zip code, the code of letters and digits added to a postal address to aid in sorting mail, is a good indicator of patient origin. Zip code maps are readily available from a variety of sources, allowing management to easily assess patient demographics. Zip code is referred to as Postal code in some countries.

The CMI is the severity statistic used as a weight for Medicare patients. CMI varies from 0.4 to over 16.0, with an average of 1.0. The CMI is used to categorize patients into statistically and clinically homogeneous groups of acuity and resource requirements. By increasing payments to a medical facility for those patients with increased care needs, the case mix system is intended to provide more appropriate care, with payment accurately based on the care needs. Similarly, the Wage Index measures relative differences in the average hourly wage for the hospitals in each labor market area compared to the national average hourly wage. See the Centers for Medicare and Medicaid Services (CMS) portal (*www.cms.gov*) for more information on the use and derivation of the CMI and Wage Index.

The APC is a payment group under the Hospital OPPS that is composed of procedures that are clinically similar and associated with similar resource requirements. The OPPS is a prospective payment system (i.e., a reimbursement program in which Medicare pays a predetermined amount for each inpatient discharge) established by the Balanced Budget Act of 1997. All services paid by Medicare are classified into APC groups, and a payment rate is established for each APC.

Table 6.4   Patient and Payer Mix Performance Indicators

Patient and Payer Mix
Admissions by patient origin
Admissions increase/decrease by patient origin
Average cost by medical service adjusted by CMI
Average inpatient charges by DRG
Average inpatient charges by medical service
Average inpatient cost by DRG
Average inpatient cost by Medical Service
Average inpatient payment by medical service
Average inpatient reimbursed by DRG
Average length of stay by DRG
Average length of stay by medical service
Average outpatient cost by ambulatory patient classification
Average outpatient cost by medical diagnosis
Average outpatient cost by medical procedure
Average outpatient payment by ambulatory patient classification
Average outpatient payment by medical diagnosis
Average outpatient payment by medical procedure
Average total inpatient charge by medical service
Average total outpatient charge by ambulatory patient classification
Average total outpatient charge by medical diagnosis
Average total outpatient charge by medical procedure
Cost per (adjusted) discharge
Days of inpatient care by patient origin
Inpatient case mix index trend
Inpatient charges by patient origin
Inpatient medical DRGs (%) trend

(Continued)

Table 6.4 (Continued)   Patient and Payer Mix
Performance Indicators

Patient and Payer Mix
Inpatient service mix index (SMI) by medical service
Inpatient surgical DRGs (%) trend
Market share by patient origin
Medicare case mix index by medical service
Deaths trend
Medicare inpatients by DRG
Medicare inpatients by medical service
Outpatient claims by ambulatory patient classification
Outpatient claims by medical diagnosis
Outpatient claims by medical procedure
Paid hours per adjusted discharge
Patient claims by medical service
Supply cost per adjusted discharge
Total outpatient outlier amount by medical diagnosis
Total outpatient payment by ambulatory patient classification
Total outpatient payment by medical diagnosis (ICD-9/ ICD-10)
Total outpatient payment by medical procedure (HCPCS/ CPT code)
Units of inpatient service by medical service
Units of outpatient service by ambulatory patient classification
Units of outpatient service by medical procedure

The ICD-9-CM was developed in the United States by modifying the ICD-9 coding system developed by the World Health Organization. Although the ICD-10 has been available for years, in some organizations, the ICD-9-CM is still the standard for comparison of birth, death, and disease data. The ICD-9-CM consists of a tabular list of disease codes, an alphabetical diseases index, and a list of surgical, diagnostic, and therapeutic procedures. Downloads of complete listings of the two-part numeric code and frequent addenda are available through the CMS website.

The DRG is a case-mix classification system that groups together patients who are similar clinically in terms of diagnosis and treatment, and in their consumption of hospital resources.

The classification system is so named because it organizes a grouping of the more than 10,000 ICD-9 codes into a more manageable, approximately 500 groups. As a component of performance indicators, DRGs allow comparisons of resource use across hospitals with varying mixes of patients.

The HCPCS/CPT coding system for medical procedures is the preferred system of coding and describing healthcare services in the United States. The purpose of CPT is to provide a uniform language that accurately describes medical, surgical, and diagnostic services, and thereby serves as an effective means for reliable nationwide communication among physicians and other healthcare providers, patients, and third parties. CPT coding assigns a five-digit code to each service or procedure provided by a physician.

- **Admissions by Patient Origin:** Total admissions by Zip code.
- **Admissions Increase/Decrease by Patient Origin:** Percent change in admissions, by Zip code, relative to the prior year.
- **Average Cost by Medical Service Adjusted by CMI:** Average cost of medical service adjusted by CMI.
- **Average Inpatient Charges by DRG:** A tabulation of inpatient charges, keyed to DRG code.
- **Average Inpatient Charges by Medical Service:** A tabulation of average inpatient charges by hospital medical service.
- **Average Inpatient Cost by DRG:** A tabulation of average inpatient cost by DRG. Average inpatient cost is calculated using the costs-to-charge ratios established for inpatient services.
- **Average Inpatient Cost by Medical Service:** A tabulation of average inpatient cost by medical service, adjusted using cost-to-charge ratios. Medicare has explicit guidelines for establishing cost-to-charge ratios.
- **Average Inpatient Payment by Medical Service:** A tabulation of average inpatient payments, by medical services.
- **Average Inpatient Reimbursement by DRG:** A tabulation of inpatient reimbursements by DRG. Excludes deductibles, coinsurance, or reimbursement for patients covered under Medicare HMOs.
- **Average Length of Stay by DRG:** A tabulation of ALOS by DRG.
- **Average Length of Stay by Medical Service:** A tabulation of ALOS by medical service.
- **Average Outpatient Cost by Ambulatory Patient Classification:** A tabulation of average outpatient cost, by Medicare APC, adjusted using hospital's cost-to-charge ratio.
- **Average Outpatient Cost by Medical Diagnosis:** A tabulation of average outpatient cost, by ICD-9/ICD-10 code, adjusted using hospital's cost-to-charge ratio.
- **Average Outpatient Cost by Medical Procedure:** A tabulation of average outpatient cost, by CPT code, adjusted using hospital's cost-to-charge ratio.
- **Average Outpatient Payment by Ambulatory Patient Classification:** A tabulation of average outpatient payment, by Medicare APC.
- **Average Outpatient Payment by Medical Diagnosis:** A tabulation of average outpatient payment, by ICD-9/ICD-10 code.
- **Average Outpatient Payment by Medical Procedure:** A tabulation of average outpatient payment, by CPT code.
- **Average Total Inpatient Charge by Medical Service:** A tabulation of average total inpatient charges by medical service, before adjustments for cost of service, deductible, or coinsurance.
- **Average Total Outpatient Charge by Ambulatory Patient Classification:** A tabulation of average total outpatient charges by APC code, before adjustments for cost of service, deductible, or coinsurance.

- **Average Total Outpatient Charge by Medical Diagnosis:** A tabulation of average total outpatient charges by ICD-9/ICD-10 code, before adjustments for cost of service, deductible, or coinsurance.
- **Average Total Outpatient Charge by Medical Procedure:** A tabulation of average total outpatient charges by CPT code, before adjustments for cost of service, deductible, or coinsurance.
- **Cost per (Adjusted) Discharge:** Cost per inpatient discharge, CMI, and Wage Index Adjusted.
- **Days of Inpatient Care by Patient Origin:** A tabulation of days of inpatient care (days of care) by patient Zip code of residence. A day of care is a day of service between the census-taking hours on two successive calendar days, the day of discharge being counted only when the patient was admitted the same day.
- **Inpatient CMI Trend:** The inpatient CMI, referenced to prior years. The CMI is a severity statistic used as a weight for Medicare patients. CMI varies from 0.4 to over 16.0, with an average of 1.0.
- **Inpatient Charges by Patient Origin:** A tabulation of inpatient charges by Zip code of patient residence.
- **Inpatient Medical DRGs (%) Trend:** The percentage of inpatients classified with medical (as opposed to surgical) DRGs, referenced to prior years.
- **Inpatient Service Mix Index (SMI) by Medical Service:** A tabulation of the average relative weight of the procedures billed for a service (SMI), by service.
- **Inpatient Surgical DRGs (%) Trend:** The percentage of inpatients classified with surgical (as opposed to medical) DRGs, referenced to prior years.
- **Market Share by Patient Origin:** Percentage of total hospital admissions (for all hospitals) with a Zip code.
- **Medicare CMI by Medical Service:** A tabulation of CMI by medical service.
- **Deaths Trend:** Number of inpatient deaths, referenced to prior years.
- **Medicare Inpatients by DRG:** A tabular listing of Medicare inpatient totals by DRG.
- **Medicare Inpatients by Medical Service:** A tabulation of Medicare inpatients, listed by medical service.
- **Outpatient Claims by Ambulatory Patient Classification:** A tabulation of outpatient claim totals by APC.
- **Outpatient Claims by Medical Diagnosis:** A tabulation of outpatient claim totals by ICD-9/ICD-10 coding.
- **Outpatient Claims by Medical Procedure:** A tabulation of outpatient claim totals by CPT code.
- **Paid Hours per Adjusted Discharge:** Paid hours per discharge, CMI Adjusted. A lower value is preferred.
- **Patient Claims by Medical Service:** A tabulation of patient claim totals by medical service.
- **Supply Cost per Adjusted Discharge:** A tabulation of supply costs per discharge, Case Mix and Wage Index Adjusted.
- **Total Outpatient Outlier Amount by Medical Diagnosis:** A tabulation of total outpatient outlier amount by ICD-9/ICD-10 code. Outlier payments are supplements to prospective payments to defray some of the expenses in caring for the most costly cases.
- **Total Outpatient Payment by Ambulatory Patient Classification:** A tabulation of total outpatient payment by APC.

- **Total Outpatient Payment by Medical Diagnosis (ICD-9/ICD-10):** A tabulation of total outpatient payment by ICD-9/ICD-10 code.
- **Total Outpatient Payment by Medical Procedure (HCPCS/CPT Code):** A tabulation of total outpatient payment by CPT code.
- **Units of Inpatient Service by Medical Service:** A tabulation of total number of units of inpatient service delivered, ordered by medical service.
- **Units of Outpatient Service by Ambulatory Patient Classification:** A tabulation of total number of units of inpatient service delivered, ordered by APC.
- **Units of Outpatient Service by Medical Procedure:** A tabulation of total number of units of inpatient service delivered, ordered by CPT code.

6.6 Pricing Strategy

- **Procedure Markup Ratios:** The ratio of cost to charge for medical supplies, laboratory, diagnostic radiology, and ancillary services.

6.7 Productivity and Efficiency

The productivity and efficiency performance indicators described here are all ratio measures that reflect administrative overhead, employee performance, and how well assets are being put to use (see Table 6.5).

Table 6.5   Productivity and Efficiency Performance Indicators

Productivity and Efficiency
Administrative expense ratio
Benefits as percentage of total salary and wages
Coding specificity rate
FTEs per adjusted patient day (occupied bed)
Inventory turnover
Operating ratio
Overtime as a percentage of production hours
Revenue per FTE
Relative value units dispensed
Total asset turnover ratio
Total available staff hours
Total procedures performed

6.7.1 Administrative Expense Ratio

The percentage of operating revenue consumed by administrative costs, sometimes referred to as indirect costs. Measures the percentage of the organization's revenue needed to meet its administrative costs.

Formula: (Total administration cost/Operating revenue) × 100

6.7.2 Benefits as Percentage of Total Salary and Wages

Employee benefits over salary and wages. The regional benchmarks are often more important than actual values, especially in tight labor markets where benefits are one way of attracting and retaining healthcare personnel.

Formula: [Benefits/(Salary + Wages)] × 100

6.7.3 Coding Specificity Rate

A measure of the accuracy and efficiency with which a hospital acquires and records clinical data. Specificity is the degree to which the principal diagnosis is specific, for example, as opposed to "other."

Formula: Number of patient records that are specific/Total number of patient records

6.7.4 FTEs per Adjusted Patient Day (Occupied Bed)

The ratio of FTEs to an approximation of patient days. The ratio can be misleading if outsourced labor and contract labor are not considered. Furthermore, inpatient revenue may be a poor denominator, depending on the ratio of inpatient to outpatient services supported by the organization. One FTE is commonly defined as 8 hours per day, 5 days per week, but local definitions may differ.

Formula: (FTEs × 365)/[(Total revenue × Patient days)/(Inpatient revenue)]

6.7.5 Inventory Turnover

The ratio of annual revenue to inventory. Low Inventory Turnover is a sign of inefficiency because inventory usually has a return rate of zero.

Formula: (Total operating revenue + Nonoperating revenue)/Inventory

Note: Total operating revenue = Net patient revenue; Nonoperating revenue = Nonpatient revenue.

6.7.6 Operating Ratio

Operating expenses over operating revenues. A measure of operating efficiency.

Formula: (Total operating expenses − Depreciation and amortization expense)/
(Total revenue − Amortization of advance fees)

6.7.7 Overtime as a Percentage of Production Hours

The percentage of overtime hours worked per reporting period. Significant overtime is an indicator of poor resource management and planning.

Formula: (Overtime/Total production hours) × 100

6.7.8 Relative Value Units Dispensed

Number of relative value units (RVUs) dispensed during physician office visit, pharmacy visit, or other clinical encounter. An RVU can be a composite measure of the time, difficulty, and resources associated with a procedure or a time measure. RVUs can be specialty-specific. For example, in the early 1990s, the Health Care Financing Administration (HCFA) adapted the Relative Value Scale from the American College of Radiology and created a comprehensive Resource-Based Relative Value Scale. The professional component of each RVU on the scale is used as the basis for measuring the work output by radiologists.

6.7.9 Revenue per FTE

Revenue generated per full-time employee equivalent is a raw measure of productivity that can be used against benchmarks, including those outside of the healthcare industry.

Formula: Total revenues/Total FTEs

6.7.10 Total Asset Turnover Ratio

Total operating revenue and nonoperating revenue divided by total assets. A measure of how well assets are being used to generate revenue. A higher Total Asset Turnover Ratio indicates more revenue is generated from every dollar invested.

Formula 1: (Total operating revenue + Nonoperating revenue)/Total assets

Formula 2: (Total operating revenue)/Total assets

Note: Total operating revenue = Net patient revenue; Nonoperating revenue = Nonpatient revenue.

6.7.11 Total Available Staff Hours (TASH)

The total staff hours available for patient care duties, which may be markedly different from payroll hours. Managerial responsibilities, staff meetings, lectures, continuing medical education (CME) workshops, and other activities reduce staff hours available for patient care. Typically averaged for a department or service.

Formula: (Payroll time − Time spent in nonclinical duties)

6.7.12 Total Procedures Performed

The sum of all CPT codes billed during a period. These codes can be linked to reimbursement to obtain revenue per physician or service, and to RVUs to obtain a productivity measure.

One of the most difficult challenges in the area of performance and efficiency is quantifying clinician productivity, especially as it relates to clinical outcomes. Consider how a pharmacist's clinical performance might be measured. Simply counting the number of prescriptions per hour provides a measure of efficiency, but there is no tie to clinical outcomes. The number of potential drug–drug interactions discovered by a pharmacist before drug administration has a clear clinical benefit, but a relatively high number of interventions might reflect a poorly trained or functioning physician and not necessarily the pharmacist's performance.

The two clinical areas in which productivity and efficiency metrics are relatively mature are radiology and pathology. The productivity of physicians and technicians in both specialties is often measured by metrics linked to CPT codes. In Radiology, CMS maintains a freely available list of CPT codes linked to the relative professional and technical work associated with each procedure. Using a plain chest film as the basic unit of measure, radiology procedures are ranked in a way that allows radiologists performing different volumes of various procedures to be compared equitably. For example, a radiologist who reads 35 chest films in one day may be less productive than a radiologist who performs only 10 more complex, time-consuming procedures, such as a brain computed tomography with contrast agents. More information on how the CPT-linked RVUs can be used to measure radiologists' productivity is available from the Radiology Business Management Association (*www.rbma.org*).

The College of American Pathologists (CAP) provides a fee-for-service productivity measurement system called Laboratory Management Index Program (LMIP). The system is a simplified version of the RVU system available to radiologists. CAP provides a table of CPT codes linked to Standard Billable Test (SBT) units—essentially RVUs—that reflect the work associated with a given procedure. More information on LMIP is available from the CAP (*www.CAP.org*).

6.8 Revenues, Expenses, and Profitability

Revenues, expenses, and profitability indicators, as listed in Table 6.6, include many of the core measures that appear in a healthcare organization's annual report.

6.8.1 Bad Debt as a Percentage of Gross Revenues

Bad debt is accounts receivables that will likely remain uncollectible and will be written off; this does not include charity debt.

Formula: (Bad debt/Gross revenues) × 100

Table 6.6   Revenues, Expenses, and Profitability Performance Indicators

Revenues, Expenses and Profitability
Bad debt as a percentage of gross revenues
Earnings before interest, taxes, depreciation, amortization and rent (EBITDAR)
Excess margin
Expenses per adjusted patient day (EPAPD)
Expenses per adjusted discharge (EPAD)
Investment turnover ratio
Medical expense ratio
Net margin
Net profit (loss)
Net profit ratio
Operating revenue
Operating profit (loss)
Operating profit margin
Overall expense ratio
Operating margin

6.8.2 Earnings before Interest, Taxes, Depreciation, Amortization, and Rent (EBITDAR)

This indicator is an approximate measure of operating cash flow, calculated by examining earnings before the deduction of interest expenses, taxes, depreciation, amortization, and rent.

Formula: Net income + Interest + Depreciation and amortization + Lease cost

6.8.3 Excess Margin

The proportion of total revenue that exceeds total expenses before taxes. Excess Margin considers nonoperating revenues such as contributions and income from investments and auxiliary operations, as well as operating sources. It indicates a major source of revenue available to the organization for replacing capital, acquiring technology, and expanding services.

Formula: (Total revenue − Total expense)/

(Total operating revenue + Nonoperating revenue)

6.8.4 Expenses per Adjusted Patient Day (EPAPD)

Expenses per patient days adjusted for outpatient services provided. This is an indicator of actual cost performance that can be benchmarked and trended to reveal performance relative to past performance and similar organizations.

Formula: Total expenses/Adjusted patient days

6.8.5 Expenses per Adjusted Discharge (EPAD)

Total operating expenses divided by the number of adjusted discharges is a measure of the average cost of delivering care on a per-unit basis.

Formula: Total operating expenses/Adjusted discharges

Note: Discharges are adjusted for CMI and wages by factoring in data from Medicare Case Mix and the CMS Wage Index.

6.8.6 Investment Turnover Ratio

Net revenue over total assets indicates amount of revenue generated by assets. Low ratio may indicate too many assets and/or insufficient revenue.

Formula: (Net revenue/Total assets)

6.8.7 Medical Expense Ratio

The percentage of the organization's premium revenue needed to meet its direct medical costs.

Formula: [(Medical + Hospital expenses)/Operating revenue] × 100

6.8.8 Net Margin

Net results as a function of net revenue. An indicator of profitability, useful when trended against itself or compared with external benchmarks.

Formula: [(Total operating revenue − Total operating expense + Nonoperating revenue)/

(Total operating revenue + Nonoperating revenue)] × 100

Note: Total operating revenue = Net patient revenue; Nonoperating revenue = Nonpatient revenue.

6.8.9 Net Profit (Loss)

The operating surplus (or deficit) after considering taxes and extraordinary costs.

Formula: Total Revenue − (Direct medical costs −
Administrative costs − Taxes and extraordinary expenses)

6.8.10 Net Profit Ratio

Earnings over net revenue, ignoring the effects of debt and taxes. Net Profit Ratio is a measure of management's effectiveness. Debt and taxes are ignored to facilitate comparison with other organizations because they can distort earnings. A high Net Profit Ratio suggests that expenses are being held down or the organization is getting more out of its assets and debt.

Formula: (Earnings before interest and taxes/Net revenue)

6.8.11 Operating Revenue

An indicator of how much revenue the organization generated from its primary lines of business.

Formula: Total revenue − (Revenue from investments,
interest, and other miscellaneous sources)

6.8.12 Operating Profit (Loss)

The money the organization has after covering its direct medical and administrative expenses. Operating Profit is an indicator of how well the organization is covering all of its costs of operations.

Formula: Operating revenue − (Direct medical costs + Administrative costs)

6.8.13 Operating Profit Margin

The percentage of return the organization achieved on its operations. Operating Profit Margin indicates how effectively the organization performed with respect to its ability to cover its fixed and variable expenses.

Formula: [(Operating revenue − (Direct medical +
Administrative costs))/Operating revenue] × 100

6.8.14 Overall Expense Ratio

The percentage of the organization's premium revenue needed to meet its direct medical and administrative costs.

Formula: [(Direct medical costs + Administrative costs)/(Operating revenue)] × 100

6.8.15 Operating Margin

A measure of profit or loss per unit operating revenue. Operating Margin is trended to determine the organization's financial direction. A positive trend suggests that resources are available for growth and service expansion, the purchase of replacement equipment, acquisition of new technology, and maintenance of the physical plants.

Formula: [(Total operating revenue − Total operating expense)/
Total operating revenue)] × 100

Note: Total operating revenue = Net patient revenue. Excludes investment income.

6.8.16 Personnel Expense as a Percentage of Total Operating Revenue

A better measure of overall productivity than FTEs per Adjusted Patient Day because it considers contract labor. However, outsourced services can distort the indicator. A downward trend is desirable.

Formula: [(Salary expense + Contract labor + Fringe benefits)/Total operating revenue] × 100

Note: Total operating revenue = Net patient revenue.

6.8.17 Rate of Return on Revenue

Net profit over net revenue. An indicator of profitability derived from each dollar in revenue. A low ratio suggests that expenses are being held down.

Formula: (Net profit/Net revenue)

6.8.18 Rate of Return on Assets

A measure of profitability generated by the use of assets. Rate of Return on Assets measures how much profit (or excess revenue over expenses for a not-for-profit) is generated for each dollar invested in assets.

Formula 1: (Net profits/Total assets) × 100

Formula 2: (Excess revenues/Total assets)

Note: Formula 2 applies to not-for-profit organizations.

6.8.19 *Rate of Return on Investment*

Indicates profitability, in terms of how much net profit was derived from a shareholder's investment in the organization. A low Rate of Return on Investment suggests that management is inefficient or the organization is too conservative and not earning up to its potential. A high rate of return suggests that management is efficient, the organization is undercapitalized, or borrowing is the source of much of the capitalization.

Formula: (Net profit/Net worth) × 100

6.8.20 *Return on Assets (ROA)*

A fundamental measure of the efficiency with which the organization manages its assets. ROA, which shows the amount of income for every dollar tied up in assets, is normally computed on a pre-tax basis so that the figure can be compared with organizations having different financing strategies.

Formula: (Net income/Total assets) × 100

6.8.21 *Return on Equity*

A measure of the return rate for each dollar of owners' equity. Equivalent to Return on Net Assets for not-for-profits.

Formula 1: (Earnings after tax/Shareholders' equity) × 100

Formula 2: [Net income/(Total assets − Total liabilities)] × 100

6.8.22 *Return on Net Assets*

A measure of the return rate for each dollar of net assets in not-for-profit organizations. Equivalent to Return on Equity used with for-profits.

Formula: (Excess revenues over expenses/Net assets)

6.9 Further Thinking

Financial performance indicators as benchmarks are useful for intra-organization comparisons of performance. However, financial benchmarks should be viewed as guidelines subject to interpretation. The limitations of using performance indicators as benchmarks include the following:

- **A cyclical financial environment.** Many indicators ignore the normal fluctuations in the economy.
- **Different case mix.** Patient demographics and disease patterns may differ significantly from one hospital to the next.
- **Hospital size.** Economy of scale may improve financial ratios for larger hospitals.
- **Hospital age.** Debt load and start-up problems favor established organizations.
- **Geographical differences.** Local conditions may affect indicators in subtle ways.
- **Parent organization influence.** Parent organizations may cover expenses and provide financial backing, hiding, or confounding economic problems.
- **Offsetting indicators.** Heavy reserves can offset current medical and administrative expense ratios.

One of the greatest challenges associated with benchmarks and nonclinical performance indicators is selecting the ones that make the most sense for the organization. One of several good commercial references for financial, operational, and utilization performance indicators that can be used as benchmarks is the annual *Almanac of Hospital Financial and Operating Indicators*, published by Optum360. The 2017 copy contains a review of more than 70 financial ratios and operating indicators.

Another source of nonclinical performance indicators is the various quality organizations that focus primarily on clinical performance. For example, the Agency for Healthcare Research and Quality (AHRQ) lists several utilization indicators. England's National Health Service (NHS) defines a comprehensive set of performance indicators, including a number of Capacity and Utilization indicators. Both the AHRQ and NHS provide detailed descriptions of their nonclinical performance indicators on their websites. Additional resources are cited below.

Sources and Further Reading

2017 Almanac of Hospital Financial & Operating Indicators. Optum360Coding.com.

American Hospital Association (AHA). *www.aha.org.*

Berger, S. *Fundamentals of Health Care Financial Management: A Practical Guide to Fiscal Issues and Activities.* 2002, San Francisco: Jossey-Bass.

Healthcare Financial Management Association (HFMA). *www.hfma.org.*

Hospital Nurse Staffing and Quality of Care. Research in Action, Issue 14. AHRQ Publication No. 04-0029, March 2004. Rockville, MD: Agency for Healthcare Research and Quality.

Radiologist Productivity Measurement. Radiology Business Management Association. *www.rbma.org.*

Silbiger, S. *The Ten Day MBA.* 1999. New York: William Morrow and Company.

Tracy, J. *The Fast-Forward MBA in Finance.* 2nd ed. 2002, New York: John Wiley & Sons.

Zelman, W. et al. *Financial Management of Health Care Organizations: An Introduction to Fundamental Tools, Concepts, and Applications.* 2nd ed. 2003. Cornwall, Great Britain: Blackwell Publishing.

Chapter 7

Clinical Indicators

At first glance, a healthcare organization could be defined by a handful of nonclinical indicators, such as capacity and utilization, and a few clinical indicators, such as mortality, readmission rate, and complication rate. In reality, the appropriateness of these broad quality indicators is a function of the healthcare organization, the environment, and the patient load. Often, the issue is the degree of applicability.

Consider that mortality may be a more meaningful indicator in a "surgical" hospital, compared with a medical hospital. In an OB/GYN hospital focused on labor and delivery in which the mortality rate is presumably low, there is less information to be gained from a mortality indicator than, say, the rate of severe lacerations with vaginal delivery. Similarly, not-for-profit organizations, which are generally more complex than for-profits, place greater emphasis on indicators that reflect patient satisfaction.

Because of the need for specific clinical indicators that have been validated for particular uses, there are dozens of organizations promoting clinical quality standards (see Appendix A). The Agency for Healthcare Research and Quality (AHRQ), the National Committee for Quality Assurance (NCQA), Centers for Medicare and Medicaid Services (CMS), and the Joint Commission on Accreditation of Healthcare Organizations (JCAHO) are prominent in the United States. England's National Health Service (NHS) and Australia's Victoria Health Service are significant forces in the healthcare quality movement outside of the United States.

This chapter provides an overview of the major quality standards in healthcare that are sources for clinical Performance Management indicators, including a synopsis of the indicators developed by the major healthcare quality groups. In addition to the sources discussed here, readers are encouraged to explore the literature for information on indicators developed at major US and Canadian centers of excellence.

7.1 Definitions

Because of space limitations, only indicator titles—sometimes supplemented with high-level definitions—are provided here. As noted in Chapter 5, the complete definition of a clinical indicator should be exhaustive. Many of the indicators defined here are risk-adjusted using a reference model based on patient demographics and other factors beyond the healthcare organization's control that affect the quality of care. The adjustment allows more meaningful comparison among organizations.

Often, the adjustments offered by the quality organizations are adequate. However, markedly different patient demographics or clinical specialties may require the development of local adjustments. For example, for its long-term care facilities, the Department of Veterans Affairs (VA) developed a model of decline in functional status in patients as an adjustment to distinguish facilities in terms of quality of care. The empirically derived model includes age, time between assessments, baseline functional status, terminal illness, pressure ulcers, pulmonary disease, cancer, arthritis, congestive heart failure, substance-related disorders, and neurologic disorders. With the adjustment, the ranking of VA facilities changed to reflect the risk-adjusted outcomes. A discussion of various modeling techniques that can be used to adjust raw Key Performance Indicator (KPI) data, such as weighted averages, appears in Chapter 11.

Following is a catalog of primarily clinical KPIs, arranged by source. As noted earlier, please refer to the complete definition before using an indicator. Often, an indicator is much more complex than the name suggests. More information is provided for the major clinical indicators in the appendices.

7.2 Agency for Healthcare Research and Quality

The AHRQ is the health services research arm of the US Department of Health and Human Services. It publishes four quality indicator modules that can be used as a source of clinical performance indicators: Inpatient Quality Indicators, Prevention Quality Indicators, Patient Safety Indicators, and Pediatric Quality Indicators. These indicators, which are defined in Appendix B, are listed below.

7.2.1 Inpatient Quality Indicators

Inpatient Quality Indicators (IQIs) reflect the quality of care inside hospitals. IQIs include inpatient mortality; utilization of procedures for which there are questions of overuse, underuse, or misuse; and volume of procedures for which there is evidence that a higher volume is associated with lower mortality. The IQIs, listed in Table 7.1, are of four types:

- Volume
- Mortality for inpatient procedures
- Mortality for inpatient conditions
- Utilization

Volume indicators are based on the assumption that hospitals performing more of certain intensive, complex procedures may have better outcomes for those procedures. Mortality indicators for inpatient procedures include those procedures for which high mortality may be associated with poorer quality of care. Mortality indicators for inpatient conditions include conditions for which high mortality may be associated with deficiencies in the quality of care. Utilization indicators examine procedures that may be overused, underused, or misused.

High or low rates for these indicators may represent inappropriate or inefficient delivery of care. As with the other indicators discussed here, these are simply tools that, when used correctly and in the environments in which they were intended, can provide meaningful data to decision makers.

Table 7.1 AHRQ Inpatient Quality Indicators (IQIs)

Inpatient Quality Indicators
PQI 01 Diabetes short-term complications admission rate
PQI 02 Perforated appendix admission rate
PQI 03 Diabetes long-term complications admission rate
PQI 05 Chronic obstructive pulmonary disease (COPD) or asthma in older adults admission rate
PQI 07 Hypertension admission rate
PQI 08 Heart failure admission rate
PQI 09 Low birth weight rate
PQI 10 Dehydration admission rate
PQI 11 Bacterial pneumonia admission rate
PQI 12 Urinary tract infection admission rate
PQI 14 Uncontrolled diabetes admission rate
PQI 15 Asthma in younger adults admission rate
PQI 16 Lower-extremity amputation among patients with diabetes rate
PQI 90 Prevention quality overall composite
PQI 91 Prevention quality acute composite
PQI 92 Prevention quality chronic composite
PQI 93 Prevention quality diabetes composite
PQI Appendix A—Admission codes for transfers
PQI Appendix B—Cardiac procedure codes
PQI Appendix C—Immuno-compromised state diagnosis and procedure codes
PQI Appendix D—Definitions of neonate, newborn, normal newborn, and outborn
PQI 01 Diabetes short-term complications admission rate
PQI 02 Perforated appendix admission rate
PQI 03 Diabetes long-term complications admission rate
PQI 05 Chronic obstructive pulmonary disease (COPD) or asthma in older adults admission rate
PQI 07 Hypertension admission rate
PQI 08 Heart failure admission rate

(Continued)

Table 7.1 (Continued)   AHRQ Inpatient Quality Indicators (IQIs)

PQI 09 Low birth weight rate
PQI 10 Dehydration admission rate
PQI 11 Bacterial pneumonia admission rate
PQI 12 Urinary tract infection admission rate
PQI 14 Uncontrolled diabetes admission rate
PQI 15 Asthma in younger adults admission rate
PQI 16 Lower-extremity amputation among patients with diabetes rate
PQI 90 Prevention quality overall composite
PQI 91 Prevention quality acute composite
PQI 92 Prevention quality chronic composite
PQI 93 Prevention quality diabetes composite
PQI Appendix A—Admission codes for transfers

Source: Inpatient Quality Indicators Overview. qualityindicators.ahrq.gov/Modules/iqi_resources
.aspx. Accessed April 16, 2017.

7.2.2 Prevention Quality Indicators

Prevention Quality Indicators (PQIs) (see Table 7.2) consist of ambulatory care sensitive conditions and hospital admissions that evidence suggests could have been avoided through high-quality outpatient care or that reflect conditions that could be less severe if treated early and appropriately. For example, several of the PQIs are related to diabetes, a condition controllable through diet, exercise, medication, and care of the lower extremities. With proper outpatient care, including patient education, the uncontrolled diabetes admission rate should be very low.

7.2.3 Patient Safety Indicators

Patient Safety Indicators (PSIs), listed in Table 7.3, focus on potentially preventable instances of complications and other iatrogenic events resulting from exposure to the healthcare system. These include presumably avoidable complications of anesthesia, such as aspiration of broken teeth and other objects, decubitus ulcers due to neglect, and surgical instruments left in the body after surgery.

7.2.4 Pediatric Quality Indicators

Pediatric Quality Indicators (PDIs/NQIs), which are specific to children, are shown in Table 7.4. They reflect the quality of outpatient and other healthcare services in an area. For example, the Pediatric Asthma Admission Rate PQI is defined by the AHRQ as the admission rate for pediatric asthma per 100,000 population of children under age 18, excluding newborns and other neonates, within a geographic area.

Table 7.2   AHRQ Prevention Quality Indicators (PQIs)

Prevention Quality Indicators
PQI 01 Diabetes short-term complications admission rate
PQI 02 Perforated appendix admission rate
PQI 03 Diabetes long-term complications admission rate
PQI 05 Chronic obstructive pulmonary disease (COPD) or asthma in older adults admission rate
PQI 07 Hypertension admission rate
PQI 08 Heart failure admission rate
PQI 09 Low birth weight rate
PQI 10 Dehydration admission rate
PQI 11 Bacterial pneumonia admission rate
PQI 12 Urinary tract infection admission rate
PQI 14 Uncontrolled diabetes admission rate
PQI 15 Asthma in younger adults admission rate
PQI 16 Lower-extremity amputation among patients with diabetes rate
PQI 90 Prevention quality overall composite
PQI 91 Prevention quality acute composite
PQI 92 Prevention quality chronic composite

Source: Prevention Quality Indicators Overview. qualityindicators.ahrq.gov/Modules/pqi_resources .aspx. Accessed April 17, 2017.

7.2.5 *AHRQ National Healthcare Quality and Disparities Report Measures*

In addition to IQIs, PQIs, and PSIs, AHRQ relies on many more quality measures from a variety of sources for its annual National Healthcare Quality and Disparities Report. Information on individual measures is available through chartbooks, accessible on the AHRQ website. The chartbooks, and the measures they describe, are in the following areas:

- ■ Access to healthcare
- ■ Patient safety
- ■ Person- and family-centered care
- ■ Care coordination
- ■ Care affordability
- ■ Healthy living
- ■ Effective treatment

Table 7.3 AHRQ Patient Safety Indicators (PSIs)

Patient Safety Indicators
PSI 02 Death rate in low-mortality diagnosis related groups (DRGs)
PSI 03 Pressure ulcer rate
PSI 04 Death rate among surgical inpatients with serious treatable conditions
PSI 05 Retained surgical item or unretrieved device fragment count
PSI 06 Iatrogenic pneumothorax rate
PSI 07 Central venous catheter-related blood stream infection rate
PSI 08 In-hospital fall with hip fracture rate
PSI 09 Perioperative hemorrhage or hematoma rate
PSI 10 Postoperative acute kidney injury requiring dialysis
PSI 11 Postoperative respiratory failure rate
PSI 12 Perioperative pulmonary embolism or deep vein thrombosis rate
PSI 13 Postoperative sepsis rate
PSI 14 Postoperative wound dehiscence rate
PSI 15 Unrecognized abdominopelvic accidental puncture/laceration rate
PSI 16 Transfusion reaction count
PSI 17 Birth trauma rate—injury to neonate
PSI 18 Obstetric trauma rate—vaginal delivery with instrument
PSI 19 Obstetric trauma rate—vaginal delivery without instrument
PSI 21 Retained surgical item or unretrieved device fragment rate
PSI 22 Iatrogenic pneumothorax rate

Source: Patient Safety Indicators Overview. qualityindicators.ahrq.gov/Modules/psi_resources .aspx. Accessed April 16, 2017.

- ■ Rural healthcare
- ■ Women's healthcare
- ■ Hispanic healthcare

A list of the types of measures in each of these 10 areas, summarized from the corresponding chartbooks, is shown in Table 7.5. For details on the actual measures in each category, see Appendix E.

Table 7.4 AHRQ Pediatric Quality Indicators

Pediatric Quality Indicators
NQI 01 Neonatal iatrogenic pneumothorax rate
NQI 02 Neonatal mortality rate
NQI 03 Neonatal blood stream infection rate
PDI 01 Accidental puncture or laceration rate
PDI 02 Pressure ulcer rate
PDI 03 Retained surgical item or unretrieved device fragment count
PDI 05 Iatrogenic pneumothorax rate
PDI 08 Perioperative hemorrhage or hematoma rate
PDI 09 Postoperative respiratory failure rate
PDI 10 Postoperative sepsis rate
PDI 11 Postoperative wound dehiscence rate
PDI 12 Central venous catheter-related blood stream infection rate
PDI 13 Transfusion reaction count
PDI 14 Asthma admission rate
PDI 15 Diabetes short-term complications admission rate
PDI 16 Gastroenteritis admission rate
PDI 17 Perforated appendix admission rate
PDI 18 Urinary tract infection admission rate
PDI 90 Pediatric quality overall composite
PDI 91 Pediatric quality acute composite
PDI 92 Pediatric quality chronic composite
PDI Appendix A—Operating room procedure codes
PDI Appendix C—Surgical MS-DRGs
PDI Appendix E—Medical MS-DRGs
PDI Appendix F—High-risk immuno-compromised state diagnosis and procedure codes
PDI Appendix G—Intermediate-risk immuno-compromised state diagnosis codes
PDI Appendix H—Infection diagnosis codes
PDI Appendix I—Definitions of neonate newborn normal newborn and outborn

(*Continued*)

Table 7.4 (Continued)   AHRQ Pediatric Quality Indicators

PDI Appendix J—Admission codes for transfers
PDI Appendix K—Stratification
PDI Appendix L—Low birth weight categories
PDI Appendix M—Cancer

Source: Patient Safety Indicators Overview. qualityindicators.ahrq.gov/Modules/pdi_resources .aspx. Accessed April 16, 2017.

Table 7.5   AHRQ's Annual National Healthcare Quality and Disparities Report Measure Categories

Access
Health insurance
Service
Infrastructure
Affordability
Access problems due to healthcare costs
Inefficiency
Supplemental
Care Coordination
Transitions
Potentially avoidable ER visits
Integration of medical information
Electronic health record
Effective Treatment
Cardiovascular disease
Cancer
Chronic kidney disease
Diabetes
HIV and AIDS
Mental health and substance abuse
Musculoskeletal disease
Respiratory disease

(Continued)

Table 7.5 (Continued) AHRQ's Annual National Healthcare Quality and Disparities Report Measure Categories

Healthy Living
Maternal and child healthcare
Access
Effectiveness
Person-centered care
Care coordination
Lifestyle modification
Clinical preventive services
Immunization
Rehabilitation
Supportive and palliative care
Relief of suffering
High-quality palliative care
Hispanic Healthcare
Breast cancer
Colorectal cancer
Other cancer
Cardiovascular care
Substance abuse
Diabetes
Mental health
Infant mortality and maternity care
Patient Safety
Healthcare-associated infections
Procedure-related events
Nursing home setting
Home health setting
Ambulatory setting
Culture

(Continued)

Table 7.5 (Continued)   AHRQ's Annual National Healthcare Quality and Disparities Report Measure Categories

Organizations
Person- and Family-Centered Care
Communications doctor's office
Communications hospital
Communications home health
Engagement in decision making
End of life
Rural Healthcare
Access to healthcare
Patient safety
Person- and family-centered care
Communication and care coordination
Prevention and treatment of leading causes of morbidity and mortality
Healthy living
Affordability
Women's Healthcare
Access to healthcare
Patient safety
Person- and family-centered care
Communication and care coordination
Prevention and treatment of leading causes of morbidity and mortality
Healthy living
Affordability

Source: 2014 National Healthcare Quality & Disparities Report Chartbooks. Content last reviewed October 2015. Agency for Healthcare Research and Quality, Rockville, MD. www.ahrq .gov/research/findings/nhqrdr/2014chartbooks/index.html

7.3 The National Quality Measures Clearinghouse

The National Quality Measures Clearinghouse (NQMC), sponsored by the AHRQ, provides online information on how to select, apply, and interpret various quality measures submitted to the AHRQ. The NQMC website (*www.qualitymeasures.ahrq.gov/browse/mesh-tag*) supports a database of measures organized by domain, measurement setting, MeSH tag, and organization. As of

April 2017, NMC offers a total of 2296 measure summaries, 2151 of which are healthcare delivery and 145 of which are population health measures. Because quality measures often overlap in what they attempt to measure, the website provides a means of comparing and contrasting measures in four different views: Measure Domain, Measurement Setting, MeSH Tag, and Organization.

The Measure Domain view provides access to measures in the categories shown in Table 7.6. Most of the measures are Clinical Quality measures, with the largest contribution from process measures, followed by patient experience.

The Measurement Setting view provides access to the measures in the settings shown in Table 7.7. Most of the measures are associated with ambulatory/office-based care, followed by hospital outpatient. The listing in Table 7.7 is ranked by the number of measures contributed to by the setting.

Table 7.6   NQMC Holding, Indexed by Measure Domain, Ranked by Contribution

Measure Domain
Clinical Quality Measures
Process
Patient experience
Outcome
Structure access
Related Healthcare Delivery Measures
Use of services
User-enrollee
Health state
Cost management
Population Health Quality
Population process
Population structure
Population outcome
Population access
Population experience
Related Population Health Measures
Population health state
Population use of services
Environment
Population management
Population cost

Table 7.7 Partial Listing of NQMC Holding, Indexed by Measurement Setting, Ranked by Contribution

Measure Setting
Ambulatory/office-based care
Hospital inpatient
Hospital outpatient
Managed care plans
Ambulatory procedure/imaging center
Community healthcare
Skilled nursing facilities/nursing homes
Emergency department
Intensive care units
Behavioral healthcare
Home care
State/provincial public health programs
Transition
Assisted living facilities
National public health programs
Hospices
Rehabilitation centers
Emergency medical services
Patient-centered medical homes
Residential care facilities
Accountable care organizations
Substance use treatment programs/centers
Ancillary services

The MeSh Tag view uses terms derived from the US National Library of Medicine's Medical Subject Headings (MeSH) classification for diseases and conditions and provides access to the measures in three major categories: Disease/Condition, Treatment/Intervention, and Health Services Administration. The breakdown of this view, ranked by contribution, is provided in Table 7.8.

Table 7.8 Partial Listing of NQMC Holding, Indexed by MeSH Tag, Ranked by Contribution

MeSH Tag
Healthcare
Diseases
Analytical, diagnostic, and therapeutic techniques and equipment
Disciplines and occupation
Psychiatry and psychology
Anthropology, education, sociology, and social phenomena
Chemicals and drugs
Disciplines and occupations
Information science
Health services administration
Phenomena and processes

The Organization view provides access to measures by contributing organization. Not surprisingly, the contributor with the greatest number of measures is the AHRQ, with 117 quality measures. Table 7.9 lists the top contributing organizations, ranked by number of measures contributed. See the AHRQ website for the complete list of organizations.

Table 7.9 Partial Listing of NQMC Holding, Indexed by Organization, Ranked by Contribution

Organization
Institute for Clinical Systems Improvement
Agency for Healthcare Research and Quality
Centers for Medicare and Medicaid Services
American College of Surgeons
Centers for Disease Control
Council of State and Territorial Epidemiologists
American College of Radiology
American Medical Directors Association
The Joint Commission
American Academy of Neurology

7.4 National Committee for Quality Assurance

The NCQA is a not-for-profit organization that acts as a watchdog for the quality of care delivered by managed care plans and physician organizations. Its accreditation process includes the Healthcare Effectiveness Data and Information Set (HEDIS) and patient satisfaction surveys. HEDIS, NCQA's tool used by health plans to collect data about the quality of care and service they provide, consists of a set of performance measures that indicate how well health plans perform in key areas such as quality of care, access to care, and member satisfaction with the health plan and its physicians. HEDIS requires health plans to collect data in a standardized way so that comparisons are fair and valid. The 2017 HEDIS specification describes 81 measures across five domains of care. An overview of these quality measures is shown in Table 7.10.

There is also a smaller set of HEDIS measures targeting physicians. A listing of the Physician Measures 2017 is provided in Appendix F. NCQA emphasizes that HEDIS measures are not clinical guidelines, and should not be used as such.

7.5 CMS Outcomes and Assesment Information Set (OASIS-C2)

The CMS maintains an Outcomes and Assessment Information Set (OASIS-C2) to assess the quality of home health agencies (HHAs). CMS requires Medicare-certified HHAs to collect and transmit OASIS data for all adult patients whose care is reimbursed by Medicare and Medicaid. There are outcomes measures as well as process measures, summarized in Tables 7.11 and 7.12, respectively. For full descriptions of the measures, including numerator, denominator, and exceptions, see Appendices G and H. In addition, see the CMS website for manuals on Home Health Quality Reporting and the associated measures.

7.6 Centers for Medicare and Medicaid Services and Joint Commission on Accreditation of Healthcare Organizations

In 2003, CMS and JCAHO released a joint specifications manual, the Specifications Manual for National Hospital Inpatient Quality Measures. The goal was to align their common national performance measures and to share one set of documentation. The measures common to CMS and JCAHO were confined to five areas: acute myocardial infarction, heart failure, surgical infection prevention, pneumonia, and pregnancy. In the years since then, the common set has periodically morphed into the measures listed in Table 7.13.

Note that behind the quality measures listed in Table 7.13 is a data dictionary, detailed description of numerator and denominator, population algorithms, associated ICD-10 (International Classification of Diseases, 10th Revision) codes, and exceptions to the use of each measure. These and other parameters associated with each of the common measures are detailed in the periodically updated Specifications Manual.

In addition to developing standards for domestic healthcare organizations, JCAHO has an international presence, in the form of the Joint Commission International (JCI). The JCI has established standards for clinical laboratories, hospitals, academic medical center hospitals, primary care centers, long-term care centers, medical transport organizations, and facilities involved

Table 7.10 HEDIS Performance Measures: ECHO—Experience of Care and Health Outcomes

Health Plan Employer Data and Information Set (HEDIS)
Effectiveness of Care
Adherence to antipsychotic medications for individuals with schizophrenia
Adult BMI assessment
Annual monitoring for patients on persistent medications
Antidepressant medication management
Appropriate testing for children with pharyngitis
Appropriate treatment for children with upper respiratory infection
Aspirin use and discussion
Asthma medication ratio
Breast cancer screening
Cardiovascular monitoring for people with cardiovascular disease and schizophrenia
Care for older adults
Cervical cancer screening
Childhood immunization status
Chlamydia screening in women
Colorectal cancer screening
Comprehensive diabetes care
Controlling high blood pressure
Diabetes monitoring for people with diabetes and schizophrenia
Diabetes screening for people with schizophrenia or bipolar disorder who are using antipsychotic medications
Disease-modifying anti-rheumatic drug therapy for rheumatoid arthritis
Fall risk management
Flu vaccinations for adults ages 18–64
Flu vaccinations for adults ages 65 and older
Follow-up after emergency department visit for alcohol and other drug dependence
Follow-up after emergency department visit for mental illness
Follow-up after hospitalization for mental illness

(Continued)

Table 7.10 (Continued)   HEDIS Performance Measures: ECHO—Experience of Care and Health Outcomes

Follow-up care for children prescribed ADHD medication
Immunizations for adolescents
Lead screening in children
Management of urinary incontinence in older adults
Medical assistance with smoking and tobacco use cessation
Medicare health outcomes survey
Medication management for people with asthma
Medication reconciliation post-discharge
Metabolic monitoring for children and adolescents on antipsychotics
Non-recommended cervical cancer screening in adolescent females
Non-recommended PSA-based screening in older men
Osteoporosis management in women who had a fracture
Osteoporosis testing in older women
Persistence of beta-blocker treatment after a heart attack
Pharmacotherapy management of COPD exacerbation
Physical activity in older adults
Pneumococcal vaccination status for older adults
Potentially harmful drug–disease interactions in the elderly
Statin therapy for patients with cardiovascular disease
Statin therapy for patients with diabetes
Use of high-risk medications in the elderly
Use of multiple concurrent antipsychotics in children and adolescents
Use of spirometry testing in the assessment and diagnosis of COPD
Weight assessment and counseling for nutrition and physical activity for children/ adolescents
Access/Availability
Adults' access to preventive/ambulatory health services
Annual dental visit
CAHPS Health Plan Survey 5.0H, Adult Version

(Continued)

Table 7.10 (Continued)   HEDIS Performance Measures: ECHO—Experience of Care and Health Outcomes

CAHPS Health Plan Survey 5.0H, Child Version
Call answer timeliness
Children with chronic conditions
Children's and adolescents' access to primary care practitioners
Initiation and engagement of alcohol and other drug dependence treatment
Prenatal and postpartum care
Use of first-line psychosocial care for children and adolescents on antipsychotics
Utilization
Adolescent well-care visits
Ambulatory care
Antibiotic utilization
Frequency of ongoing prenatal care
Frequency of selected procedures
Identification of alcohol and other drug services
Inpatient utilization—general hospital/acute care
Mental health utilization
Standardized healthcare-associated infection ratio
Well-child visits in the first 15 months of life
Well-child visits in the third, fourth, fifth and sixth years of life
Risk Adjusted Utilization Measures
Emergency department utilization
Hospitalization for potentially preventable complications
Inpatient hospital utilization
Plan all-cause readmissions
Relative Resource Use
Relative resource use for people with:
Asthma
Cardiovascular conditions

(Continued)

Table 7.10 (Continued)   HEDIS Performance Measures: ECHO—Experience of Care and Health Outcomes

COPD
Diabetes
Hypertension
Health Plan Descriptive Information
Board certification
Enrollment by product line
Enrollment by state
Language diversity of membership
Race/ethnicity diversity of membership
Total membership
Weeks of pregnancy at time of enrollment

Source: The 2017 HEDIS Technical Specifications Manual. www.ncqa.org/hedis-quality-mea surement/hedis-measures/hedis-2017

in the care continuum. Unlike the JCAHO standards, which involve specific indicators, JCI standards are intended to ensure that processes are in place. It does not specify exactly what these processes must entail, however.

7.7 The NHS of England

The NHS of England publishes, generally on a monthly basis, statistics on the performance of the health service at the organization level, NHS Trusts, NHS Foundation Trusts, and independent sector organizations. The list of various indicators used as the basis for these publications is shown in Table 7.14. Moreover, the NHS provides extensive, transparent documentation for each measure on the NHS website.

7.8 Australian National Safety and Quality Health Service Standards

The Australian Commission on Safety and Quality in Health Care leads and coordinates the quality of healthcare in Australia. One product of the Commission is the Australian National Safety and Quality Health Service (NSQHS) Standards. The 10 areas covered by these standards are listed in Table 7.15. As with the NHS standards, although the NSQHS quality standards are specific to Australia, they may have applicability to a Performance Management Initiative in the

Table 7.11   Summary of OASIS Outcomes Measures by Measure Title

OASIS-Based Outcomes Measures
Acute care hospitalization
Discharged to community
Emergency department use with hospitalization
Improvement in ambulation–locomotion
Improvement in bathing
Improvement in bed transferring
Improvement in bowel incontinence
Improvement in confusion frequency
Improvement in dyspnea
Improvement in lower body dressing
Improvement in management of oral medications
Improvement in pain interfering with activity
Improvement in status of surgical wounds
Improvement in toilet transferring
Improvement in upper body dressing
Percent of residents or patients with pressure ulcers that are new or worsened
Stabilization in bathing
Stabilization in bed transferring
Stabilization in grooming
Stabilization in management of oral medications
Stabilization in toilet transferring
Stabilization in toileting hygiene

Source: Home_Health_Outcomes_Measures_Table_OASIS_C2_02_03_17_Final.pdf, downloaded from https://www.cms.gov/Medicare/Quality-Initiatives-Patient-Assessment-Instruments /HomeHealthQualityInits/HHQIQualityMeasures.html

United States. For example, one focus of the standards is preventing and controlling infection—a universal challenge in any hospital. The standards address issues such as healthcare providers cleaning their hands before and after a procedure. The full text of the standard is available in PDF form from the Australian Commission on Safety and Quality in Health Care website, *www.safetyandquality.gov.au/publications/national-safety-and-quality-health-service-standards*. A synopsis of the standards is provided in Appendix J.

Table 7.12 Summary of OASIS Process Measures by Measure Title

OASIS-Based Process Measures
Depression assessment conducted
Diabetic foot care and patient/caregiver education implemented during all episodes of care
Diabetic foot care and patient education in plan of care
Drug education on all medications provided to patient/caregiver during all episodes of care
Drug regimen review conducted with follow-up for identified issues
Influenza immunization contraindicated
Influenza immunization offered and refused for current flu season
Influenza immunization received for current flu season
Multifactor fall risk assessment conducted for all patients who can ambulate
Pneumococcal polysaccharide vaccine contraindicated
Pneumococcal polysaccharide vaccine ever received
Pneumococcal polysaccharide vaccine offered and refused
Timely initiation of care

Source: Home-Health-Process-Measures-Table_OASIS-C2_02_03_17_Final-Revised-1.pdf, downloaded from https://www.cms.gov/Medicare/Quality-Initiatives-Patient-Assessment
-Instruments/HomeHealthQualityInits/PBQIProcessMeasures.html

7.9 Commercial and Private Entities

Commercial and private entities are a useful source of ideas for grouping or developing an evolving set of clinical indicators. Before the need to demonstrate Meaningful Use, it was commonplace for EMR vendors to develop their own library of performance indicators. The problem with using these indicators was often that the definition, including the adjustments, was proprietary and not open to inspection or modification. In addition, indicators were sometimes tied to particular data collection hardware systems.

Today, the major EMR vendors target the obvious quality organizations and their standards to develop a core set of indicators, such as reporting requirements for CMS, the Joint Commission, and, of course, Meaningful Use. As noted in Chapter 2, there are also private industry awards that establish their own criteria for identifying high performing hospitals. The best example is perhaps the Truven Health 100 Top Hospitals Study, which is based on 11 indicators (5 clinical and 6 nonclinical).

7.10 Medical Specialty Groups

Many of the medical specialty groups have some type of quality or performance improvement program. The College of American Pathologists (CAP) and American College of Radiology (ACR) are examples of specialty groups that have developed comprehensive lists of quality measures or

Table 7.13   Summary of CMS and JCAHO Combined National Hospital Quality Measures

National Hospital Inpatient Quality Measures
Severe Sepsis and Shock
Early management bundle—identifies intervention within 3 hours and 6 hours of presentation of severe sepsis
Venous Thrombosis
Hospital acquired potentially preventable venous thromboembolism
Emergency Department
Median time from ED arrival to ED departure for admitted ED patients—Overall rate median Time from ED arrival to ED departure for admitted ED patients—Reporting measure
Median time from ED arrival to ED departure for admitted ED patients—Psychiatric/Mental Health Patients
Admit decision time to ED departure time for admitted patients—Overall rate
Admit decision time to ED departure time for admitted patients—Reporting measure admit Decision time to ED departure time for admitted patients—Psychiatric/mental health patients
Immunization
Influenza immunization
Substance Use
Alcohol use screening alcohol use brief intervention provided or offered
Alcohol use brief intervention
Alcohol and other drug use disorder treatment provided or offered at discharge
Alcohol and other drug use disorder treatment at discharge
Alcohol and drug use: assessing status after discharge
Tobacco Treatment
Tobacco use screening
Tobacco use treatment provided or offered
Tobacco use treatment provided or offered at discharge
Status assessment after discharge

Source: Specifications Manual for National Hospital Inpatient Quality Measures Discharges 01-01-17 (1Q17) through 12-31-17 (4Q17).

Table 7.14 NHS Statistical Publications

Accident and emergency attendances and emergency admissions
Ambulance quality indicators
Bed availability and occupancy
Cancelled elective operations
Cancer patient experience survey
Cancer waiting times
Combined performance summary
Consultant-led referral to treatment (RTT) waiting times
Critical care bed capacity and urgent operations cancelled
Delayed transfers of care
Dementia assessment and referral
Dental commissioning
Diagnostic imaging dataset
Diagnostic test waiting times and activity
Direct access audiology waiting times
Early intervention in psychosis waiting times
Extended access to general practice
General practice (GP) patient survey
General practice patient survey: dental results
Hospital activity
Mental health community teams activity
Mixed sex accommodation breaches
National patient and staff surveys
NHS 111 minimum data set
NHS staff survey in England
Overall patient experience scores
Patient reported outcome measures (PROMs)
Venous thromboembolism (VTE) risk assessment
Winter daily situation reports

Source: https://www.england.nhs.uk/statistics/statistical-work-areas.

Table 7.15   List of Ten NSQHS Standards

NSQHS Standards
Governance
Partnering with consumers
Preventing and controlling infection
Medication safety
Patient ID and procedure matching
Clinical handover
Blood and blood products
Pressure injuries
Clinical deterioration in acute healthcare
Preventing falls

Source: Australian Commission on Safety and Quality in Health Care (ACSQHC). Vital Signs 2013: The State of Safety and Quality in Australian Health Care. Sydney: ACSQHC, 2013.

indicators that can serve as the basis for department-level clinical indicators. Other groups, with focuses ranging from the ER and infection control to pediatrics, oncology, and cardiology, can be located on the web (see Appendix A).

7.10.1 College of American Pathologists

In 1989, the CAP introduced Q-probes, a modular quality improvement program aimed at identifying and describing key indicators in anatomic pathology and laboratory medicine. Ten years later, the CAP introduced Q-Tracks, a voluntary program that required quarterly data submission with renewal on an annual basis. Studies on individual indicators, such as patient wristband error rates, have shown Q-Tracks to be effective in reducing medication errors. Misidentification of patients for lab testing is a major cause of medical errors. Table 7.16 lists examples of the 2017 Q-Tracks indicators or quality monitors. Most of the quality tracks, which embody multiple indicators, are focused on clinical pathology. Extensive details of these and additional measures are available online at *www.cap.org*.

7.10.2 American College of Radiology

The ACR Appropriateness Criteria are intended as a best-practices guide for radiologists, radiation oncologists, and referring physicians in making decisions regarding radiologic imaging and treatment. As of 2017, the ACR Appropriateness Criteria include nearly 250 clinical topics with more than 1000 variants. The criteria under each category are a potential basis for clinical indicators. Table 7.17 lists major categories of the ACR Appropriateness Criteria.

The resources available through the ACR are considerable. Each of the categories listed in Table 7.17 contains 10–30 topics, each topic associated with a narrative and rating table, evidence table, and literature search. Moreover, each of the nearly 250 variants can be extensive. For example, the Cardiac diagnostic category is associated with a dozen topics, from suspected aortic dissection to suspected infective

Table 7.16 Examples of Q-Tracks Measures

2017 Q-TRACKS
Patient Identification Accuracy—QT1
Wristband error rate (%)
Blood Product Wastage—QT4
Overall blood wastage rate (%)
Wastage rates by blood component type (%)
Gynecologic Cytology Outcomes—QT5
Predictive value of positive cytology (%)
Sensitivity (%)
Screening/interpretation sensitivity (%)
Critical Values Reporting—QT10
Total critical values reporting rate (%)
Inpatient critical values reporting rate (%)
Outpatient critical values reporting rate (%)
Turnaround Time of Troponin—QT15
Median troponin order-to-report turnaround time (minutes)
Troponin turnaround time compliance rate (%)

Source: American College of Pathologists, *www.cap.org.*

endocarditis. Suspected Aortic Dissection is linked to a table of appropriate radiologic procedures, a discussion of the disease and appropriate imaging, and a list of 65 references. In short, the ACR provides ample material that can be used to form the basis for a performance indicator.

7.11 Centers of Excellence

The numerous centers of excellence in the United States, Canada, England, and Australia are a good source of clinical indicators, as long as the source organization is similar to the target organization. For example, the Mayo Clinic (www.mayoclinic.org) focuses on quality measures in three areas: outcomes, process, and patient satisfaction. Outcomes measures include mortality ratio, patient safety, readmission rates, and transplant quality indicators. Process measure areas include stroke and venous thromboembolism. Patient satisfaction measures cover both inpatient and outpatient areas.

In searching for indicators used at regional and national centers of excellence, the nature of the organization and patient population are as critical as the organization's reputation. Often, a local

Table 7.17 ACR Appropriateness Criteria Major Diagnostic and Interventional Categories

ACR Criteria Diagnostic Categories
Breast
Cardiac
Gastrointestinal
Musculoskeletal
Neurologic
Pediatric
Thoracic
Urologic
Vascular
Women's
ACR Criteria Interventional Categories
Interventional radiology
ACR Criteria Radiation Oncology
Bone
Brain
Breast
Gastrointestinal
Gynecology
Head and neck
Lung
Lymphoma
Prostate

Source: American College of Radiology, *www.acr.org.*

hospital with similar patient demographics and services can provide insight into the indicators most applicable to the organization's needs. Also, at the department level, there are likely to be indicators that can be applied locally, regardless of the particulars at the organization level.

Consider the perioperative services indicators listed in Table 7.18. Virtually every anesthesia unit in the United States, regardless of size, patient demographics, profit or not-for-profit, has to deal with cancelled cases, surgical delays, and OR turnover time. There may be local differences

Table 7.18 Perioperative Services Indicators

Block scheduling utilization
Cancellation rate and count
First case of the day start time
Hospital admissions after "day" surgery
Inventory utilization
OR hours per anesthetist
Patient temperature on arrival in PACU
Supply and equipment utilization
Surgical delays
Surgical schedule management
Turnover time (OR)
Unexpected admissions to ICU
Unexpected readmissions after surgery
Utilization (OR)

Source: Michael Bailin, MD, Chief of Anesthesia, Tenet Healthcare Group.

such as surgical schedule management, but most of the indicators listed in Table 7.18 can be applied to US hospitals. The challenges are defining each indicator exactly and then determining how to capture and manage the data accurately and in a timely manner. In this regard, it is often worth a site visit to a hospital with a similar infrastructure and budget to investigate how the information technology (IT) department supports the hospital's Performance Management Initiative.

7.12 Further Thinking

In reviewing the sources of clinical performance indicators above, it is important to keep in mind that they may or may not be aligned with the needs of a particular healthcare organization. Furthermore, what constitutes the "best" indicators for a department or healthcare enterprise may change from year to year. Each of the batteries of indicators listed above has been revised since their introduction. Some indicators have been dropped, while others have been added. Reasons for change include the following:

■ Poor planning. The initial indicators were chosen without regard to local practices or validity.
■ A shift in patient demographics.
■ A change in management's focus.

In planning for the automated collection of performance indicator data, readers should consider making provision for ease in modifying the data flow so that little or no IT infrastructure reengineering is required to meet future indicator data collection and reporting.

Sources and Further Reading

2014 National Healthcare Quality and Disparities Report Chartbooks. Content last reviewed October 2015. Rockville, MD: Agency for Healthcare Research and Quality. *www.ahrq.gov/research/findings /nhqrdr/2014chartbooks/index.html*

2014 National Healthcare Quality and Disparities Report Data Query Tool. *nhqrnet.ahrq.gov/inhqrdr/data /query*

2015 National Healthcare Quality and Disparities Report and 5th Anniversary Update on the National Quality Strategy. Rockville, MD: Agency for Healthcare Research and Quality. AHRQ; April 2016. AHRQ Pub. No. 16-0015.

American Journal of Medical Quality. us.sagepub.com/en-us/nam/american-journal-of-medical-quality /journal201749

Commission for Health Improvement (CHI), *www.chi.nhs.uk/Ratings/more_information.asp*

Healthy People 2020. Access to Health Services. Washington, DC: U.S. Department of Health and Human Services, Office of Disease Prevention and Health Promotion. www.healthypeople.gov/2020/topics -objectives/topic/Access-to-Health-Services. Accessed April 17, 2017.

NCQA, Health Plan Accreditation (HPA)—1016 Standards. *www.ncqa.org/programs/accreditation /health-plan-accreditation-2016-standards.*

NHS performance indicators. *Br J Healthcare Comput Info Manage* 2002, 19(5): 18–20.

NIST, 2004 Criteria for Performance Excellence Baldrige National Quality Program. 2004, Gaithersburg, MD: National Institute of Standards and Technology.

Quality and Mayo Clinic. *www.mayoclinic.org/about-mayo-clinic/quality/quality-measures.* Accessed April 22, 2017.

Specifications Manual for Joint Commission National Quality Measures Version 2017A is periodically updated by The Joint Commission. Users of the Specifications Manual for Joint Commission National Quality Measures must update their software and associated documentation based on the published manual production timelines.

Chapter 8

Benchmarks

Benchmarks are indicator values that a healthcare organization should use as a reference point to validate best practices. That is, the goal is not to achieve benchmarks, but to implement the necessary process improvements or best practices that are reflected in the benchmarks. With this caveat in mind, identifying benchmarks relevant to an organization should entail much more than simply selecting indicators for which there are national or regional benchmarks.

Consider the process used by the management at Mayo Clinic to identify its benchmark indicators. First, it gathered data from published articles on indicators developed at peer academic healthcare organizations, including Allina Health Systems, Kaiser Permanente, Henry Ford Health Systems, Group Health Northwest, and Lahey Hitchcock Clinic. Mayo also commissioned a healthcare research and consulting firm to study indicators and measurement systems used by other leading academic healthcare centers. Moreover, Mayo did not limit its research to healthcare, but studied the literature on Performance Management systems used in leading organizations in multiple industries and those devised by business school academics. In searching for relevant benchmarks, readers should consider this approach.

8.1 Sources

Several ratings and financial management organizations collect and disseminate financial and utilization benchmarks that are useful for external comparison of performance indicators. The myriad medical benchmark and reporting organizations include the following:

- American Hospital Directory (*www.ahd.com*)
- Data Advantage Group (*www.dag.com*)
- Fitch Ratings (*www.fitchratings.com*)
- Healthcare Financial Management Association (*www.hfma.org*)
- McKesson (*www.mckesson.com*)
- Moody's (*www.moodys.com*)
- Standard & Poor's (*www.standardandpoors.com*)
- Truven Health Analytics (*100tophospitals.com*)

Each benchmark organization has a different focus, ranging from evaluating healthcare organizations as investment vehicles to serving as purveyors of quality healthcare.

Most benchmarking and assessment organizations require a fee for access to the latest figures. The American Hospital Association (*www.aha.org*), for example, is an often-cited membership organization that provides benchmark definitions to subscribers. A readily available (and free) source of unadjusted data on hospitals in the United States is the Medicare Cost Report, available from CMS (*www.cms.gov/research-statistics-data-and-systems/downloadable-public-use-files/cost-reports/*).

8.2 American Hospital Directory

The commercial American Hospital Directory (AHD) provides online information for more than 7000 hospitals, based on data compiled from public data sources, such as Medicare claims, hospital cost reports, Hospital Compare, and CMS. It also relies on a number of proprietary sources, such as accreditation status with the Joint Commission, teaching status with the American Medical Association (AMA), and DNV Healthcare accreditation status. The AHD offers half-dozen reports using indicators compiled for individual hospitals, including financial, inpatient utilization, and outpatient utilization reports.

Because these indicator values reported by the AHD are based on a large sample of hospitals, they serve as readily available benchmarks. The AHD offers free hospital profiles through the AHD website (*www.ahd.com*) that essentially establish benchmarks for hospitals of a given size and patient load. For example, the AHD report lists hospitals by type of facility total staffed beds, total patient days, total discharges, and total patient revenue. From these parameters, it's easy to identify a comparable hospital for comparing clinical and financial indicators.

A sample of the indicators used in each of the 10 areas of the AHD reports is listed in Table 8.1.

8.3 Healthcare Financial Management Association

The Healthcare Financial Management Association (HFMA) developed MapKeys—Key Performance Indicators (KPIs) to track revenue cycle performance—for both hospitals and physician practices. Hospital MapKeys focus on patient access, pre-billing, claims, account resolution, and financial management. Physician practice MapKeys are in the areas of patient access, revenue integrity, claims adjudication, and management.

Table 8.2 provides a partial listing of the MapKeys associated with hospital account resolution and financial management. Each MapKey is linked to a purpose, value, equation and data source, and points of clarification, such as patients or situations to exclude from the indicator.

Even though indicators and warning signs may serve as benchmarks for industry norms, they may not reflect local realities. For example, even though a benefit package worth 30% of total salary and wages may be out of line with national norms, it may reflect a local nursing shortage. This is true of the Northeast, for example, where many nurses can command six-figure incomes because of the shortage of qualified nursing staff.

Table 8.1 American Hospital Directory Report Indicators

AHD Report Indicators
Characteristics
Type of facility and control
Staffed beds
Total patient revenue
Total discharges
Total patient days
Total performance score quality score
Patient experience
Clinical Services
Services by department
Joint Commission Accreditation
Accreditation status
Verified Trauma Program
American College of Surgeons Committee on Trauma Verification Program
Teaching Status
From AMA and Association of Medical Colleges
Inpatient Utilization by Medical Service
Average length of stay
Average charges
Medicare case mix
Inpatient Origin
By zip codes
Outpatient utilization by ambulatory payment classification (APC)
APC number
Number patient claims
Average charge
Average cost

(*Continued*)

Table 8.1 (Continued)   American Hospital Directory Report Indicators

AHD Report Indicators
Bed and Patient Days by Unit
Routine
Special care
Nursery
Total hospital
Financial Statistics
Gross patient revenue
Nonpatient revenue
Total revenue
Net income/loss

Source: American Hospital Directory, *www.ahd.com.*

Table 8.2   Examples of HFMA MapKeys for Hospital Account Resolution and Financial Management

MapKeys for Account Resolution
Aged A/R as % of total billed
Denial rate
Denial write offs
Bad debt
Charity care
Net days in credit balance
MapKeys for Financial Management
Net days in accounts receivable
Cash collection as % net patient revenue
Uninsured discount
Uncompensated care
Case mix index
Cost to collect

Source: www.hfma.org/MAP/MapKeys. Accessed April 23, 2017.

8.4 Safety Benchmarks

Improved safety is one of the drivers of Performance Management in healthcare. As highlighted by the Institute of Medicine, medical errors are unfortunately a common component of the modern medical practice—almost 100,000 Americans die every year because of avoidable medical errors such as wrong medications, wrong dose, and poor surgical technique. Furthermore, the challenge of addressing and limiting the number and severity of errors is everything but straightforward. Not only do physicians resist change, but the economics of the healthcare system do not reward investment in systems to reduce errors.

There is a false perception that medical errors are limited to rural hospitals staffed by physicians far removed from academic medicine circles. In reality, medical errors are pervasive in every healthcare organization. Consider the Partners HealthCare System, which include the prestigious Harvard teaching hospitals and a number of satellite clinics. Of the incredible load of 15,000 patients seen daily, 1.4% are there because of a life-threatening drug interaction, 4% have medication errors—wrong drug or incorrect dose—attributed to an illegible written prescription, and 9% are there because of drug complications.

One reason for the seemingly high rate of medication errors is that patients at the Partners-affiliated hospitals tend to be sicker than patients at less well-known hospitals, and patients are often on multiple medications. However, poly-pharmacy is becoming the national norm as America ages. According to the Institute of Medicine, by the end of the decade, 80% of all healthcare expenditures will be spent toward chronic diseases associated with an aging population, from diabetes and Alzheimer's to hypertension and osteoporosis.

8.4.1 Leapfrog Group

The Leapfrog Group (*www.leapfroggroup.org*) is a coalition of public and private organizations that provide healthcare benefits. The voluntary program was created to mobilize employer purchasing power to improve the healthcare safety. The Leapfrog Group focuses on four hospital quality and safety practices: computerized provider order entry, evidence-based hospital referral, intensive care unit (ICU) physician staffing, and the Leapfrog Quality Index.

8.5 Further Thinking

Benchmarks are useful in gauging how an organization is doing, relative to best practices. The danger in using benchmarks is that they can lead to complacency. Benchmarks should be considered minimum standards, not necessarily good enough for local practices. For example, a pathology lab may be CAP (College of American Pathologists) certified, with Stat Test Turnaround Time Outlier Rate well within the acceptable range, and yet the local impression of the lab may be that the outlier rate is woefully inadequate. Complacency with benchmark values can also lead to poor patient care. Consider that, according to the Center for Information Technology Leadership (CITL) report, the average outpatient physician creates 38 adverse drug events per year, of which 14 are preventable and 2 of which are potentially fatal. In this context, average physician performance is inadequate, even if it does satisfy benchmark requirements.

Focusing on benchmark values to the exclusion of the objective data is like having a goal of achieving a passing grade—but no more. In this regard, benchmarks can impede the development of new and improved processes and approaches to local performance improvement. Resources allowing, it is generally better to set goals one standard deviation or more above established benchmarks.

Blindly following benchmarks can cause decision makers to overlook significant problems. For example, consider an outpatient diabetes clinic in which 90% of diabetes patients have their HbA1c values checked every 6 months. If this compliance figure is comparable to the national benchmark, the head of the clinic might be tempted to look at some other area in which the performance indicator of overall performance is below benchmark. However, the 10% of patients who are not tested biannually may share a physician who is careless about scheduling HbA1c lab tests. Providing the responsible physician with education, incentives, or even disincentives may be all that is required to bring the clinic into near full compliance—significantly better than the national or internal benchmark. In this example, the return on a modest investment in time and effort is significant, especially from the patient's perspective. As the motivational speaker Earl Nightingale said, "If you always play follow the leader, you'll always be second best."

Sources and Further Reading

Ash, J., P. Gorman, and W. Hersh. Physician order entry in US hospitals. In *AMIA Annual Symposium.* 1998, Washington, DC: AMIA.

Bates, D. et al. Effect of computerized physician order entry and a team intervention on prevention of serious medication errors. *JAMA* 1998, 280(15): 1311–6.

Bates, D. Frequency, consequences and prevention of adverse drug events. *J Qual Clin Pract* 1999, 19(1): 13–7.

Bates, D. and S.P. Slight. Medication errors: What is their impact? *Mayo Clinic Proceedings* 2014, 89(8): 1027–9.

Birkmeyer, J. and J. Dimick. *Leapfrog Safety Standard: Potential Benefits of Universal Adoption.* 2004, Washington, DC: The Leapfrog Group.

Center for Information Technology Leadership. *www.CITL.org.*

Computer Physician Order Entry. The Leapfrog Group Factsheet, 2004 (August).

Dudley, R. et al. Selective referral to high-volume hospitals. *JAMA* 2000, 283: 1159–66.

Edell, E. Strategic performance management: Development of a performance management system at the Mayo Clinic. *Journal of Healthcare Management,* 2000 (January): 27–34.

Kohn, L., J. Corrigan, and M. Donaldson, eds. *To Err Is Human: Building a Safer Health System.* 2000, Washington, DC: National Academy Press.

Leape, L. et al. Preventing medical injury. *Qual Rev Bull* 1993, 19(5): 144–9.

Morley, E., S. Bryant, and H. Hatry. *Comparative Performance Measurement.* 2001, Washington, DC: Urban Institute Press.

Pronovost, P. et al. Physician staffing patterns and clinical outcomes in critically ill patients: A systematic review. *JAMA* 2002, 288: 2151–62.

Semel, M.E. et al. Rates and patterns of death after surgery in the United States, 1996–2006. *Surgery* 2012 Feb, 151(2): 171–82.

Chapter 9

Reporting

Key Performance Indicator (KPI) data are of greatest value when the intended recipients are able to quickly understand their meaning and apply them to decision making. In this regard, reporting is at least as important as defining the KPIs and creating the information technology (IT) infrastructure required to extract and transform the data from the various data sources. This chapter provides an overview of the issues relevant to generating meaningful reports.

9.1 Reporting Options

Reporting indicator values may be the culmination of a complex process of linking to disparate databases with an ETL (extraction, transformation, and loading) tool, developing a data warehouse with data marts, and integrating a business intelligence (BI) charting front end to the system. In addition to the usual IT issues such as handling fragmented and distributed data in a variety of data formats from multiple platforms, and achieving Health Insurance Portability and Accountability Act (HIPAA) compliance, the report type, frequency, and response times are key variables.

The most common report types used in Performance Management are predefined and ad hoc queries, statistical analysis, and drill-down or multidimensional reporting, as shown in Figure 9.1. Ad hoc reports—often referred to as a form of data mining—require a BI toolset that allows users to define free-form queries. The IT infrastructure burden for timely ad hoc reports may be significant unless the system architecture is optimized for mining. The burden associated with predefined or canned reports can be mitigated through the use of cubes and other data management technologies.

The example in Figure 9.1 assumes that disparate data sources, a data warehouse, and an online analytical processing (OLAP) server provide KPI data and report generation mechanisms.

Statistical reports, which are statistical summaries of KPI data, typically use specialized statistical reporting software that goes beyond the modest statistical capabilities of most BI reporting software. Statistical reports may be ad hoc or predefined. Furthermore, all three report types can be processed in a batch mode, with the output sent to a printer or a computer screen.

In contrast, drill-down reports, which are hierarchically linked reports wherein supporting data can be accessed through a summary report, are limited to live, on-screen reporting. With

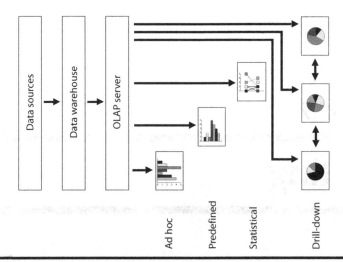

Figure 9.1 KPI report types: predefined reports, ad hoc queries, statistical analysis, and multi-dimensional reporting (drill down).

the click of a mouse, a decision maker can access summary data, such as hospital-wide mortality rate, and drill down to the mortality data at the department level. Drill-down reports, often in the form of graphical dashboards, highlight the system's response time limitations. An executive decision maker is not going to wait more than a few seconds for his or her screen to refresh with the requested KPI data.

One of the greatest concerns at the system architecture level is the report frequency. At a smaller institution, monthly reporting may be adequate. In a large, bustling healthcare enterprise, however, reports may be needed on a daily, weekly, biweekly, and monthly basis. Both large and small institutions would likely generate quarterly and annual reports.

Specific reports, designed to suit the specific authority and responsibility of a particular department or service head, tend to be required at the greatest frequency. For example, the head of surgery might require a report that details OR turnover times and complication rates on a weekly or even daily basis. Periodic Limited Reports, which are intended for hospital management, are generally required less frequently. Summaries of combined departmental data may be required on a monthly basis. Periodic Comprehensive Reports, which are executive summaries of organization-wide activity, such as profit, cash flow, and occupancy rate, tend to be required quarterly or semiannually. Quarterly, monthly, and even weekly reports may place minimal demands on the IT infrastructure. However, if a large number of KPIs must be reported on a daily basis, then tuning the data marts and other elements of the infrastructure take on increasing relevance.

9.2 Report Design

Although addressing issues such as response time and hardware requirements are part of the core competency of every successful IT shop, where BI tools are concerned, there is often a temptation to develop screen-based reports with little forethought. Designing graphic displays, especially groups of charts or dashboards, is a specialty in itself. A good chart or dashboard design should reflect the end user's view of the organization and the types of questions he or she will ask. Simply assigning someone from IT to pull together graphs that are colorful and arranged symmetrically on a screen without knowledge of the clinical and business decisions that the data must support is ill advised. See Figure 9.2 for a dashboard I developed for a Performance Management Initiative at the King Faisal Specialist Hospital and Research Centre (KFSH&RC), Riyadh.

Dashboards are a popular form of a Performance Management report. When properly designed, a dashboard can present a large number of key indicators—often an entire scorecard—in one consolidated, easily understood view. In a way, dashboards mirror the backend operations illustrated in Figure 9.1.

The backend data aggregation that forms the basis of a scorecard display need not span the organization or entire application suite to be effective. For example, St. Luke's Episcopal Health System in Houston initially consolidated its financials by developing a financial portal through which it could import financial data from all of its financial applications. Decision makers could in turn interact with the employee turnover, patient wait times, supply expenses, and other financial data through financial dashboards.

The most useful dashboards are not simply displays of indicator values, but they serve as a bidirectional user interface to the data. These so-called "analytical dashboards" allow drill-down as well as sideways exploration of indicator data. In this regard, drill-down exploration is a means of acquiring finer detail, contributing data. For example, a decision maker could drill down on the overall mortality figure to view mortality by department or physician. Sideways exploration allows moving from, say, mortality by physician to number of procedures by physician.

Just as in an aircraft or automobile dashboard, the type, size, and placement of charts on a dashboard display should be carefully planned to match the decision maker's needs. As such, a professional information architect may add significantly to the success of a Performance Management Initiative. The best approach is to develop in-house expertise in dashboard design because the dashboard will necessarily change with time. Adjustments to the dashboard should be possible without third-party intervention.

Even without the aid of an interface specialist, decision maker acceptance of dashboards can be facilitated by using graphs within BI tools that support the analytical needs of the decision makers. A pie chart is of little value, for example, in identifying potential sources of nonrandom error in a process; a process chart is more appropriate. This brings up a timing issue. If the BI reporting suite is selected before the KPIs and the most appropriate reporting formats have been defined, then there is a chance that the software suite may be inadequate. Because most BI reporting suites are focused on the general business environments, reporting may be inadequate for all but high-level KPIs in a healthcare organization. For this reason, it is a good idea to understand the types of charts and statistical analysis that may be required for various medical decision makers before deciding on a BI solution.

9.3 Charting Requirements

Much of the commercial activity in BI reporting is focused on supporting graphical charts ranging in complexity from simple line graphs to sophisticated control and spider charts. Although colorful, three-dimensional charts make for eye-catching advertising and may even have a place in presenting medical KPI information to decision makers, graphics do not obviate the need for traditional tabular reports. Not everyone is comfortable with graphics, and graphics are not necessarily the best way to present data. An accountant with decades of experience reading tabular financial statements may be able to assess a department's financial status in a glance, without the need to drill down through layers of charts or continually refer to the axis on the chart to determine exact dollar values. That is, graphics often lack the resolution of tabular data.

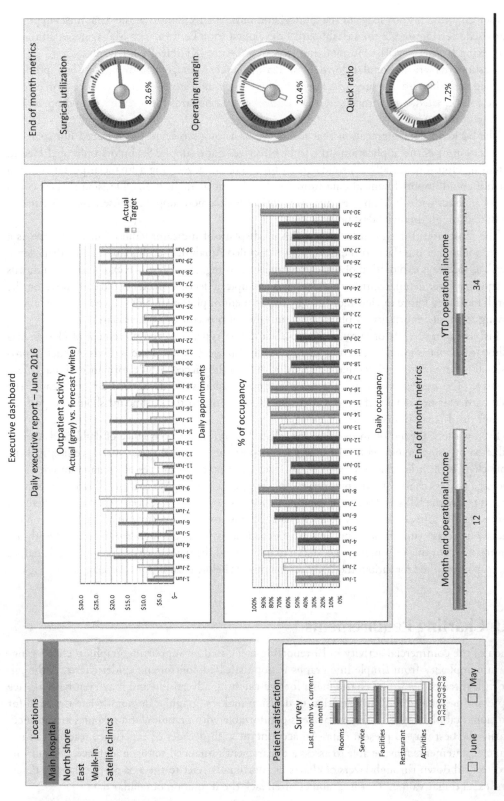

Figure 9.2   Dashboard showing multiple performance measures.

For many decision makers, graphics can provide added insight into certain trends that may not be obvious from tabular reports, especially clinical phenomena associated with an unstable process. As such, the reporting capabilities of a Performance Management system should include traditional tabular and graphical formats, with the relative weighting determined by end-user preferences and analytical requirements.

Software allowing, tabular data and graphical charts can be combined in a single report to cover all user preferences. For example, when decision makers access indicator web-based reports, the initial view can show aggregate level data for the entire organization. Data in this view can be presented as a list of indicator values. By clicking on a specific indicator, the decision maker can drill down to region-specific data for the last 3 years, displayed in the form of a histogram and a tabular listing of the source data. By clicking on the graph for a particular region, the decision maker can continue drilling down to a control chart and the source data for that indicator.

The histogram and control charts are two of the major chart types used in Performance Management. The other chart types and the analysis they support are listed in Table 9.1. For example, boxplot and comparison charts are useful in comparing data sets, such as the discharge rates of two hospitals. A histogram of patients by age would reveal whether the distribution of patients is normal (central peak), bimodal (two separate peaks), or skewed (peaks left or right of center). The common line graph is useful in identifying trends.

There is overlap in and difference in degree in the utility or application of each chart type. Furthermore, there are drawbacks associated with each type of chart. Consider the run chart (Figure 9.3, top) and one type of control chart (Figure 9.3, bottom), both of which can be used to determine if variability is attributed to common cause (random) or statistically significant special cause (nonrandom) variation. The run chart is less complex than the control chart and therefore more likely to be available in a BI reporting package, but is less sensitive to common cause variation. Both chart types require data points over a considerable period of time to be useful. In addition, the charts highlight common cause variation over the time sequence in which it occurs.

The statistical analysis associated with a run chart is simply a median line computed from the data points shown in the chart. Even so, the rules for interpreting a run chart are a function of the number of data points on the chart. With 10 points, only five consecutive data points on one side

Table 9.1 Chart Type and Type of Analysis Supported

Chart Type	Analysis Supported
Boxplot and comparison	Compare data sets, including benchmarking
Control and run	Determine if a variation is statistically significant
Histogram	Reveal distribution of a variable
Line graph	Identify trends in a process
Pareto	Identify causes of a problem
Performance matrix	Combines priorities with performance
Radar	View many variables simultaneously
Scatter diagram	Identify correlation between two variables
Stratum	Visualize component data

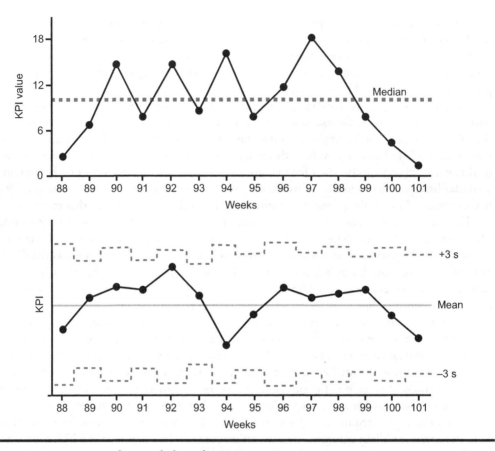

Figure 9.3   Run (top) and control chart (bottom).

of the median line (run length) are allowed before the variation is considered statically significant. If the number of data points is increased to 20, the maximum run length is seven.

The more sophisticated control chart includes control limits based on plus or minus three standard deviations or sigmas from the centerline. Like the run chart, there are heuristics for determining when an observed variation is statistically significant, including maximum run length. A control chart can be thought of as a graphical statistical analysis tool. Instead of dealing with square roots and variance equations, the decision maker simply notes the plotted data pattern relative to the mean and three sigma limits. Just as there are mathematical statistical operations for different types of data, there are seven types of control charts, all similar to the one in Figure 9.3, but appropriate for different types of data and requiring different interpretation.

An overriding consideration in selecting among the various chart types for the best fit between data, type of analysis to be supported, and limitations of BI reporting software is training end users. Although a given user or class of user may interact with three or four types of charts, organization-wide, a dozen or more chart types may be in use. As such, there must be provision for training end users on how to interpret the range of charts supported. Furthermore, the most appropriate chart for a given user or indicator may evolve over time. For example, the more powerful control and run charts may not be appropriate for a dashboard until after a year of data collection. A simple line chart may be used until there are enough data points to support a run or control chart.

There are a number of excellent publications available on the subject of charting and Performance Management. One of the best is the Joint Commission's *Tools for Performance Measurement in Health Care: A Quick Reference Guide, 2nd Edition*. Additional references are in the Sources and Further Reading section.

9.4 Charting Software

Informative charts and dashboards can be created with built-in graphics in MS Excel and statistical analysis packages such as SPSS. However, PC-based graphical rendering of tabular data are usually inappropriate for all but small, department-level KPI reporting projects. Listed in Table 9.2 is a small sampling of graphical report generation tools and toolkits that can be used to aid decision makers in their analysis of KPI data. Products range from stand-alone PC-based systems to

Table 9.2 Software for Graphical Report Generation

Product	Company	Note
OpenViz Data Visualization API	Advanced Visual Systems, Inc, *www.avs.com*	Data visualization toolkit
Crystal Enterprise (Crystal Reports)	SAP, *www.sap.com*	A toolkit for integrating reports within other systems
Cognos Analytics	IBM Cognos, *www.ibm.com*	Enterprise-level solution
Rocket HyperVu	Rocket Software, *www.rocketsoftware.com*	Enterprise-level reporting
eRoom	Dell EMC, *www.dellemc.com*	Enterprise-level suite
Oracle Hyperion Performance Scorecard, PeopleSoft and Siebel	Oracle, *www.oracle.com*	Wide range of products from acquisitions
SAP Dashboard Design	SAP, *www.sap.com*	Formerly Crystal Xcelsius
Informatica Information Platform	Informatica, *www.informatica.com*	Enterprise-level solution within a data integration suite
Omni-HealthData Insights, WebFocus	Information Builders, *www.informationbuilders.com*	Integrated with Information Builders suite
Logi	Logi Analytics, *www.logianalytics.com*	Development toolkit; server-based
Microsoft Power BI	Microsoft, *www.microsoft.com*	Complete BI platform

(Continued)

Table 9.2 (Continued)   Software for Graphical Report Generation

Product	Company	Note
PerformancePoint Services in SharePoint Server 2013	Microsoft, *www.microsoft.com*	Server-based business Performance Management scorecard application
MicroStrategy 10	MicroStrategy, Inc., *www.microstrategy .com*	Specific solutions for healthcare
Netsuite 10.0	Netsuite, *www.netsuite.com*	Cloud based
Easy Charts	Object Planet, *www.objectplanet.com*	Toolkit for chart building
Showcase Reporting Solution	SPSS, *www.spss.com*	Comprehensive statistical analysis; one component in a suite of tools
NetCharts Reporting Suite	Visual Mining, *www.visualmining .com*	Server-based toolkit that can be used to extend existing reporting
IBM Watson Analytics	IBM, *www.ibm.com*	Predictive analysis and data visualization
Tableau Desktop	Tableau, *www.Tableau.com*	Supports drag and drop
Looker	Looker, *www.looker.com*	Healthcare-targeted products
	Domo, *www.domo.com*	Multiple user platforms
Qlik Sense Enterprise Server	Qlik, *www.qlik.com*	Easy-to-use report toolset
Zoho Reports	Zoho, *www.zoho.com*	Free trial

cloud-based enterprise-wide solutions. Enterprise-level packages, such as Rocket HyperVu, IBM Cognos Analytics, Informatica Healthcare Analytics, and Oracle Hyperion, combine elements of data mining and data integration with report generation.

9.5 The Balanced Scorecard

KPIs are seldom used alone, but are combined in a scorecard or table listing various indicator values. Often, these listings are arranged by department, service, or area of interest to the organization's decision makers. When the scorecard covers a broad range of departments or areas, it is often called balanced, meaning that the indicators are representative of various aspects of the organization, as opposed to a single area or domain. Sometimes a dashboard is referred to as a balanced scorecard (BSC).

However, as defined by Kaplan and Nolan in their seminal article, "The Balanced Scorecard—Measures that Drive Performance," the BSC is much more than an arrangement of performance indicators dashboards with generic indicators grouped into four categories. Rather, it is a strategic Performance Management methodology that translates strategy into action throughout every level of the organization. Following a BSC *strategy* entails carefully selecting performance indicators across four balanced perspectives: financial, customer, internal business process, and employee learning and growth (see Figure 9.4). The figure pairs the original BSC drivers with healthcare indicators.

Following Kaplan and Norton's definition, the process of creating a BSC begins with a statement of vision, which leads to a stakeholder analysis along the four perspectives. This, in turn, leads to identifying critical success factors, which then define the critical measurements or KPIs. In this regard, the BSC is a form of process reengineering.

The original BSC quadrants were designed for business, but they can be easily remapped to indicators relevant to a healthcare organization, as in Table 9.3. For example, the financial perspective examines how the organization looks to shareholders and stakeholders. In business, this translates to indicators such as return on investment (ROI) and net income. In healthcare, relevant indicators for the financial quadrant include in/outpatient revenue mix, occupancy rate, average length of stay, cost per adjusted discharge, and discounts as a percentage of operating patient revenues.

The innovation/learning perspective originally used indicators of employee satisfaction, motivation, and empowerment. In healthcare, this perspective includes indicators such as employee turnover, the creation of new services and products, availability of continuing medical education (CME) and other training, and advancement opportunities. For example, at Mayo Clinic, innovation/learning indicators have included the number of peer-reviewed papers published, the number of presentations, the number of grants awarded by the National Institutes of Health (NIH) and industry, and breakthroughs in treatments and medicines.

The internal perspective, as defined by the original BSC design, is intended to quantify how well the organization performs on key internal operational processes. Indicators such as cycle time, safety ratings, and percentage of on-time deliveries are used in business. Parallel indicators in healthcare include surgical capacity utilization and full-time equivalents (FTEs) per average daily

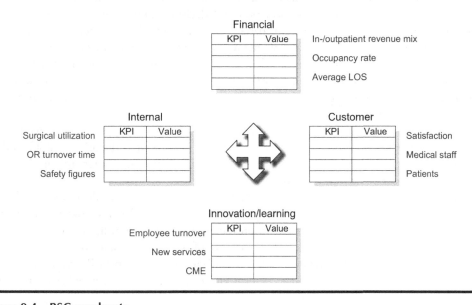

Figure 9.4   BSC quadrants.

Table 9.3 BSC Quadrants That Have Been Used in Prominent Healthcare Organizations, Contrasted with the Original Quadrants Defined by Kaplan and Norton

Strategy	Q1	Q2	Q3	Q4
Kaplan and Norton	Financial	Customer	Internal	Innovation and learning
Duke Medical Center	Cost	Patient satisfaction	Functional health status	Education and research
Henry Ford Health Service	Low-cost provider	Customer satisfaction	Growth	System integration
Johns Hopkins	Financial goals	Patient satisfaction	Clinical outcomes	Research and teaching
New Zealand HHS	Financial	Patient and quality	Process and efficiency	Organizational health and learning
Ontario Hospitals Association	Financial performance and condition	Patient satisfaction	Clinical utilization and outcomes	System integration and change

Sources: Duke Medical Center, Henry Ford Health Service, Johns Hopkins, New Zealand HHS, and Ontario Hospitals Association.

census. Balancing the internal perspective is the customer perspective, which focuses on how well the organization satisfies the customer's needs. In healthcare, this quadrant is typically focused on the primary stakeholders—patients, payers, and medical staff.

Common BSC drivers or quadrants in healthcare include community health promotion, facility quality, image and reputation, information and decision support, market share, operating efficiency, patient and family satisfaction, patient outcomes, physician outcomes, and physician satisfaction. According to the original BSC definition, changing the names of the original quadrants not only changes the indicators used in each quadrant but also redefines the healthcare organization's strategy. Whether the institutions listed in Table 9.3 follow a management strategy keyed to their BSC or simply group their indicators in a balanced way is open for interpretation. Most likely, it is a question of degree.

Just as the names of the four BSC quadrants can be renamed, there is nothing magic about the number of perspectives. Although it would not map directly onto the original BSC model, a Performance Management strategy that attempts to balance the organization among three, five, or even six dimensions can work equally as well.

Consider the United Kingdom performance assessment framework developed by the Department of Health to measure each hospital trust in England. The framework initially measured performance from six perspectives: improvement in people's health, fair access across services, delivery of effective care, efficiency, experiences of patient and their caregivers, and health outcomes. Similarly, the 2003 World Health Organization Workshop in Barcelona established six dimensions of hospital performance: clinical effectiveness, patient centeredness, production efficiency, safety, staff, and responsive government.

Even the basic "flat" quadrant structure can be modified to suggest a hierarchy of focus areas. For example, a BSC may be rearranged into a pyramidal structure, with the customer domain at the top. This "unbalanced" arrangement reflects the priority the healthcare organization gives to patients.

The first major BSC effort in healthcare was undertaken by the Ontario Hospital Association (OHA), as reported in *Hospital Report '99: A Balanced Scorecard for Ontario Acute Care Hospital* by the University of Toronto. According to the report, the approach was more of a means of creating a comprehensive scorecard than of defining a management strategy. Nonetheless, the BSC consisted of 39 indicators arranged in the traditional four quadrants. According to the OHA, the BSC was composed of 10 clinical utilization and outcomes indicators, 5 financial performance and condition indicators, 12 indicators focused on patient satisfaction, and 7 indicators dealing with system integration and change.

Clinical Utilization and Outcomes indicators included acute myocardial infarction (AMI), asthma, gastrointestinal bleeding, heart failure, community-acquired pneumonia, and stroke. Financial Performance and Condition indicators included measures of financial viability, efficiency, liquidity, capital, and human resources. Indicators from the patient satisfaction perspective included global and process quality, admissions, and indicators of nursing, physician, and housekeeping staff quality. System integration and change indicators reflected three general areas: increased use of information to improve service, better internal coordination of care to improve outcomes, and higher levels of hospital integration with community services. Whereas the indicators in the other three quadrants were based on indicators used in other institutions, most of the indicators for system integration and change were developed specifically for the BSC project.

The BSCs for Acute, Ambulance, and Mental Health trusts share three focus areas: clinical, patient, and capacity and capability. The BSC for primary care trusts is focused on access to quality service, health improvement, and service provision.

9.6 Further Thinking

In addition to user-directed reporting, KPIs can serve as the basis for automated alerts and for predictive modeling or forecasting. Automated alert mechanisms use predefined KPI trigger values to determine when to send an e-mail, SMS message, or other form of alert to the appropriate decision makers. Example trigger values include full occupancy, days cash on hand below a specific number of days, and OR turnaround times greater than a predetermined number of hours.

The most advanced form of reporting is predictive modeling. Consider the system used at William Beaumont Hospital, a system consisting of a large tertiary care hospital, a smaller community hospital, and several nonhospital facilities. The hospital's management engineering group developed a model to predict nursing unit occupancies over a 3-day horizon. The objective of the predictive model is to provide decision makers involved in staffing, discharge planning, and patient placement with information on how busy the hospital is likely to be over the next 72 hours. The model was shown to be 85% accurate at 24-hour forecasts.

Sources and Further Reading

Balanced Scorecard Institute. *www.balancedscorecard.org*.

Bendall-Lyon, D. and T. Powers. The role of complaint management in the service recovery process. *Joint Commission Journal on Quality Improvement* 2001, 27(5): 278–86.

Enwere, E.N. et al. Balanced Scorecards As a Tool for Developing Patient-Centered Pharmacy Services. *Hospital Pharmacy* 2014, 49(6): 579–84.

Evans, R.S. et al. Clinical use of an enterprise data warehouse. *AMIA Annual Symposium Proceedings* 2012: 189–98.

Genovich-Richards, J. and J. Wyzkiewicz. Consumers: From perceptions to participation. *Journal of Healthcare Quality* 2002, 24(6): 39–41.

Gilmore, J. and B. Pine. The four faces of mass customization. *Harvard Bus Rev* 1997, 75(1): 91–101.

Guptil, J. Knowledge management in healthcare. *Journal of Health Care Finance* 2005, 31(3): 10–4.

Isken, M., S. Littig, and M. West. A data mart for operations analysis. *Journal of Healthcare Information Management* 2001, 15(2): 143–53.

Jamie, W. Scorecards, dashboards, and KPIs: Keys to integrated performance measurement. *Healthcare Financial Management* 2004 (Feb): 14–9.

Kaplan, R. and D. Norton. Putting The Balanced Scorecard To Work. *Harvard Bus Rev* 1992 (Sept–Oct): 2–15.

Kaplan, R. and D. Norton. The balanced scorecard—Measures that drive performance. *Harvard Bus Rev* 1992 (Jan–Feb): 71–9.

Kaplan, R. *The Balanced Scorecard for Public Sector Organizations*. 2000, Cambridge: Harvard Business School Press.

Memel, D. et al. Development and implementation of an information management and information technology strategy for improving healthcare services: A case study. *Journal of Healthcare Information Management* 2001, 15(3): 261–85.

Pink, G. et al. Creating a balanced scorecard for a hospital system. *Journal of Health Care Finance* 2001, 27(3): 1–20.

Rimar, S. Strategic planning and the balanced scorecard for faculty practice plans. *Academic Medicine* 2000, 75(12): 1186–8.

Schneiderman, A. Why balanced scorecards fail. *Journal of Strategic Performance Management* 1999 (Jan): 6–11.

Sunnybrook Health Sciences Centre, University of Toronto Faculty of Medicine, Sunnybrook's Strategic Balanced Scorecard. December, 2016.

Tiwana, A. *Knowledge Management Toolkit: Orchestrating IT, Strategy, and Knowledge Platforms*, 2nd ed. 2002, Englewood Cliffs, NJ: Prentice Hall.

Tools for Performance Measurement in Health Care: A Quick Reference Guide, 2nd ed. 2008, Oakbrook Terrace, Illinois: Joint Commission Resources.

Tufte, E. *The Visual Display of Quantitative Information*, 2nd ed. 2001, Cheshire, CT: Graphics Press.

Weintraub, P. *Planning for Healthcare Reform: Using the Balanced Scorecard Approach to Strategic Planning*. Hospital Planning for Healthcare Reform, 2010. *www.healthcarereformmagazine.com/business/planning-for-healthcare-reform-using-the-balanced-scorecard-approach-to-strategic-planning*. Accessed April 16, 2017.

Zelman, W., G. Pink, and C. Matthias. Use of a balanced scorecard in health care. *Journal of Health Care Finance* 2003, 29(4): 31–3.

Chapter 10

Behavior Change

Management, in general, is about getting people to do what you want and need them to do. And this holds for a Performance Management Initiative, where the impediments to change come in a variety of political, cultural, and sociological flavors. There is the initial hurdle of getting multiple administrative groups together from different departments and divisions to establish common performance indicators. Once this obstacle has been overcome, there often remains the challenge of enticing clinicians to comply with additional data gathering and documentation activities. Then, there is the push to convince decision makers to actually use the new information in a meaningful way. There is also the task of training IT staff so that the Performance Management Initiative can be maintained without constant intervention from an outside vendor.

There are various ways to go about understanding and then promoting behavior change. I sometimes follow a simple heuristic that 10% of the staff are going to dig in their heels and refuse to change. Another 10% are going to be more excited than you about bringing about change (the evangelists). The remaining 80% can be sold on the benefits of changing, if you provide the appropriate leadership and incentives. However, this simplistic view of management and behavior change doesn't provide much of a road map for administrators who are invested in bringing about change as quickly and as efficiently as possible. For example, it doesn't support a model for training, for how and when to best incentivize behavior change, or for estimating the long-term return on investment from a training program.

The focus of this chapter is one road map that I have used successfully in a Performance Management Initiative, a modified version of the Stages of Change Model, also referred to as the Transtheoretical Model. In addition, this chapter covers the role of incentive programs and training in a Performance Management Initiative. As you read through the chapter, keep in mind that the goal isn't to develop the psychoanalytical skills to get into the heads of your clinical staff, but rather to be able to intelligently communicate with your trainers, to assess the clinical staff's readiness to change, and, once the behavior change process is underway, to quantify the progress of the desired behavior change. Of note is that one of the seven components of the AHRQ's QI Toolkit is devoted to assessing readiness to change. Included in the toolkit is a survey to self-assess readiness to change.

10.1 Stages of Change Model

The Stages of Change Model, developed by two clinical psychologists (James Prochaska and Carlo DiClemente) to treat patients with addictions, is depicted in Figure 10.1. The model assumes that everyone goes through five discrete, predictable of stages when making a behavior change: (1) Pre-contemplation, (2) Contemplation, (3) Preparation, (4) Action, and (5) Maintenance. According to the original model, the changes in behavior are associated with energy expenditure. I've modified the model slightly to reflect expenditure of personal resources, in terms of energy and/or time. In an ideal world, fewer personal resources, in terms of energy and/or time, are expended after people change their behavior, compared to their previous behavior, as illustrated in Figure 10.1.

Assuming the term "decision makers" includes administrators, clinicians, and everyone else in the organization who must change his or her behavior to adopt the Performance Management Initiative, the stages of change are discussed in the subsequent sections.

10.1.1 Pre-contemplation

Pre-contemplation is the initial steady state in which decision makers are unaware of the Performance Management Initiative. This is the initial state of decision makers in the healthcare organization, extending back to the start of their affiliation with the organization. Typically, the amount of personal resources expended by decision makers in carrying out their daily activities at this stage of the model is stable. Although this resource expenditure level may be primarily subjective and therefore difficult to quantify, it is nonetheless a critical determinant of the initiative's eventual success or failure.

10.1.2 Contemplation

At the Contemplation stage, decision makers are aware of the initiative and consider the benefits—and drawbacks—associated with adopting the Performance Management Initiative. Although no observable activity is involved in the mental exercise of contemplation, subjective resource expenditure can be substantial.

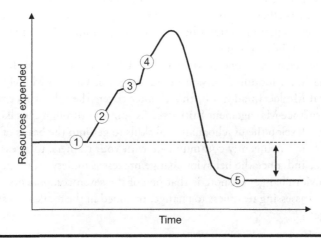

Figure 10.1   Ideal stages of change model. (1) Pre-contemplation. (2) Contemplation. (3) Preparation. (4) Action. (5) Maintenance.

The duration of this stage, like that of the other five stages, is a function of the environment and the individual. For example, clinical decision makers may resist incorporating the computer-based dashboards in their decision-making process. Even today, there remain clinicians who are resistant to certain technologies. These technophobes, who tend to be older clinicians, will not directly use a computer system, but will instead have their secretary or resident interact with the system for them. There are also variable users, clinicians who will only use a computer system for a specific purpose, such as checking their e-mail or to look up drug–drug interactions. These clinicians tend to be younger than technophobes. The remaining clinicians, many of whom have been exposed to computing before or during their medical training, will generally use a computer system if it provides some reasonable time or energy savings.

The Contemplation stage may be extended because decision makers formerly in control of the information—a form of power—realize that they will lose some of that control. When senior management can drill down through data at the department or physician level without interacting with a department head, for example, that department head can do little to regulate or color the reports of department activity.

10.1.3 Preparation

Preparation is the stage in which decision makers decide to change or, rather, adopt components of Performance Management, and they mentally prepare for the changes ahead. This stage of the Change Model, which is still mental, is typically shorter in duration than Contemplation. The relative duration is a function of the decision maker's personality and experience with similar initiatives. A clinician or administrator who has been burned by a similar initiative that failed—a relatively common experience in healthcare—is likely to have a prolonged Preparation stage. Furthermore, these tainted decision makers may expend considerable resources during the Preparation stage to formulate a "Plan B" that will allow them to continue working productively if the Performance Management Initiative fails.

10.1.4 Action

The Change Model's Action stage marks the time when decision makers become active participants in the Performance Management Initiative. The change is no longer mental, but is obvious in external, visible activity. Decision makers may become involved in the Performance Management Committee, attend classes on how to interpret statistical graphs imbedded in dashboards, and begin to incorporate scorecards in their decision-making processes.

As shown in Figure 10.1, the resources expended during this stage of change can be significant, especially initially. The underlying promise, whether implied or stated, is that after the initial "hump" in resource expenditure, things will be better, meaning the time and/or energy required to complete a given task will be less than before. This is indicated by the resource shift below the dashed energy baseline in the figure.

10.1.5 Maintenance

The fifth stage of change, Maintenance, is achieved when Performance Management becomes an integral part of the decision maker's routine. The Maintenance phase may be short-lived, however, and lead to extinction of the new behavior, if the resources required to maintain the new behavior are greater than that required during Pre-contemplation, as in Figure 10.2. The figure shows an

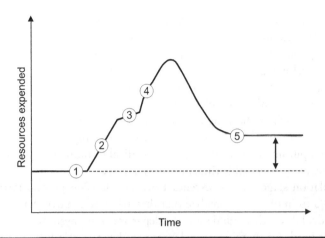

Figure 10.2 Stages of change model with higher maintenance energy requirements. (1) Precontemplation. (2) Contemplation. (3) Preparation. (4) Action. (5) Maintenance.

increased resource requirement that will tend to lead to recidivism. That said, it's possible that the increased resource requirements associated with the new behavior can be overcome by appropriately rewarding maintenance of the new behavior.

For example, a Performance Management Initiative may result in more work for individual decision makers, with little or no positive impact on their ability to provide patient care, and yet provide an overall benefit to the organization. Consider that physicians and nurses working in a clinic may be required to capture additional patient information regarding medication history, allergies, and other data related to medication errors. To these clinicians, the initiative may be little more than a bother and compliance with the required additional data capture may suffer. In such cases, to avoid extinction of the new behavior, it may be in the organization's best interest to compensate these decision makers for the extra resources they are requested to expend to support an ongoing Performance Management Initiative.

10.2 Incentive Programs

As noted above, a popular means of ensuring against recidivism is to incentivize those negatively affected by a Performance Management Initiative. I've seen bonuses, new tablet computers, large-screen desktop computers, and similar bribes work wonders for compensation. Although this may seem like bribery—and it is—it is a practice with a long history in healthcare. For example, in the early 1990s, physician-operated voice recognition systems developed by Kurzweil AI seemed like a valid replacement for traditional transcription. Because it was an arduous task with a steep learning curve on the early systems as well as time consuming for physicians, many physicians simply opted out of the programs. In order to get the physicians back on board, many hospitals adopted a policy in which physicians who used voice recognition instead of the transcription pool were compensated $5 per report. In this profit sharing model, the hospital administration acknowledged the greater work burden placed on clinicians.

WellSpan Health System, an integrated delivery system that serves south central Pennsylvania and northern Maryland, was able to enjoin primary care physicians in its Performance Management Initiative by using a dual approach. Not only did WellSpan link clinical performance indicators to physician compensation, it provided physicians with feedback on their practice management performance with statistical process charts. Similarly, Yale New Haven Health System implemented a performance incentive program that enabled all of its employees—not only physicians—to earn up to 3% of additional compensation annually, based on indicators related to finance, patient satisfaction, and costs.

Inducements to follow a Performance Management Initiative have also been applied at the institution level; some payers and organizations have decided to stimulate adoption of technology in support of better patient outcomes. For example, Verizon, IBM, PepsiCo, and others incentivized New York hospitals to adopt more stringent patient safety standards. Similarly, at Partners Community HealthCare in Boston, physicians received bonus payments based on their attainment of benchmark compliance rates for specific interventions and practices.

10.3 Training

One of the primary means of catalyzing the change of individual and group decision-maker behavior is to offer or mandate training. The training requirements associated with a comprehensive Performance Management Initiative can be significant, spanning topics from indicator selection, indicator development, report design, and report analysis to change management. Furthermore, not only is attending training often the first objective sign of user buy-in—the Action stage in the Change Model discussed earlier—but it can help lower the energy "hump" characteristic of the Action stage.

From the perspective of achieving maximum buy-in, the training program should focus not simply on the information that must be conveyed to decision makers, but how information is presented, the environment in which the information will be used, and the characteristics of decision makers who will be trained. For example, while the chief operating officer (COO) may require personal hand-holding when he or she is taught how to interpret the organization-wide dashboard, nursing staff tasked with added data collection duties will probably receive group training. These and other key issues related to developing an effective Performance Management training program that will achieve maximum buy-in are summarized in Table 10.1.

10.3.1 User Profiles

Training should reflect the profiles of decision makers and other users of the data collection and display systems as well as provide for users with special needs and particular learning issues. For example, occasional users, such as hospital board members who review dashboards on a quarterly basis, have training needs that are different from department heads (mainstream users) that are expected to use the system on a daily or weekly basis. Some users may have specific needs that affect their ability to learn and use components of the system, even though they are able to perform their clinical or administrative duties. For example, a visually impaired administrator may benefit from a text-to-speech (TTS) utility, and a decision maker suffering from carpal tunnel syndrome might benefit from the installation of voice recognition software on their computing platform of choice.

10.3.2 Platform Profiles

Training should reflect the popularity of alternatives to the desktop or bedside computer platform. Today, a department administrator is more likely to check performance statistics on their

Table 10.1   Issues in Developing a Performance Management Training Program That Maximizes Buy-in for Decision Makers and Staff with an Active Role in the Initiative

Training Issues	
User profiles	Mainstream users, learning issues users, special needs users
Environment profiles	Work space, home, commute
Platform profiles	Desktop, bedside, tablet, smartphone platforms
Usage pattern profiles	Work usage patterns, home usage patterns
Training design	Methodology, visual–spatial skill levels, cognitive skill levels, prior system experiences
Passing criteria	Absolute, curve, attendance
Ongoing training	New hires, transfers, new feature sets

smartphone than on their desktop computer. As such, training should reflect the range of hardware and software platforms most likely to be used to access Performance Management data.

10.3.3 Environmental Profiles

Profiles of the work and home environments are critical to successful training. The head of the emergency room (ER) likely has very different time pressures compared with the head of the dermatology department, and training should reflect this difference. The head of the ER may need to know how to quickly access data, with little interest in drilling down, sideways, or otherwise exploring the data available through a dashboard. Similarly, as noted above, some decision makers may wish to review their department's performance from home, during their commute, or otherwise during their off time, using hardware that is different from the standard office configuration. Ideally, training should reflect these and similar differences in environmental profiles.

10.3.4 Usage Pattern Profiles

Usage pattern profiles are a function of the environment, the workload, and the individual decision maker's work habits. For example, many department heads check their e-mail and other computer-based data early in the morning, before attending meetings, participating in morning rounds, and tending to their other responsibilities. Often, this is earlier than technical support is available in the hospital. Training should recognize the unique support needs of these decision makers.

10.3.5 Training Design

The overall training design methodology should reflect individual needs. A major decision in training design is whether to use professional trainers or in-house staff. Another is whether to offer one-on-one training as an alternative to group training. For example, the schedules of high-level decision makers may not allow for fixed time group training. Similarly, other executives may not feel comfortable in a remedial statistics class, surrounded by staff charged with data collection.

The methodology employed in the training design should reflect the visual–spatial and cognitive skill levels of the decision makers and others involved in the Performance Management Initiative, as well as their previous experience with decision support systems. Staff with a negative Performance Management experience at their former places of employment, or from prior administrations, may present particular training challenges because of negative transference. Surveys conducted before training can help determine the skill level of those to be trained and their relevant prior experience with Performance Management.

10.3.6 Passing Criteria

Often a key issue in training is whether to establish an absolute passing grade for participation, grade on a curve, or, as is commonly practiced with CME programs, provide a passing grade to everyone who shows up for training. The choice usually depends on the level of self-motivation in the group to be trained as well as the skills being taught. Complex data collection skills, such as coding clinical events, may require training with passing grade criteria to ensure that the staff are adequately trained. In contrast, simply showing up for training may be sufficient for high-level administrators learning to interpret dashboards. The point here is to have a training plan that at least considers individual needs.

10.3.7 Ongoing Training

Training, like Performance Management, is an ongoing process. As such, the training program should provide for new hires, transfers, and changes to the Performance Management system, and simple knowledge decay. Consider instituting an open door policy wherein employees can schedule training on an as-needed basis, with the appropriate administrative sign-off.

10.4 IT and Training

The IT department can become a major facilitator in training by supporting the development of web-based tutorials and online help. This support should go beyond the usual help desk function and incorporate elements of training discussed above that are rolled into just-in-time end-user training programs.

In my experience, a major stumbling block for upper-level decision makers is a lack of statistical analysis skills related to the proper analysis of the various chart types used in dashboards. These decision makers can often benefit from short, online tutorials that are available on demand. As noted in the chapter on reporting, proper statistical analysis of certain charting types requires knowledge of statistical methods as well as seemingly arbitrary rules of what constitutes a statistically significant pattern. Online references that address these rules can be of benefit to even the most statistically savvy decision makers.

Online training and references can also go a long way in assuring compliance with the standards established by the Performance Management Initiative. Staff involved in data collection can benefit from an online portal that provides one-stop access to the list of Key Performance Indicators (KPIs), including their detailed definitions, lists of relevant ICD-10 (International Classification of Diseases, 10th Revision) codes, contact information for indicator owners, and schedules of additional training. The portal can also serve as a community bulletin board for information on performance indicators used at other institutions and other news on the use of performance management in healthcare. For example, at King Faisal Specialist Hospital and Research Centre in Saudi Arabia, the IT department supports a Quality Portal that lists scorecards, current indicator values, and definitions of each indicator. The portal is open to administrators and clinicians with access to the hospital's intranet.

10.5 Further Thinking

One of the behavior issues to consider when implementing a Performance Management Initiative is how to deal with negative feedback. Consider what happened when St. Luke's Medical Center made medication errors one of its KPIs. The 650-bed general medical/surgical hospital in Quezon City, Philippines, was confronted with a sudden increase in the reporting of medication errors. Although the increased awareness of medication errors eventually enabled the hospital to identify and address the system failures responsible for the medication errors, the initial rise in reported medical errors was a disincentive for many hospital employees involved in the initiative. Few people respond positively to negative feedback.

The experience at St. Luke's illustrates the need to manage expectations. If the medical staff follow a Performance Management Initiative with the expectation that the system will initially establish a baseline of errors as a starting point for improvement, they will be less likely to resist reporting errors. Management should also assure staff that the Performance Management Initiative is not punitive, but is in line with the organization's mission of delivering quality healthcare.

On the topic of incentivizing behavior change, in contrast to success stories above, I've also been a part of failed compensation-based incentive program. In a 2015–2017 initiative, physicians were offered what seemed to everyone in management as a financial incentives package impossible to turn down. However, the incentive simply wasn't big enough for most physicians. As a result, what was planned as an 18-month initiative required nearly 3 years to complete.

It turned out that physicians valued their time more than the marginal increase in income, possibly a reflection of the time pressure of the modern medical practice. More likely, the initiative was simply poorly designed and/or executed, and the new, desired behavior overly burdened the clinical staff. The bottom line is that you shouldn't count on being able to buy—that is, bribe—your way out of a poorly executed Performance Management Initiative.

Sources and Further Reading

Blander, J. and B. Bergeron. *Clinical Management Systems: A Guide for Systems Deployment.* 2004. Chicago, IL: HIMSS.

Gagon, M. et al. Electronic health record acceptance by physicians: Testing an integrated theoretical model. *Journal of Biomedical Informatics* 2014, 48(4): 17–27.

Garvin, D. *Learning in Action: A Guide to Putting the Learning Organization to Work.* 2000. Cambridge, MA: HBS Press.

Hutton, D. *From Baldrige to the Bottom Line: A Road Map for Organizational Change and Improvement.* 2000. San Francisco: Jossey-Bass.

Nambisan, P. et al. *Understanding electronic medical record adoption in the United States: Communication and sociocultural perspectives. Interact J Med Res* 2013 Jan–Jun, 2(1): e5.

Office of the National Coordinator for Health Information Technology. Office-based Physician Electronic Health Record Adoption, Health IT Quick-Stat #50. dashboard.healthit.gov/quickstats/pages/physician -ehr-adoption-trends.php. December 2016.

Prochaska, J. Helping patients at every stage of change. *Behavioral Approaches to Addiction Journal* 1992, 1(1): 2–7.

Prochaska, J. and C. DiClemente. Transtheoretical therapy: Toward a more integrative model of change. *Psychotherapy: Theory, Research and Practice* 1982 (19): 276–88.

Prochaska, J. and J. Norcross. *Changing for Good.* 1994. New York: William Morrow and Company.

Prochaska, J.O. and J.M. Prochaska. *Changing to Thrive.* 2016. Center City, MN: Hazeldon Publishing.

Spotlight on Success: St. Luke's Medical Center, Quezon City, Philippines. *Joint Commission International Newsletter* 2004, 2(3): 4–6.

Transtheoretical Model. *https://en.wikipedia.org/wiki/Transtheoretical_model.* Accessed April 7, 2017.

Chapter 11

Statistics

Performance Management is fundamentally about making decisions based on the analysis of outcomes and process measures, and much of this analysis is statistical in nature. As noted in Chapter 9 (Reporting), even when the task of statistical manipulation for charting purposes is performed automatically, the end user has to have an appreciation for how to interpret the charts. This chapter provides a review of data types and statistical methods relevant to performance indicator development and analysis.

11.1 Data Types

Valid statistical analysis requires underlying data that are timely, accurate, and appropriate for the decision at hand. The four basic types of indicator data are nominal, ordinal, interval, and ratio, and each type supports different degrees of statistical analysis, as listed in Table 11.1. Nominal data, such as simple presence/absence or yes/no responses, are useful for simple classification. Ordinal data, such as relative time or quantity, are useful for qualitative ranking. Interval data, which indicate the difference between measurement values, can provide the basis for limited statistical analysis. Ratio data, which are expressed using an absolute scale, support the full spectrum of statistical analyses.

The data types are supersets of each other, following the hierarchy ratio, interval, ordinal, and nominal. That is, interval data can be derived from ratio data, ordinal data can be derived from interval data, and nominal data can be derived from any of the other data types. In most cases, the data type with the most information is captured and stored whenever feasible.

As an illustration of how data types affect analysis, consider the blood pressure data captured from two patients who appear in a high blood pressure clinic. One patient has a systolic blood pressure of 145 mmHg and the other, 140 mmHg. If the clinician records absolute blood pressure values (ratio data), then the full range of statistical analysis can be applied to the data. For example, the average or mean blood pressure can be calculated as [(145 + 140)/2)] = 142.5 mmHg. However, if the difference in blood pressure values is recorded (interval data), only limited statistical techniques can be applied during analysis. The difference of 5 mmHg may be all that is required to quantify, for example, the effectiveness of an anti-hypertensive drug, but even a simple calculation of average blood pressure is no longer possible.

Table 11.1   Data Types and the Analysis They Support

Type	Example	Analysis Possible
Nominal	Yes, no	Simple classification
Ordinal	First, second	Qualitative ranking
Interval	5 mg more	Limited statistical analysis
Ratio	140 and 145 mm	Full statistical analysis

The two patients could be ranked in terms of systolic blood pressure, with "First" and "Second" recorded for each patient (ordinal data). No information on absolute blood pressure or even the range differentiating the patients is available for analysis, however. Finally, the blood pressure values could be recorded as "High" for hypertensive and "Normal" for pressure values below the cutoff value (nominal data). Even the simplest statistical operations are not available to assist the decision maker with data analysis. Furthermore, if the definition of hypertension changes in the future, the data on the two patients probably will not be useful in a study. Even today, some physicians would argue over whether both patients would/should be considered borderline hypertensive.

Given the utility of ratio data, why bother to record anything less? There are many valid reasons. The practical limitation of time is one. Ratio data may not be available, and the easily accessed nominal data may be all that is required for a given set of Key Performance Indicators (KPIs). Expense is another issue. Recording ratio data often cost more to acquire, store, and access, compared with data of other types. The take-away message is that the decision of when to invest in recording data of one type over another should be made with consideration of the costs as well as the potential future data application.

11.2 Data Quality

Another characteristic of data, regardless of type, is that they are imperfect. Finite limits on reproducibility, accuracy, and precision, owing to equipment limitations, human error, environmental factors, and deficiencies in the overall data acquisition process, all introduce errors in the quantity the data represent. Furthermore, this variability is cumulative, in that it propagates through subsequent measurement and analysis activities. Even with the most advanced statistical techniques, errors can at best be reduced and never eliminated. Determining the magnitude and pervasiveness of error is one reason for employing statistical techniques.

The inherent imperfections in data are described in terms of accuracy, repeatability, sensitivity, and stability. Accuracy is the degree to which a value being measured is correct. All instruments are subject to changes in accuracy over time, whether or not they are operating. For example, the mercury sphygmomanometer used to measure blood pressure is subject to a change in accuracy because of changes in the glass column, which crystallizes and contracts over time. Many accuracy specifications are stated in terms of time since calibration. The accuracy of a calibration standard limits the maximum accuracy of the equipment being calibrated.

Precision, also referred to as resolution, is the ability of an instrument to resolve small differences. Repeatability, the ability of an instrument or system to provide consistent results, is affected by any changes in the data source caused by the measurement process. An instrument may provide highly repeatable results, but the results may be inaccurate unless the instrument is properly calibrated.

Sensitivity, the ability of a device to detect low-level signals, is a function of the resolution and the amount of noise or random variability in the system. Stability is the ability of an instrument or device to provide repeatable results over time, assuming certain environmental conditions.

Data quality issues are not limited to laboratory or clinical measurements. Everything from the data capture systems used to determine pathology lab turnaround time, the computer system timers used to determine average wait times at admitting, and OR inventory figures are subject to data quality limitations. A common finding in using data to determine KPI values is that there are several, different values for a given measurement. For example, OR turnaround time as recorded by the anesthesia team may be significantly different from the time recorded by OR technicians. The challenge is determining which measurements are the most valid, accurate, and error-free— and that is where statistics come into play.

11.3 Statistical Analysis

The two broad categories of statistics are inferential and descriptive. Inferential statistics are used to infer population parameters based on sample data, while descriptive statistics are used to organize and present data in a convenient, useable form. Both categories of statistics are based on the idea that there is a complete set of actual or potential observations (the population) and that population characteristics can be inferred by sampling a subset of the population. The sample should be random, in that each member of the population has an equal opportunity to be selected. This randomness refers not to the data, but how they are obtained.

11.4 Descriptive Statistics

Much of descriptive statistics deals with obtaining as much information as possible from small samples of the population data. Population parameters are estimated by sampling population data and drawing inferences from the sample data, based in part on assumptions of how the data are distributed in the population. Another assumption is that sample parameters tend to approach the population parameters, given a large enough sample size or enough smaller samples. The most important of these parameters is the mean, weighted mean, mode, median, and variance.

Mean. The mean ($\bar{x}$) is the average value of a sample, calculated by dividing the sum of sample values (x) by the number of measures (n):

$$\bar{x} = \frac{\sum(x)}{n}$$

The mean is usually the best indicator of central tendency—the tendency of the sample mean to approach the population mean. However, because the mean is very sensitive to outliers that are not distributed symmetrically around the mean, alternative measures of central tendency may provide better information about population mean.

Weighted Mean. The weighted mean is the sum of the weighted scores over the sum of the weights, calculated as

$$\text{Weighted Mean} = \frac{\sum (w^i x^i)}{\sum w^i}.$$

In this calculation, w^i is the weight corresponding to a data value x^i. This measure of central tendency is used to combine two or more measurements of the same quantity but with differing accuracy in such as way that the more accurate sample data contribute more to the measure than less accurate data. Weighted mean is useful when working with data from different sources when the relative accuracy of each source is known. Weight is given to a source in proportion to its accuracy.

The weighted mean is also useful in calculating the mean value of a series of average values taken from groups of differing size. For example, when average values from groups of 10, 100, and 500 patients are computed, without a weighting, the average from the group of 10 patients would have just as much influence (weight) as the group of 500. With weighting, the contribution of each group could be proportional to the number of samples.

Assume, for example, that the average age of patients from samples of 10, 100, and 500 patients is 20, 30, and 40 years. A simple average or mean calculation results in a mean age of 30 years:

$$\text{Mean Age} = \frac{20 + 30 + 40}{3} = 30$$

In contrast, the weighted mean age, in which the weights are simply the group sizes, is 38 years:

$$\text{Weighted Mean Age} = \frac{(20 \times 10) + (30 \times 100) + (40 \times 500)}{10 + 100 + 500} = 38$$

The weighted mean can also be used to combine indicator values to create another global indicator. For example, consider a hospital in which each department calculates staff productivity using different metrics. In Radiology, productivity may be measured in terms of the number of relative value units associated with the current procedural terminology (CPT) code of each procedure, as defined by the Centers for Medicare and Medicaid Services (CMS). The Pathology department measures productivity in terms of the volume of tests completed within College of American Pathologists (CAP) guidelines. Pediatrics assesses productivity in terms of case load. One way to combine these disparate measures of productivity, each using different metrics and numbers of full-time equivalents (FTEs), is to use a weighted mean based on the number of FTEs in each department. First, the productivity units are normalized on a work output scale that applies equally to all clinicians. The measures are then combined using a weighted mean that uses the relative number of FTEs in each department as the basis for the weight applied to each department's work output. In this way, each clinician's relative contribution to the hospital's productivity measure is equal.

Mode. Another measure of central tendency, the mode is the sample data value that occurs most often. If the data are distributed normally with one peak, the mode corresponds to the value represented by the peak in the single "hump" of data. Because of this feature, unlike the mean, the mode is relatively resistant to outlier values. A major limitation of using the mode as a measure of central tendency it that it is unstable when the distribution has two peaks—a distribution referred to as bimodal (see Figure 11.1). The mode could be markedly different from one sample to the next, as the mode shifts randomly from the peak value of data in one hump to the next. Most descriptive statistical analyses assume sample data are distributed normally.

Median. The median is the middle value when the numbers in a sample are arranged in order of magnitude. The median is the best measure for measuring central tendency with nominal data or ratio data with a few extreme outliers.

Distributions. Although descriptive statistical analysis often assumes a normal (bell shaped) distribution of sample data, the distribution of sample data may take a variety of forms, including skewed and bimodal. Note that these measures of central tendency apply to the sample data. There is only one true or population mean. On a graph, the population mean would be indicated by a single vertical line; the concept of a normal or skewed distribution does not apply.

Variability. In addition to central tendency, descriptive statistics are commonly used to describe variability or dispersion of sample data. The most common measures of variability, range, variance, and standard deviation are typically paired with a measure of central tendency.

Range. Range, the difference between the largest and smallest value in a sample, is the simplest measure of variability. This easily calculated measure highlights the presence of outlier values in a sample, but provides little information on the data within the range. For this reason, the more sophisticated measures of variability are commonly used to describe data.

Variance. Variance (s^2), a measure of dispersion of data values in a sample, is calculated by taking the average of squared differences between sample data values (x) and their mean ($\bar{x}$). Note that the average is computed by dividing by the sample size (n) minus 1:

$$s^2 = \frac{\sum (x - \bar{x})^2}{n-1}$$

When variance is used to describe data variability, it is usually paired with a more intuitive transformation, standard deviation.

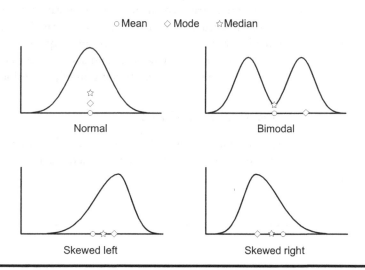

Figure 11.1 **Distributions of sample data.**

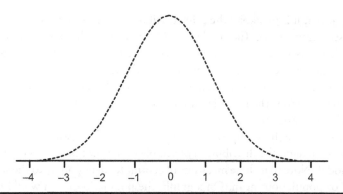

Figure 11.2 Z-distribution with a mean of zero and a standard deviation of one.

Standard Deviation. Standard deviation, the most common measure of dispersion in sample data, is calculated by taking the square root of the variance:

$$s = \sqrt{\frac{\sum (x - \bar{x})^2}{n-1}}$$

The standard deviation of sample data can be appreciated graphically by examining the z-distribution, a special case of the normal distribution. The z-distribution has a mean of 0 and a standard deviation of 1 (see Figure 11.2).

Numbers along the x-axis represent standard deviations from the mean.

As noted earlier, measures of variability are often paired with measures of central tendency to provide a complete picture of the data. Variance and standard deviation are typically used to summarize the dispersion of data values around the mean, for example, the average length of stay can be summarized as 5.6 ± 2.1 days, where 2.1 days is understood to represent one standard deviation.

A smaller standard deviation or variance suggests that data are clustered about the mean. A larger standard deviation means data are distributed farther from the mean and are more variable. A reduction in the outcome variability is usually associated with an increase in quality.

Unlike measures of central tendency, measures of variability apply equally to population and sample data. Although the formulas for population variance and standard deviation are slightly different from those presented here, the concept of a z-distribution of population data holds.

11.4.1 Application of Descriptive Statistics

Consider three samples of a variable, with values 6, 7, and 10, graphed on a line segment, as in Figure 11.3. At question is the range of values that should be considered statistically similar to the values of these samples.

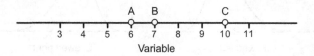

Figure 11.3 Observed sample values, labeled A, B, and C.

Additional samples will be taken, and at issue is which values can be considered statistically different from the values represented by samples A, B, and C. In other words, which range of values can be considered to be different from A, B, and C by change alone. One way to answer this question is to determine the z-distribution of the sample values represented by A, B, and C. First, the mean and standard deviation of the sample data are computed:

$$\bar{x} = \frac{\sum (x)}{n} = \frac{6+7+10}{3} = 7.67$$

$$s^2 = \frac{1}{n-1}\sum_{i-1}^{n}(X_i - \bar{X})^2 = \frac{1}{2}[(6-10)^2 + (7-10)^2 + (10-10)^2]$$

$$s^2 = \frac{1}{2}[(-4)^2 + (-3)^2 + (0)^2] = \frac{1}{2}[16+9] = 12.5$$

$$s = \sqrt{12.5} = 3.54$$

The calculation results appear graphically in Figure 11.4, which shows the samples along a z-distribution. Given a standard deviation (s) of 3.54, the three samples are all within about one standard deviation of the mean (7.67). The typical criterion for statistical significance is greater than plus or minus three standard deviation from the mean, or greater than 18.3 and less than –2.9. That is, a sample value of 20 would be considered significantly different from the current sample values, and therefore not due to chance variation alone. Similarly, if the criterion is relaxed to only plus or minus two standard deviations from the mean, then values less than 0.6 and greater than 14.6 would be considered statistically significant. This method of establishing the range of allowable values has application in control charts, described in Chapter 9 (Reporting).

Assuming a cutoff of plus or minus three standard deviations, additional sample values less than approximately –2.9 and 18.3 should be considered significantly different from the values of samples A, B, and C.

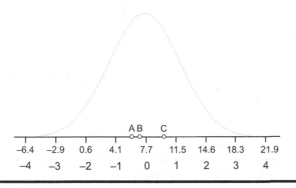

Figure 11.4   *Z*-scores of sample values.

11.5 Inferential Statistics

Inferential statistics, like descriptive statistics, are used to infer qualities in a population based on random samples taken from the population. Linear regression, Bayes' theorem, and contingency tables are three inferential statistics methods useful in Performance Management.

Linear regression is useful when it is desirable to uncover linear relationships between two continuous interval or ratio variables. The degree to which one variable can be used to predict the other is expressed as the correlation coefficient (r). The correlation coefficient is a measure that expresses the extent to which two variables co-relate, where r varies between –1 and +1.

Figure 11.5 illustrates a positive correlation of 0.9 between variables A and B and a positive correlation of 0.2 between variables A and C. A correlation of 0.9 means that $(0.9)^2$ or 81% of the value of variable A can be attributed to variable B. In contrast, only $(0.2)^2$ or 4% of variable A can be attributable to variable C. The term "attributed" does not constitute causality, but only predictive value. Even a correlation coefficient of 1.0 should not be confused with one variable causing another. The frequency of hospital admissions may correlate highly with the phases of the moon, for example.

Correlation is useful in determining whether there is overlap in performance indicators—suggesting one of the indicators can be dropped without affecting decision making. For example, if two utilization measures based on bed occupancy have a correlation coefficient of 0.9, then one of the measures can probably be dropped and another can be used in its place. The cutoff value for statistically significant correlation (i.e., $r = 0.9$ vs. 0.8) depends on the number of data points and the desired level of certainty.

Because it takes time to collect sufficient data for a meaningful correlation calculation (20 or more data points are typical), correlation analysis is useful in assessing indicator value only after several months of weekly indicator data have been collected. Similarly, if indicator data are collected daily, correlation can be assessed after a few weeks.

11.5.1 Bayes' Theorem

Bayes' theorem combines prior probabilities of outcomes with the conditional probabilities of input features to reach a conclusion. Probability is useful in quantifying, for example, the odds that a 45 year-old overweight business executive presenting to the emergency room (ER) with chest pain is suffering from an acute myocardial infarction (AMI). Using the odds-likelihood form of Bayes' theorem, the probability that the patient is suffering from an AMI (posttest odds)

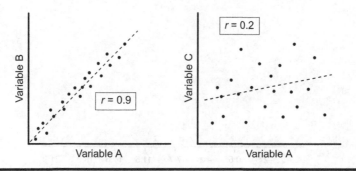

Figure 11.5   Correlation of continuous variables.

can be calculated from three parameters: the probability of a 45-year-old overweight business executive having an AMI (pretest probability), the probability that chest pain is present in people suffering from an AMI, and the probability that chest pain is present in someone not suffering from an AMI.

Probability (p) and odds are related as follows:

$$\text{odds} = \frac{p}{1-p}$$

$$p = \frac{\text{odds}}{1+\text{odds}}$$

The relationship between pretest and posttest odds is

Posttest odds = pretest odds × likelihood ratio.

Now, assume that the pretest odds of the executive having an AMI is 50%, that the probability that chest pain is present in people suffering from an AMI is 65%, and that the probability that chest pain is present in executives not suffering from an AMI is 20%. The posttest odds that the executive is having an AMI are calculated as

$$\text{Pretest odds} = \frac{0.50}{1-0.50} = \frac{0.50}{0.50} = 1$$

$$\text{Likelihood ratio} = \frac{0.65}{0.20} = 3.25$$

$$\text{Posttest odds} = 1 \times 3.25 = 3.25 : 1$$

Converting odds to probability:

$$p = \frac{\text{odds}}{1+\text{odds}} = \frac{3.25}{1+3.25} = 0.77$$

That is, the odds that the business executive is suffering from an AMI are 0.77. A better indicator than chest pain, such as an abnormal EKG (electrocardiogram), would have a greater likelihood ratio and more of an influence on the odds determination.

Bayes' theorem also has an application in classification: using data and heuristics to assign measurements to groups. Consider two groups of patients, low-cost and high-cost, as defined by length of stay and number of clinician contacts. The task is to classify three patients, A, B, and C, as member of one of the two groups (see Figure 11.6). This classification is represented by open and closed circles using Bayes' theorem.

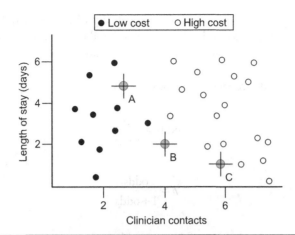

Figure 11.6   Classification of patients A, B, and C in one of two cost groups.

Using Bayes' theorem to determine whether a given patient should be classified as a member of the high-cost group, the following equation applies:

$$p(\text{High Cost} \mid X_i Y_i) = p(\text{High Cost} \mid X_i) \times p(\text{High Cost} \mid Y_i)$$

That is, the probability of a patient belonging to the high-cost group, given his or her number of clinical contacts and length of stay (X and Y coordinates) is equal to the product of the independent probabilities of the patient belonging to the high-cost group, given length of stay and number of clinician contacts.

Whereas patients A and C can be reasonably assigned to the low- and high-cost groups by visual inspection, patient B is less clear. Given the probability values for the above equation, patient B can be assigned to one of the two groups in an objective manner. In practice, Bayes' theorem is reserved for much more complex categorization problems that cannot be solved easily by alternative methods.

11.5.2 Contingency Tables

Although a variety of statistical methods can be applied to index and ratio data, a few methods are also available for nominal data such as gender, patient preferences, and other non-numerical data that may appear in a balanced scorecard. One statistical method that can be used on nominal data is the contingency table, which can be thought of as a spreadsheet in which two nominal variables are mapped onto each other (see Table 11.2).

The purpose of contingency tables, which are also known as cross-tabulations, is to discover the relationships between nominal concepts. This contingency table above is designed to explore the relationship of gender and approval or disapproval of physician care. The rows represent gender (Male or Female) and columns represent patient responses on a questionnaire (Approval or Disapproval). A chi-square test for independence or Fisher's exact test (both beyond the scope of this discussion) can be used to determine whether there is a statistically significant linkage between the two variables. The point is there are a few statistical methods available for index and ratio data.

Table 11.2   2 × 2 Contingency Table with Factors of Gender and Approval of Physician Care at a Large Community Hospital

	Approval	*Disapproval*
Male	44	14
Female	26	36

11.6 Sensitivity and Specificity

Tests and tools used to collect data vary considerably in sensitivity and specificity. Sensitivity is the percentage of actual positives that are counted as positive. Specificity is the percentage of actual negatives that are rejected. Ideally, specificity and sensitivity are both 100%. A completely sensitive test for AMI, for example, would detect every patient presenting to the ER with an AMI. Furthermore, a completely selective test would classify patients not having an AMI as such 100% of the time. In practice, there are no completely sensitive and selective tests, and there is a trade-off between the two characteristics. For a test to identify 100% of AMI patients, for example, it will necessarily include overweight, middle-aged business executives with a bad case of heartburn.

Expressed in the vernacular of statisticians, sensitivity is the number of true positives divided by the sum of true positives and false negatives, and specificity is the number of true negatives divided by the sum of false positives and true negatives:

$$\text{Sensitivity} = \frac{\text{True Positives}}{\text{True Positives} + \text{False Negatives}}$$

$$\text{Specificity} = \frac{\text{True Negatives}}{\text{True Negatives} + \text{False Positives}}$$

For the less mathematically inclined, the relationship between sensitivity and specificity is illustrated in Figure 11.7.

TP—True Positive
TN—True Negative
FP—False Positive
FN—False Negative

As shown in Figure 11.7, a test with cutoff at position "A" includes nearly all of the true positives (high sensitivity), at the expense of including about a quarter of the false positives (low selectivity). Moving the cutoff to position "B" eliminates the false positives (high selectivity) but misses half of the true positives as well (low sensitivity). Following the example of patients presenting to the ER with chest pain, moving the cutoff from "A" to "B" would result in turning away half of the patients actually suffering from an AMI. Because of the considerable cost of turning away patients with an AMI from the ER, even cutoff "A" may be too severe. Without a better test (one with greater sensitivity and selectivity), it may be necessary to admit virtually every patient for observation.

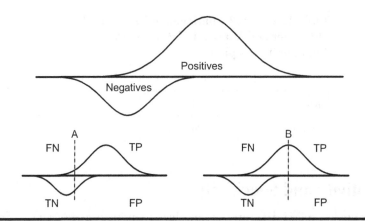

Figure 11.7 **Sensitivity and specificity as a function of the number of true and false positives and negatives.**

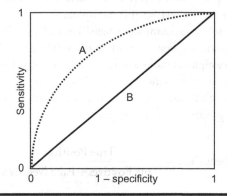

Figure 11.8 **Receiver operating characteristic (ROC) curves for two tests.**

Another way to visualize the sensitivity and specificity of a test is to determine its receiver operating characteristic (ROC) curve, as in Figure 11.8. The ROC curve is a plot of a test's sensitivity versus specificity, or true-positive rate versus false-positive rate. Every point along an ROC curve corresponds to test sensitivity and specificity at a given threshold of abnormal. All else being equal, a test with the greatest discriminative ability (Test A) is superior to a test with lower discriminative ability (Test B).

The sensitivity and specificity (or discrimination capabilities) of a test come into play when calculating performance indicators. For example, one of the performance indicators promoted by JCAHO (Joint Commission on Accreditation of Healthcare Organizations)/CMS is the administration of aspirin to AMI patients within 24 hours of arrival. The test criteria used to determine whether patients are in fact having an AMI can profoundly influence the validity of the indicator.

11.7 Missing Data

Invariably, in the process of preparing data for analysis, it will become evident that some data were never collected, lost, corrupted, or otherwise unavailable. Possible ways of dealing with missing data include listwise deletion, pairwise deletion, and mean estimation.

Listwise deletion is the method of choice if it can be applied. In listwise deletion, if a variable value is missing, all other variables associated with the patient or other source of data are eliminated from all calculations, even if there are valid values for some variables. This approach is limited to situations in which sample size is adequate and cases where missing data do not differ significantly from those with complete data (this later constraint being impossible to verify). In other words, if every physician in a large teaching hospital contributed data on three variables—for example, job satisfaction, years with the hospital, and academic rank—and the information on years with the hospital is missing for one physician, the data on rank and job satisfaction should be discarded.

In pairwise deletion, the data from a case are used in all calculations except those in which data are missing. Pairwise deletion, which is considered inferior to listwise deletion, is sometimes used when sample size is limited and there are not enough samples to throw out any sources. Following the previous example, if the physician survey on job satisfaction is limited to a dozen physicians in a department, then years with the hospital and academic rank would be included in summary statistics.

In mean estimation, missing values are replaced by the mean of the variable. This is considered a conservative approach because it reduces the probability of obtaining significant results. For example, if the average job satisfaction for all physicians in the hospital is 3.2 on a scale of 1–5, then the missing job satisfaction value of 3 would be assigned to the physician, regardless of his or her actual satisfaction score.

11.8 Trending

Trending, the analysis of the positive or negative movement of indicator value over time, is computed with the formula:

Percent Change = [(Value in subsequent year − Value in base year)/Value in base year] × 100.

Trend analysis looks at the percentage change in indicator value from a reference or base year. Horizontal analysis is a special case of trend analysis in which the base year is the previous year. The formula for horizontal analysis is

Percent Change = [(Value in subsequent year − Value in previous year)/Value in previous year] × 100.

When indicators are "trended," the term generally implies horizontal analysis. Even so, true trend analysis may be more appropriate in certain circumstances. For example, the opening of a new department, major renovation, or acquisition may be more relevant than the previous year as the basis for analysis.

11.9 Predictive Modeling

While trending and horizontal analysis provide a view of the past, predictive modeling is an analytical method with which future indicator values can be determined with some degree of accuracy (80% is considered good). The actual accuracy depends on how far out into the future the prediction is made, the time-varying nature of the data, and the accuracy and quality of the data used in the prediction. The farther out in time, the more erratic the nature of the data, and the poorer the data, the lower the prediction accuracy.

Before the introduction of modern business intelligence (BI) tools from companies such as SAS, SPSS, and Cognos, predictive modeling required the end user to select a curve fitting function (e.g., a second-degree polynomial expression), adjust the variables and constants, run the equation, and observe how closely the equation described the existing data. Today, software agents try multiple algorithms and curve fitting functions until the best match is found. However, it is up to the user to determine which variables to use in predicting the indicator values.

An example from the public health arena is the relationship between salmonella outbreaks and the sale of ice cream. Because ice cream is a common cause of salmonella poisoning, ice cream sales and the weather can be used to predict salmonella cases admitted to the ER. Ice cream sales lead such poisoning by one to several days, depending on how quickly the ice cream is eaten after purchase (assuming packaged ice cream). Similarly, the sale of ice cream is partially dependent on the weather. Hot weather generally results in greater sales and the consumption of ice cream already purchased. Given accurate data on ice cream sales and the weather, it should be possible, with some degree of accuracy, to predict admissions. The ability to predict admissions with, say, 80% accuracy, is a significant improvement over simply waiting to see what walks in the ER door.

Of course, an experienced ER physician is aware of the relationship between ice cream consumption, hot summers, and salmonella. However, many healthcare decision makers may not be aware of the predictors of average length of stay or bed turnover rate. It is possible to use an educated guess as to what are the possible predictors of an indicator and select other predictors if the predictive modeling tool does not come up with an acceptable prediction accuracy. Another approach is to search the literature on predictors that have been used by others. A good source for accessing peer-reviewed material on modeling and other scientific issues is Highwire Press (www.highwirepress.com), which offers a monthly subscription model for accessing published articles online.

11.10 Indicator Adjustments

Indicators are often "adjusted" or subject to a statistical process for reducing, removing, or clarifying the influences of confounding factors. The rationale for adjusting an indicator is to allow for more useful inter-organization indicator comparisons. For example, evaluating the performance of two hospitals based on a comparison of average length of stay figures can be misleading if the hospitals have markedly different patient demographics.

Differences in patient age, sex, and disease severity can profoundly affect length of stay, independent of the underlying processes in place at each hospital. An adjustment for these differences, such as a multiplier based on the weighted mean of patient age, sex, and disease severity, could be used to provide a more meaningful comparison.

11.11 Further Thinking

It is possible to spend months on a data collection design and end up with worthless data on a dashboard because the data are invalid in the context of answering the question at hand. For example, if the people entrusted to capture data can be affected by the analysis results, the data may be biased positively or negatively. Similarly, unless there are clear rules on how certain findings are handed, results may be invalid. For example, does a patient admitted with a myocardial infarction (MI) and diabetes count for two patients in some calculations or one? Handling of comorbidities is only one of several data acquisition issues that can invalidate analytical results.

It is possible to draw erroneous conclusions from accurate, timely data unless the limitation of statistical methods is understood and accounted for. Furthermore, statistical significance does not necessarily translate to clinical significance. Consider the limitations of the seemingly straight-forward contingency table, which was briefly introduced above. Categories cannot overlap, meaning a patient may be included in only one category. Furthermore, categories must include all possibilities (e.g., what of transgender, chromosomally abnormal, and other patients who may not be classified as either male or female?). The observations must also be independent. Then, there are non-intuitive limitations on the types of statistical tools that can be used with the table, for example, the result of a chi-square analysis is suspect if the number in any cell in the contingency table is less than 1 and the value in more than 20% of cells is less than 5.

Many of these conditions cannot be met with data that can influence indicator values. For example, in a contingency table representing AMI patients and diabetic patients, there is a good likelihood that some MI patients are also diabetic. Because people with diabetes have increased incidence of cardiovascular disease, including MI, the two disease presentations are linked. Not only do the contingency table categories overlap, but they fail to pass the independence test.

The takeaway message is that readers should understand the types of data they intend to collect and make certain the statistical methods used in analysis are correct and appropriately applied.

Sources and Further Reading

Carey, R. and R. Lloyd. *Measuring Quality Improvement in Healthcare: A Guide to Statistical Process Control Applications.* 2001, Milwaukee: ASQ Press.

Enders, C.K. *Applied Missing Data Analysis.* 2010, New York: The Guilford Press.

Ewens, E. and G. Grant. *Statistical Methods in Bioinformatics*, 2nd ed. 2005, New York: Springer.

Kellar, S.P. and E. Kelvin. *Munro's Statistical Methods for Health Care Research*, 6th ed. 2012, Philadelphia: Lippincott Williams & Wilkins.

Quality Indicator Empirical Methods (Revised by Truven Health Analytics, Stanford University (prime contractor), under Contract No. HHSA290201200003I). Rockville, MD: Agency for Healthcare Research and Quality. November 2014.

Smith, G.M. *Statistical Process Control and Quality Improvement.* 2003, London: Pearson.

Wheeler, D. and D. Chambers. *Understanding Statistical Process Control.* 1992, Knoxville, TN: SPC Press.

Appendix A: Healthcare Quality Organizations

The major healthcare quality organizations that have a bearing on the US Healthcare system are listed below. Exemplary Australian, Canadian, and UK organizations are included because US policymakers often reference them for either positive or negative examples of how healthcare should be managed.

United States

Accreditation Association for Ambulatory Health Care (AAAHC) *www.aaahc.org*
Agency for Healthcare Research and Quality (AHRQ) *www.ahrq.gov*
America's Health Insurance Plans (AHIP) *www.ahip.org*
American Association of Blood Banks (AABB) *www.aabb.org*
American Board of Medical Quality (ABMQ) *www.abmq.org*
American College of Emergency Physicians (ACEP) *www.acep.org*
American College of Surgeons (ACS) *www.facs.org*
American Dental Association (ADA) *www.ada.org*
American Health Information Management Association (AHIMA) *www.ahima.org*
American Health Quality Association (AHQA) www.ahqa.org
American Hospital Association (AHA) *www.aha.org*
American Medical Association (AMA) *www.ama-assn.org*
American Nurses Association (ANA) *www.ana.org*
American Optometric Association (AOA) *www.aoa.org*
American Organization of Nurse Executives (AONE) *www.aone.org*
American Osteopathic Association (AOA) *www.aoa-net.org*
American Pharmacists Association (APhA) *www.aphanet.org*
American Society for Healthcare Risk Management (ASHRM) *www.ashrm.org*
American Society for Quality (ASQ) *www.asq.org*
American Society of Health-System Pharmacists (ASHP) *www.ashp.org*
American Society of Histocompatibility and Immunogenetics (ASHI) *www.ashi-hla.org*
Anesthesia Patient Safety Foundation (APSF) *www.apsf.org*
Association of American Medical Colleges (AAMC) *www.aamc.org*
Automotive Industry Action Group (AIAG) *www.aiag.org*
Aviation Safety Reporting System (ASRS) *asrs.arc.nasa.gov*

Baldrige Performance Excellence Program (BPEP) *www.nist.gov/baldrige*
Care Quality Commission (CQC) *www.cqc.com*
Centers for Disease Control (CDC) *www.cdc.gov*
CDC Division of Healthcare Quality Promotion (DHQP) *www.cdc.gov/ncezid/dhqp*
CDC Healthcare-Associated Infections *www.cdc.gov/hai*
Center for Information Technology Leadership (CITL) *www.citl.org*
Centers for Medicare and Medicaid Services (CMS) *www.cms.hhs.gov*
COLA *www.cola.org*
College of American Pathologists (CAP) *www.cap.org*
Food and Drug Administration (FDA) *www.fda.gov*
Hospital & Healthsystem Association of Pennsylvania *www.haponline.org*
Institute for Healthcare Improvement *www.ihi.org*
Institute for Safe Medication Practices *www.ismp.org*
Joint Commission International (JCI) *www.jointcommission.org*
Joint Commission on Accreditation of Healthcare Organizations (JCAHO) *www.jcaho.org*
Kaiser Permanente *www.kaiserpermanente.org*
Leapfrog Group *www.leapfroggroup.org*
Medical Group Management Association *www.mgma.com*
National Academy for State Health Policy *www.nashp.org*
National Association for Healthcare Quality *www.nahq.org*
National Association of Chain Drug Stores *www.nacds.org*
National Coalition on Health Care *www.nchc.org*
National Committee for Quality Assurance (NCQA) *www.ncqa.org*
National Coordinating Council on Medication Error Reporting and Prevention (NCCMERP) *www.nccmerp.org*
National Health Policy Forum (NHPF) *www.nhpf.org*
National Patient Safety Foundation *www.npsf.org*
National Quality Forum (NQF) *www.qualityforum.org*
Partnership for Patient Safety *www.p4ps.org*
Pharmaceutical Research and Manufacturers of America (PhRMA) *www.phrma.org*
US Department of Veterans Affairs (VA) *www.va.gov*
US Pharmacopeial Convention (USP) *www.usp.org*

Australia

Australian Association for Quality Health Care (AAQHC) *www.aaqhc.org.au*
Australian Commission on Safety and Quality in Health Care *www.safetyandquality.gov.au*
Australian Council on Healthcare Standards (ACHS) *www.achs.org.au*
Australian Healthcare & Hospitals Association (AHHA) *www.ahha.asn.au*
Australian Patient Safety Foundation (APSF) *www.apsf.net.au*

Canada

Accreditation Canada *www.accreditation.ca*
Standards Council of Canada (SCC) *www.scc.ca*

International

International Organization for Standardization (ISO) *www.iso.org*

United Kingdom

National Health Service (NHS) *www.nhs.uk*
QHA Trent Accreditation *www.qha-trent.co.uk*
UK Akkreditering Forum Limited (UKAF) *www.ukaf.org.uk*

Appendix B: Summary of AHRQ Quality Indicators

Below is a summary of the Agency for Healthcare Research and Quality (AHRQ) Quality Indicators that are available in the areas of prevention, inpatient, patient safety, and pediatrics. As noted in the list below, most of the indicators are endorsed by the National Quality Forum (NQF). For a full description of AHRQ Quality Indicators, see *qualityindicators.ahrq.gov/Modules*.

In addition to the textual versions available on the AHRQ website, AHRQ Quality Indicators are a feature of free software tools distributed by AHRQ for organizations to use in a quality improvement effort. Download SAS/STAT, SQL Server or the open source MONARQ versions of the software at *https://www.qualityindicators.ahrq.gov/Software*.

AHRQ Prevention Quality Indicators (PQIs)

This set of AHRQ Quality Indicators, based on hospital inpatient data, is used to identify quality of care for ambulatory care conditions. The AHRQ promotes Prevention Quality Indicators (PQIs) as easy-to-use, inexpensive screening tools.

PQI 01 Diabetes Short-term Complications Admission Rate

Admissions for a principal diagnosis of diabetes with short-term complications per 100,000, ages 18+. Endorsed by NQF.

PQI 02 Perforated Appendix Admission Rate

Admissions for diagnosis of perforations or abscesses of the appendix per 1000 admissions with appendicitis, ages 18+. Endorsed by NQF.

PQI 03 Diabetes Long-term Complications Admission Rate

Admissions for a principal diagnosis of diabetes with long-term complications per 100,000, ages 18+. Endorsed by NQF.

PQI 05 Chronic Obstructive Pulmonary Disease (COPD) or Asthma in Older Adults Admission Rate

Admissions with a principal diagnosis of chronic obstructive pulmonary disease (COPD) or asthma per 100,000, ages 40+. Endorsed by NQF.

PQI 07 Hypertension Admission Rate

Admissions with a principal diagnosis of hypertension per 100,000, ages 18+.

PQI 08 Heart Failure Admission Rate

Admissions with a principal diagnosis of heart failure per 100,000, ages 18+. Endorsed by NQF.

PQI 09 Low Birth Weight Rate

Low birth weight (<2500 g) infants per 1000 newborns. Endorsed by NQF.

PQI 10 Dehydration Admission Rate

Admissions with a principal diagnosis of dehydration per 100,000, ages 18+. Endorsed by NQF.

PQI 11 Bacterial Pneumonia Admission Rate

Admissions with a principal diagnosis of bacterial pneumonia per 100,000, ages 18+.

PQI 12 Urinary Tract Infection Admission Rate

Admissions with a principal diagnosis of urinary tract infection per 100,000, ages 18+. Endorsed by NQF.

PQI 14 Uncontrolled Diabetes Admission Rate

Admissions for a principal diagnosis of diabetes without mention of short-term (ketoacidosis, hyperosmolarity, or coma) or long-term (renal, eye, neurological, circulatory, or other unspecified) complications per 100,000, ages 18+. Endorsed by NQF.

PQI 15 Asthma in Younger Adults Admission Rate

Admissions for a principal diagnosis of asthma per 100,000, ages 18–39. Endorsed by NQF.

PQI 16 Lower-Extremity Amputation among Patients with Diabetes Rate

Admissions for any-listed diagnosis of diabetes and any-listed procedure of lower-extremity amputation (except toe amputations) per 100,000, ages 18+. Endorsed by NQF.

PQI 90 Prevention Quality Overall Composite

Prevention Quality Indicators (PQI) overall composite per 100,000, ages 18+. Includes admissions for one of the following conditions: diabetes with short-term complications, diabetes with long-term complications, uncontrolled diabetes without complications, diabetes with lower-extremity amputation, chronic obstructive pulmonary disease, asthma, hypertension, heart failure, dehydration, bacterial pneumonia, or urinary tract infection.

PQI 91 Prevention Quality Acute Composite

Prevention Quality Indicators (PQI) composite of acute conditions per 100,000, ages 18+. Includes admissions with a principal diagnosis of one of the following conditions: dehydration, bacterial pneumonia, or urinary tract infection.

PQI 92 Prevention Quality Chronic Composite

Prevention Quality Indicators (PQI) composite of chronic conditions per 100,000, ages 18+. Includes admissions for one of the following conditions: diabetes with short-term complications, diabetes with long-term complications, uncontrolled diabetes without complications, diabetes with lower-extremity amputation, chronic obstructive pulmonary disease, asthma, hypertension, or heart failure without a cardiac procedure.

PQI 93 Prevention Quality Diabetes Composite

Prevention Quality Indicators (PQI) composite of diabetes admissions per 100,000, ages 18+. Includes admissions for one of the following conditions: diabetes with short-term complications, diabetes with long-term complications, uncontrolled diabetes without complications, diabetes with lower-extremity amputation.

PQI Appendix A—Admission Codes for Transfers

See www.qualityindicators.ahrq.gov/Downloads/Modules/PQI/V60-ICD10/TechSpecs/PQI _Appendix_A.pdf for list.

PQI Appendix B—Cardiac Procedure Codes

See www.qualityindicators.ahrq.gov/Downloads/Modules/PQI/V60-ICD10/TechSpecs/PQI _Appendix_B.pdf for list.

PQI Appendix C—Immuno-compromised State Diagnosis and Procedure Codes

See for www.qualityindicators.ahrq.gov/Downloads/Modules/PQI/V60-ICD10/TechSpecs/PQI _Appendix_C.pdf list.

PQI Appendix D—Definitions of Neonate, Newborn, Normal Newborn, and Outborn

See www.qualityindicators.ahrq.gov/Downloads/Modules/PQI/V60-ICD10/TechSpecs/PQI _Appendix_D.pdf for definitions and lists of codes.

AHRQ Inpatient Quality Indicators (IQIs)

These AHRQ Quality Indicators, based on hospital administrative data, are used to assess hospital quality of care. The AHRQ suggests that Inpatient Quality Indicators (IQIs) are useful, for example, in identifying potential problem areas in hospitals that may need further study, based on administrative data found in typical discharge records.

IQI 01 Esophageal Resection Volume

The number of hospital discharges with a procedure for esophageal resection or gastrectomy and esophageal cancer for patients 18+ or obstetric patients.

IQI 02 Pancreatic Resection Volume

The number of hospital discharges with a procedure of partial or total pancreatic resection for patients 18+ or obstetric patients. Endorsed by NQF.

IQI 04 Abdominal Aortic Aneurysm (AAA) Repair Volume

The number of hospital discharges with a procedure for abdominal aortic aneurysm (AAA) repair for patients 18+ or obstetric patients. Includes optional metrics for the number of discharges grouped by rupture status and procedure type. Endorsed by NQF.

IQI 05 Coronary Artery Bypass Graft (CABG)

The number of hospital discharges with a coronary artery bypass graft (CABG) procedure for patients 18+ or obstetric patients.

IQI 06 Percutaneous Coronary Intervention (PCI) Volume

The number of hospital discharges with a percutaneous coronary intervention (PCI) procedure for patients 18+ or obstetric patients.

IQI 07 Carotid Endarterectomy Volume

The number of hospital discharges with a procedure for carotid endarterectomy for patients 18+ or obstetric patients.

IQI 08 Esophageal Resection Mortality Rate

In-hospital deaths per 1000 discharges with esophageal resection for cancer, ages 18+.

IQI 09 Pancreatic Resection Mortality Rate

In-hospital deaths per 1000 discharges with pancreatic resection, ages 18+. Includes metrics for discharges grouped by type of diagnosis and procedure. Endorsed by NQF.

IQI 11 Abdominal Aortic Aneurysm Repair Mortality Rate

In-hospital deaths per 1000 discharges with abdominal aortic aneurysm repair, ages 18+. Includes metrics for discharges grouped by type of diagnosis and procedure. Endorsed by NQF.

IQI 12 Coronary Artery Bypass Graft (CABG) Mortality Rate

In-hospital deaths per 1000 discharges with coronary artery bypass graft (CABG), ages 40+.

IQI 13 Craniotomy Mortality Rate

In-hospital deaths per 1000 discharges with craniotomy, ages 18+.

IQI 14 Hip Replacement Mortality Rate

In-hospital deaths per 1000 pelvic and thigh osteoarthrosis discharges with partial or full hip replacement, ages 18+.

IQI 15 Acute Myocardial Infarction (AMI) Mortality Rate

In-hospital deaths per 1000 hospital discharges with acute myocardial infarction (AMI) as a principal diagnosis for patients ages 18+. Endorsed by NQF.

IQI 16 Heart Failure Mortality Rate

In-hospital deaths per 1000 hospital discharges with heart failure as a principal diagnosis for patients ages 18+. Endorsed by NQF.

IQI 17 Acute Stroke Mortality Rate

In-hospital deaths per 1000 hospital discharges with acute stroke as a principal diagnosis for patients ages 18+. Includes metrics for discharges grouped by type of stroke. Endorsed by NQF.

IQI 18 Gastrointestinal Hemorrhage Mortality Rate

In-hospital deaths per 1000 hospital discharges with gastrointestinal hemorrhage as a principal diagnosis for patients age 18+. Endorsed by NQF.

IQI 19 Hip Fracture Mortality Rate

In-hospital deaths per 1000 hospital discharges with hip fracture as a principal diagnosis for patients ages 65+. Endorsed by NQF.

IQI 20 Pneumonia Mortality Rate

In-hospital deaths per 1000 hospital discharges with pneumonia as a principal diagnosis for patients ages 18+. Endorsed by NQF.

IQI 21 Cesarean Delivery Rate, Uncomplicated

Cesarean deliveries without a hysterotomy procedure per 1000 deliveries.

IQI 22 Vaginal Birth after Cesarean (VBAC) Delivery Rate, Uncomplicated

Vaginal births per 1000 deliveries by patients with previous Cesarean deliveries.

IQI 23 Laparoscopic Cholecystectomy Rate

Laparoscopic cholecystectomy discharges per 1000 cholecystectomy discharges for patients with cholecystitis and/or cholelithiasis ages 18+.

IQI 24 Incidental Appendectomy in the Elderly Rate

Incidental appendectomy discharges per 1000 hospital discharges with abdominal or pelvic surgery for patients ages 65+.

IQI 25 Bilateral Cardiac Catheterization Rate

Bilateral cardiac catheterization discharges per 1000 heart catheterizations discharges for coronary artery disease for patients ages 18+. Endorsed by NQF.

IQI 26 Coronary Artery Bypass Graft (CABG) Rate

Coronary artery bypass graft (CABG) discharges per 100,000, ages 40+.

IQI 27 Percutaneous Coronary Intervention (PCI) Rate

Percutaneous coronary intervention (PCI) discharges per 100,000, ages 40+.

IQI 28 Hysterectomy Rate

Hysterectomy discharges per 100,000 female, ages 18 and older.

IQI 29 Laminectomy or Spinal Fusion Rate

Laminectomies or spinal fusion discharges per 100,000, ages 18+.

IQI 30 Percutaneous Coronary Intervention (PCI) Mortality Rate

In-hospital deaths per 1000 percutaneous coronary intervention (PCI) discharges for patients 40+.

IQI 31 Carotid Endarterectomy Mortality Rate

In-hospital deaths per 1000 carotid endarterectomy (CEA) discharges for patients ages 18+.

IQI 32 Acute Myocardial Infarction (AMI) Mortality Rate, without Transfer Cases

In-hospital deaths per 1000 hospital discharges with acute myocardial infarction (AMI) as a principal diagnosis for patients ages 18+.

IQI 33 Primary Cesarean Delivery Rate, Uncomplicated

First-time Cesarean deliveries without a hysterotomy procedure per 1000 deliveries.

IQI 34 Vaginal Birth after Cesarean (VBAC) Rate, All

Vaginal births per 1000 deliveries by patients with previous Cesarean deliveries.

IQI Appendix A—Abnormal Presentation, Preterm, Fetal Death, and Multiple Gestation Diagnosis Codes

See https://www.qualityindicators.ahrq.gov/Downloads/Modules/IQI/V60-ICD10/TechSpecs/IQI_Appendix_A.pdf for list.

AHRQ Patient Safety Indicators (PSIs)

These AHRQ Quality Indicators, based on hospital administrative data, are used to assess hospital quality of care, in terms of in-hospital complications and adverse events after surgeries, procedures, and childbirth. As with Inpatient Quality Indicators (IQIs), PSIs are useful in identifying potential problem areas in hospitals that may need further study, based on administrative data found in typical discharge records.

PSI 02 Death Rate in Low-Mortality Diagnosis-Related Groups (DRGs)

In-hospital deaths per 1000 discharges for low mortality (<0.5%) Diagnosis-Related Groups (DRGs) among patients ages 18+ or obstetric patients. Endorsed by NQF.

PSI 03 Pressure Ulcer Rate

Stage III or IV pressure ulcers or unstageable (secondary diagnosis) per 1000 discharges among surgical or medical patients ages 18+.

PSI 04 Death Rate among Surgical Inpatients with Serious Treatable Conditions

In-hospital deaths per 1000 surgical discharges, among patients ages 18–89 or obstetric patients, with serious treatable complications (deep vein thrombosis/pulmonary embolism, pneumonia, sepsis, shock/cardiac arrest, or gastrointestinal hemorrhage/acute ulcer). Includes metrics for the number of discharges for each type of complication. Endorsed by NQF.

PSI 05 Retained Surgical Item or Unretrieved Device Fragment Count

The number of hospital discharges with a retained surgical item or unretrieved device fragment (secondary diagnosis) among surgical and medical patients ages 18+ or obstetric patients. Endorsed by NQF.

PSI 06 Iatrogenic Pneumothorax Rate

Iatrogenic pneumothorax cases (secondary diagnosis) per 1000 surgical and medical discharges for patients ages 18+. Endorsed by NQF.

PSI 07 Central Venous Catheter-Related Bloodstream Infection Rate

Central venous catheter-related bloodstream infections (secondary diagnosis) per 1000 medical and surgical discharges for patients ages 18+ or obstetric cases.

PSI 08 In-Hospital Fall with Hip Fracture Rate

In-hospital fall with hip fracture (secondary diagnosis) per 1000 discharges for patients ages 18+.

PSI 09 Perioperative Hemorrhage or Hematoma Rate

Perioperative hemorrhage or hematoma cases involving a procedure to treat the hemorrhage or hematoma, following surgery per 1000 surgical discharges for patients ages 18+.

PSI 10 Postoperative Acute Kidney Injury Requiring Dialysis

Postoperative acute kidney failure requiring dialysis per 1000 elective surgical discharges for patients ages 18+.

PSI 11 Postoperative Respiratory Failure Rate

Postoperative respiratory failure (secondary diagnosis), prolonged mechanical ventilation, or reintubation cases per 1000 elective surgical discharges for patients ages 18+. Endorsed by NQF.

PSI 12 Perioperative Pulmonary Embolism or Deep Vein Thrombosis Rate

Perioperative pulmonary embolism or proximal deep vein thrombosis (secondary diagnosis) per 1000 surgical discharges for patients ages 18+. Endorsed by NQF.

PSI 13 Postoperative Sepsis Rate

Postoperative sepsis cases (secondary diagnosis) per 1000 elective surgical discharges for patients ages 18+.

PSI 14 Postoperative Wound Dehiscence Rate

Postoperative reclosures of the abdominal wall per 1000 abdominopelvic surgery discharges for patients ages 18+.

PSI 15 Unrecognized Abdominopelvic Accidental Puncture/Laceration Rate

Accidental punctures or lacerations (secondary diagnosis) during a procedure of the abdomen or pelvis per 1000 discharges for patients ages 18+ that require a second abdominopelvic procedure one or more days after the index procedure. Endorsed by NQF.

PSI 16 Transfusion Reaction Count

The number of medical and surgical discharges with a secondary diagnosis of transfusion reaction for patients ages 18+ or obstetric patients. Endorsed by NQF.

PSI 17 Birth Trauma Rate—Injury to Neonate

Birth trauma injuries per 1000 newborns.

PSI 18 Obstetric Trauma Rate—Vaginal Delivery with Instrument

Third- and fourth-degree obstetric traumas per 1000 instrument-assisted vaginal deliveries.

PSI 19 Obstetric Trauma Rate—Vaginal Delivery without Instrument

Third- and fourth-degree obstetric traumas per 1000 vaginal deliveries.

PSI 21 Retained Surgical Item or Unretrieved Device Fragment Rate

Retained surgical item or unretrieved device fragment cases per 100,000, ages 18+.

PSI 22 Iatrogenic Pneumothorax Rate

Iatrogenic pneumothorax cases per 100,000, ages 18+.

PSI 23 Central Venous Catheter-Related Bloodstream Infection Rate

Central venous catheter-related bloodstream infections per 100,000, ages 18+.

PSI 24 Postoperative Wound Dehiscence Rate

Postoperative reclosures of the abdominal wall per 100,000, ages 18+.

PSI 25 Accidental Puncture or Laceration Rate

Accidental punctures or lacerations during a procedure in patients with two abdominopelvic procedures performed one or more days apart per 100,000, ages 18+.

PSI 26 Transfusion Reaction Rate

Transfusion reactions per 100,000, ages 18+.

PSI 27 Perioperative Hemorrhage or Hematoma Rate

Perioperative hemorrhage or hematoma cases with control of perioperative hemorrhage, drainage of hematoma, or a miscellaneous hemorrhage- or hematoma-related procedure after surgery per 100,000 ages 18+.

PSI Appendix A—Operating Room Procedure Codes

See www.qualityindicators.ahrq.gov/Downloads/Modules/PSI/V60-ICD10/TechSpecs/PSI_Appendix _C.pdf for list of operating room procedure codes.

PSI Appendix C—Medical Discharge MS-DRGs

See www.qualityindicators.ahrq.gov/Downloads/Modules/PSI/V60-ICD10/TechSpecs/PSI_Appendix _C.pdf for list.

PSI Appendix E—Surgical Discharge MS-DRGs

See www.qualityindicators.ahrq.gov/Downloads/Modules/PSI/V60-ICD10/TechSpecs/PSI_Appendix _E.pdf for list.

PSI Appendix F—Infection Diagnosis Codes

See www.qualityindicators.ahrq.gov/Downloads/Modules/PSI/V60-ICD10/TechSpecs/PSI_Appendix _F.pdf for list.

PSI Appendix G—Trauma Diagnosis Codes

See www.qualityindicators.ahrq.gov/Downloads/Modules/PSI/V60-ICD10/TechSpecs/PSI_Appendix_G.pdf for list.

PSI Appendix H—Cancer Diagnosis Codes

See www.qualityindicators.ahrq.gov/Downloads/Modules/PSI/V60-ICD10/TechSpecs/PSI_Appendix_H.pdf for list.

PSI Appendix I—Immuno-compromised State Diagnosis and Procedure Codes

See www.qualityindicators.ahrq.gov/Downloads/Modules/PSI/V60-ICD10/TechSpecs/PSI_Appendix_I.pdf for list.

PSI Appendix J—Admission Codes for Transfers

See www.qualityindicators.ahrq.gov/Downloads/Modules/PSI/V60-ICD10/TechSpecs/PSI_Appendix_J.pdf for list.

PSI Appendix K—Self-Inflicted Injury Diagnosis Codes

See www.qualityindicators.ahrq.gov/Downloads/Modules/PSI/V60-ICD10/TechSpecs/PSI_Appendix_K.pdf for list.

PSI Appendix M—Definitions of Neonate, Newborn, Normal Newborn, and Outborn

See www.qualityindicators.ahrq.gov/Downloads/Modules/PSI/V60-ICD10/TechSpecs/PSI_Appendix_M.pdf for list.

AHRQ Pediatric Quality Indicators (PDIs)

Pediatric Quality Indicators(PDIs), based on hospital inpatient discharge data, are used to screen for problems pediatric patients experience that are due to the healthcare system—that is, preventable iatrogenic events.

NQI 01 Neonatal Iatrogenic Pneumothorax Rate

Iatrogenic pneumothorax cases (secondary diagnosis) per 1000 discharges for neonates weighing 500 g or more but less than 2500 g.

NQI 02 Neonatal Mortality Rate

In-hospital deaths per 1000 neonates.

NQI 03 Neonatal Bloodstream Infection Rate

Discharges with healthcare-associated bloodstream infection per 1000 discharges for newborns and outborns with birth weight of 500 g or more but less than 1500 g; with gestational age between 24 and 30 weeks; or with birth weight of 1500 g or more and death, an operating room procedure, mechanical ventilation, or transferring from another hospital within 2 days of birth. Endorsed by NQF.

PDI 01 Accidental Puncture or Laceration Rate

Accidental punctures or lacerations (secondary diagnosis) during procedure per 1000 discharges for patients ages 0–17. Includes metrics for discharges grouped by risk category. Endorsed by NQF.

PDI 02 Pressure Ulcer Rate

Stage III or IV pressure ulcers (secondary diagnosis) per 1000 discharges among patients ages 0–17. Includes metrics for discharges grouped by risk category. Endorsed by NQF.

PDI 03 Retained Surgical Item or Unretrieved Device Fragment Count

The number of hospital discharges with a retained surgical item or unretrieved device fragment (secondary diagnosis) among surgical and medical patients ages 0–17.

PDI 05 Iatrogenic Pneumothorax Rate

Iatrogenic pneumothorax cases (secondary diagnosis) per 1000 surgical or medical discharges for patients ages 0–17. Endorsed by NQF.

PDI 08 Perioperative Hemorrhage or Hematoma Rate

Perioperative hemorrhage or hematoma cases with control of perioperative hemorrhage or drainage of hematoma following surgery per 1000 elective surgical discharges for patients ages 0–17. Includes metrics for discharges grouped by high and low risk.

PDI 09 Postoperative Respiratory Failure Rate

Postoperative respiratory failure (secondary diagnosis), mechanical ventilation, or reintubation cases per 1000 elective surgery discharges for patients ages 0–17.

PDI 10 Postoperative Sepsis Rate

Postoperative sepsis cases (secondary diagnosis) per 1000 surgery discharges for patients ages 0–17. Includes metrics for discharges grouped by risk category. Endorsed by NQF.

PDI 11 Postoperative Wound Dehiscence Rate

Postoperative reclosures of the abdominal wall per 1000 abdominopelvic surgery discharges for patients ages 0–17. Includes metrics for discharges grouped by risk category. Endorsed by NQF.

PDI 12 Central Venous Catheter-Related Bloodstream Infection Rate

Central venous catheter-related bloodstream infections (secondary diagnosis) per 1000 medical and surgical discharges for patients ages 0–17. Includes metrics for discharges grouped by risk category. Endorsed by NQF.

PDI 13 Transfusion Reaction Count

The number of medical and surgical discharges with a secondary diagnosis of transfusion reaction for patients ages 0–17.

PDI 14 Asthma Admission Rate

Admissions with a principal diagnosis of asthma per 100,000, ages 2–17.

PDI 15 Diabetes Short-term Complications Admission Rate

Admissions for a principal diagnosis of diabetes with short-term complications (ketoacidosis, hyperosmolarity, or coma) per 100,000, ages 6–17.

PDI 16 Gastroenteritis Admission Rate

Admissions for a principal diagnosis of gastroenteritis, or for a principal diagnosis of dehydration with a secondary diagnosis of gastroenteritis per 100,000, ages 3 months to 17 years.

PDI 17 Perforated Appendix Admission Rate

Admissions for any-listed diagnosis of perforations or abscesses of the appendix per 1000 admissions with any-listed appendicitis, ages 1–17.

PDI 18 Urinary Tract Infection Admission Rate

Admissions with a principal diagnosis of urinary tract infection per 100,000, ages 3 months to 17 years.

PDI 90 Pediatric Quality Overall Composite

Pediatric Quality Indicators (PDI) overall composite per 100,000, ages 6–17. Includes admissions for one of the following conditions: asthma, diabetes with short-term complications, gastroenteritis, or urinary tract infection.

PDI 91 Pediatric Quality Acute Composite

Pediatric Quality Indicators (PDI) composite of acute conditions per 100,000, ages 6–17. Includes admissions for gastroenteritis or urinary tract infection.

PDI 92 Pediatric Quality Chronic Composite

Pediatric Quality Indicators (PDI) composite of chronic conditions per 100,000, ages 6–17. Includes admissions for asthma or diabetes with short-term complications.

PDI Appendix A—Operating Room Procedure Codes

See www.qualityindicators.ahrq.gov/Downloads/Modules/PDI/V60-ICD10/TechSpecs/PDI _Appendix_A.pdf for list.

PDI Appendix C—Surgical MS-DRGs

See www.qualityindicators.ahrq.gov/Downloads/Modules/PDI/V60-ICD10/TechSpecs/PDI _Appendix_C.pdf for list.

PDI Appendix E—Medical MS-DRGs

See www.qualityindicators.ahrq.gov/Downloads/Modules/PDI/V60-ICD10/TechSpecs/PDI _Appendix_E.pdf for list.

PDI Appendix F—High-Risk Immuno-compromised State Diagnosis and Procedure Codes

See www.qualityindicators.ahrq.gov/Downloads/Modules/PDI/V60-ICD10/TechSpecs/PDI _Appendix_F.pdf for list.

PDI Appendix G—Intermediate-Risk Immuno-compromised State Diagnosis Codes

See www.qualityindicators.ahrq.gov/Downloads/Modules/PDI/V60-ICD10/TechSpecs/PDI _Appendix_G.pdf for list.

PDI Appendix H—Infection Diagnosis Codes

See www.qualityindicators.ahrq.gov/Downloads/Modules/PDI/V60-ICD10/TechSpecs/PDI _Appendix_G.pdf for list.

PDI Appendix I—Definitions of Neonate Newborn Normal Newborn and Outborn

See www.qualityindicators.ahrq.gov/Downloads/Modules/PDI/V60-ICD10/TechSpecs/PDI _Appendix_I.pdf for list.

PDI Appendix J—Admission Codes for Transfers

See www.qualityindicators.ahrq.gov/Downloads/Modules/PDI/V60-ICD10/TechSpecs/PDI _Appendix_J.pdf for list.

PDI Appendix K—Stratification

The PDI module reports rates stratified by age and/or birth weight and, in some cases, by specified clinical strata. Refer to the individual Technical Specifications documents for indicator-specific stratification. The values of three variables related to age and weight are used to assign cases to stratification categories: Pediatric Age in Years, Age in Days, and Birth Weight.

PDI Appendix L—Low Birth Weight Categories

See www.qualityindicators.ahrq.gov/Downloads/Modules/PDI/V60-ICD10/TechSpecs/PDI _Appendix_L.pdf for list.

PDI Appendix M—Cancer

See www.qualityindicators.ahrq.gov/Downloads/Modules/PDI/V60-ICD10/TechSpecs/PDI _Appendix_M.pdf for list.

Source: Agency for Healthcare Research and Quality, Rockville, MD. qualityindicators.ahrq.gov. Accessed April 8, 2017.

Appendix C: AHRQ Toolkits

Following is a summary of toolkits freely available from the Agency for Healthcare Research and Quality (AHRQ), with the target audience identified.

AHRQ's Making Informed Consent an Informed Choice: Training Modules for Health Care Leaders and Professionals. For hospital leaders and health care professionals.

AHRQ Safety Program for End-Stage Renal Disease (ESRD) Facilities Toolkit. For dialysis center clinicians.

Carbapenem-Resistant Enterobacteriaceae (CRE) Control and Prevention Toolkit. For clinical staff.

Communication and Optimal Resolution (CANDOR) Toolkit. For health care institutions and practitioners.

Community Connections Obesity Referral Toolkit. For clinicians and staff.

Comprehensive Unit-Based Safety Program (CUSP) Toolkit. For clinicians.

Dissemination Planning Tool. For researchers.

Electronic Health Record (EHR) Information Design and Usability Toolkit. For primary care practices.

Emergency Severity Index (ESI): A Triage Tool for Emergency Department Care, V4. For the emergency department.

Enhancing the Clinical Content of Administrative Data—Present on Admission (POA) Toolkit. For clinicians.

Falls Management Program: A Quality Improvement Initiative for Nursing Facilities. For nursing facilities.

Guide to Patient and Family Engagement in Hospital Quality and Safety. For staff and patients.

Health Information Technology (Health IT) Evaluation Toolkit. For project teams.

Improving Patient Flow and Reducing Emergency Department Crowding: A Guide for Hospitals. This guide presents step-by-step instructions for planning and implementing patient flow improvement strategies to alleviate crowded emergency departments.

Improving Medication Safety in High Risk Medicare Beneficiaries Toolkit. For clinicians and researchers.

Improving Your Office Testing Process. A Toolkit for Rapid-Cycle Patient Safety and Quality Improvement. For physicians' offices, clinics, and other ambulatory care facilities.

Informed Consent and Authorization Toolkit for Minimal Risk Research. For researchers.

Integrating Chronic Care and Business Strategies in the Safety Net: A Toolkit for Primary Care Practices and Clinics. For clinicians.

Medications at Transitions and Clinical Handoffs (MATCH) Toolkit. For hospital administration.

National Quality Strategy Stakeholder Toolkit. For organizations.

Nursing Home Antimicrobial Stewardship Modules. For nursing homes.

Pediatric Toolkit for Using the AHRQ Quality Indicators. For clinical staff and administrators. This is a stand-alone, pediatric version of the QI Toolkit.

Preventing Falls in Hospitals—A Toolkit for Improving Quality of Care. For hospital administration and staff.

Preventing Pressure Ulcers in Hospitals. For hospital staff.

Questions Are the Answer Toolkit. For clinicians.

Race and Ethnicity Data Improvement Toolkit. For hospital staff.

Re-Engineered Discharge (RED) Toolkit. For hospital administrators.

The SHARE Approach. For clinicians.

Team Strategies and Tools to Enhance Performance and Patient Safety 2.0 (TeamSTEPPS). For clinicians and clinical staff.

Toolkit for Hospitals: Improving Performance on the AHRQ Quality Indicators (QI). For hospital administrators and staff.

Toolkit for Implementing the Chronic Care Model in an Academic Environment. For administrators.

Toolkit for Reducing Catheter-Associated Urinary Tract Infections (CAUTI). For clinical staff.

Toolkit for Reduction of Clostridium difficile Infections Through Antimicrobial Stewardship. For hospital administrators and staff.

Tools for Reducing Central Line-Associated Blood Stream Infections (CLABSI). For hospital staff.

Tracking and Improving Screening for Colorectal Cancer (CRC) Intervention: A Systems Approach. For clinicians.

Transitioning Newborns from NICU to Home: A Resource Toolkit. For hospital staff and patients.

Source: Toolkits. Content last reviewed February 2017. Rockville, MD: Agency for Healthcare Research and Quality. *www.ahrq.gov/professionals/education/ahrq-toolkits.html*

Appendix D: AHRQ QI Toolkit Components

This is a summary of the AHRQ QI Toolkit components, a set of tools available free of charge from the AHRQ website. As noted in Chapter 1, the tools are grouped into six major areas, arranged in logical order of likely use. The full toolkit description, *Toolkit for Using the AHQR Quality Indicators: How to Improve Hospital Quality and Safety*, is a PDF downloadable from the AHRQ website.

Area 1: Assess Readiness to Change

Survey to self-assess readiness to change
 Infrastructure for change management
 Readiness to work on the quality indicators
 (Your) Role in quality improvement
Case studies of using the QI toolkits for quality improvements
Specific tools to support change

Area 2: Apply Quality Indicators to Hospital Data

AHRQ quality indicators
 Data requirements
 Use
Quality indicator rates
 Observed
 Expected
 Risk adjusted
 Smoothed
Interpreting hospital quality indicator rates
Assessing performance of quality indicators (trends and comparators)
Preparing to calculate rates

Area 3: Identify Priorities for Quality Improvement

Prioritization worksheet
    Own rate and national comparator
    Estimate annual cost and cost to implement
    Rate strategic alignment and regulatory mandates
    Barrier assessment (staff capability and willingness)

Area 4: Implementation

Project charter
Quality indicators best practices
Gap analysis
Implementation plan
Implementation measurement
Project evaluation and debriefing

Area 5: Monitor Progress for Sustainabile Improvement

Ongoing monitoring
    Choosing a limited set of indicators
    Establish regular reporting schedule
    Develop report formats
    Establish procedures for acting on problems
    Assess sustainability periodically

Area 6: ROI Estimation

Calculating and interpreting ROI
    Determine basic ROI design
    Calculate ROI
    Interpret ROI ratio
Additional guidance
    Understand point of view for ROI calculations
    Assembling the ROI team
    Getting ready to conduct ROI calculation
    Using existing literature to estimate ROI calculation
    Selecting the time horizon for ROI calculation
    Making adjustments for future costs and savings
    Determining differences between costs and savings
    Using micro costing versus gross costing
Implementation costs worksheet
Net returns worksheet
Case studies

Additional resources
Components of implementation costs
ROI calculators

Source: Toolkit for Using the AHRQ Quality Indicators. Content last reviewed March 2017. Rockville, MD: Agency for Healthcare Research and Quality. *www.ahrq.gov/professionals/systems /hospital/qitoolkit/index.html*

Appendix E: AHRQ National Healthare Quality and Disparities Report Measures

Access

Health Insurance

Adults 18–64 who were uninsured at the time of interview
People without health insurance coverage at the time of interview, by age
Adults 18–64 who were uninsured at the time of interview, by race/ethnicity
Adults 18–64 without health insurance at the time of interview, by region
Adults 18–64 with private health insurance coverage, by age

Service

People with a place to go for medical care, by age and sex
Age-/sex-adjusted percentage of people with a place to go for medical care, by race/ethnicity
People who were unable to get or delayed getting needed medical care, dental care, or prescription medicines in the last 12 months, by insurance (under age 65) and age
People who were unable to get or delayed getting needed medical care, dental care, or prescription medicines in the last 12 months, by perceived health status and ethnicity

Timeliness

Adults who needed care right away for an illness, injury, or condition in the last 12 months who sometimes or never got care as soon as wanted, by insurance (ages 18–64) and ethnicity
Children who needed care right away for an illness, injury, or condition in the last 12 months who sometimes or never got care as soon as wanted, by preferred language and ethnicity

Infrastructure

Physicians and surgeons per 100,000 population, by race and ethnicity
Primary care medical residents per 100,000 population, by sex and race/ethnicity

Characteristics of HRSA-supported health center population versus US population
Medicaid and uninsured discharges in US short-term acute hospitals, by facility characteristics

Affordability
Access Problems due to Healthcare Costs

People under age 65 whose family's health insurance premiums and out-of-pocket medical expenses were more than 10% of total family income

People without a usual source of care who indicate a financial or insurance reason for not having a source of care

People unable to get or delayed getting needed medical care, dental care, or prescription medicines who indicate a financial or insurance reason for the problem

Inefficiency

Ruptured appendix per 1000 adult admissions with appendicitis

Men age 40+ who had a screening prostate-specific antigen test in the past year

Supplemental

Per capita national health expenditures

Care Coordination
Transitions

Hospitalized adult patients with heart failure who were given complete written discharge instructions

Median hospital 30-day risk standardized readmission rate or certain conditions

Median hospital 30-day risk standardized readmission rate

Potentially Avoidable ER Visits

ER visits with a principal diagnosis related to mental health, alcohol, or substance abuse ED visits with a principal diagnosis of dental conditions

ER visits for asthma, ages 18–39

ER visits for asthma, ages 2–17

Integration of Medical Information

People under age 65 with a usual source of care whose health provider usually asks about prescription medications and treatments from other doctors

Hospitals with electronic exchange of patient medication history with hospitals outside their system

Hospitals with electronic exchange of patient medication history with ambulatory providers outside their system

Electronic Health Record

Patients who reported that it was very important for them to get their own medical information electronically

Patients who reported that it was very important that doctors and other health providers be able to share their medical information with other providers electronically

Hospitals with fully implemented electronic medical record system

Hospitals with computerized systems that allow for electronic clinical documentation

Hospitals with computerized systems that allow for results viewing

Hospitals with computerized systems that allow for decision support

Hospitals with computerized systems that allow for computerized provider order entry

Effective Treatment

Cardiovascular Disease

Adults with hypertension whose blood pressure is under control

Hospital patients with heart attack given fibrinolytic medication within 30 minutes of arrival

Inpatient deaths per 1000 adult hospital admissions with heart attack

Adult admissions for congestive heart failure per 100,000 population

Total national costs of hospitalizations for congestive heart failure

Cancer

Patients with colon cancer who received surgical resection of colon cancer that included at least 12 lymph nodes pathologically examined

Age-adjusted colorectal cancer deaths per 100,000 population

Chronic Kidney Disease

Nephrology care before kidney failure

Registration for transplantation

Hemodialysis death rate

Diabetes

Receipt of four recommended diabetes services

People with current diabetes who have a written diabetes management plan

Outcome:

Adults age 40+ with diagnosed diabetes with hemoglobin A1c and blood pressure under control

Hospital admissions for uncontrolled diabetes

New cases of end-stage renal disease due to diabetes

HIV and AIDS

New AIDS cases
Adult HIV patients who had at least two outpatient visits during the year
Adult HIV patients with a viral load less than 200 copies/mL
HIV infection deaths
HIV patients in Ryan White–funded care who were virally suppressed (HIV RNA <200 copies/mL)
HIV patients in Ryan White–funded care who were retained in care (at least two ambulatory visit dates 90 days apart)

Mental Health and Substance Abuse

Treatment for depression
Suicide deaths
Treatment for illicit drug use or alcohol problem
Completion of substance abuse treatment
Emergency department visits with a principal diagnosis related to mental health, alcohol or substance abuse, by age and income

Musculoskeletal Disease

Adults with chronic joint symptoms who have ever seen a doctor or health professional for joint symptoms

Respiratory Disease

Completion of tuberculosis therapy
Daily asthma medication
Written asthma management plans
Emergency department visits for asthma

Healthy Living

Maternal and Child Healthcare

Access
Periods without insurance
Effectiveness
Prenatal care
Receipt of recommended immunizations by young children
Children's vision screening
Well-child visits in the last year
Receipt of meningococcal vaccine by adolescents
Receipt of human papillomavirus (HPV) vaccination by adolescents
Person-centered care

Children who had a doctor's office or clinic visit in the last 12 months who reported poor communication with health providers

Patient Safety

Birth trauma—injury to neonates
Care Coordination
   Children and adolescents whose health provider usually asks about prescription medications and treatments from other doctors
   Emergency department (ED) visits with a principal diagnosis related to mental health, alcohol, or substance abuse
   ED visits for asthma

Lifestyle Modification

Adult current smokers with a checkup in the last 12 months who received advice to quit smoking
Adults with obesity who ever received advice from a health professional to exercise more
Adults with obesity who did not spend half an hour or more in moderate or vigorous physical activity at least five times a week
Children 2–17 for whom a health provider gave advice within the past 2 years about the amount and kind of exercise, sports, or physically active hobbies they should have
Adults with obesity who ever received advice from a health professional about eating fewer high-fat or high-cholesterol foods
Children 2–17 for whom a health provider gave advice within the past 2 years about healthy eating

Clinical Preventive Services

Women 21–65 who received a Pap smear in the last 3 years
Invasive cervical cancer incidence per 100,000 women age 20+
Adults who received a blood pressure measurement in the last 2 years and can state whether their blood pressure was normal or high

Immunization

Adults 65+ who ever received pneumococcal vaccination
Hospital patients who received
   – Pneumococcal immunization
   – Influenza immunization
Long-stay nursing home residents who were assessed and appropriately given
   – Pneumococcal immunization
   – Influenza immunization

Rehabilitation

Improvement in mobility among home healthcare patients

Nursing home residents needing more help with daily activities
Improvement in management of oral medications

Supportive and Palliative Care

Relief of suffering:
Improvement in shortness of breath among home healthcare patients
Nursing home residents with moderate to severe pain
Nursing home residents who lose too much weight
Help with emotional and spiritual needs
Worsening depression or anxiety in nursing home residents
High-quality palliative care:
Home healthcare patients with hospital admission
Home healthcare patients with urgent, unplanned medical care
Nursing home residents receiving antipsychotic medication

Hispanic Healthcare

Breast Cancer

Women 50–74 who received a mammogram in the last 2 years
Breast cancer diagnosed at advanced stage per 100,000 women age 40+
Women with clinical Stage I–IIb breast cancer who received axillary node dissection or sentinel lymph node biopsy at the time of surgery
Women under 70 treated for breast cancer with breast-conserving surgery who received radiation therapy to the breast within 1 year of diagnosis
Breast cancer deaths per 100,000 female population per year

Colorectal Cancer

Men and women 50–75 who report that they had a blood stool test in the past year, sigmoidoscopy in the past 5 years and blood stool test in the past 3 years, or colonoscopy in the past 10 years
Colorectal cancer diagnosed at advanced stage per 100,000 men and women age 50+
Patients with colon cancer who received surgical resection of colon cancer that included at least 12 lymph nodes pathologically examined
Colorectal cancer deaths per 100,000 population per year

Other Cancer

All cancer deaths per 100,000 population per year
Women 21–65 who received a Pap smear in the last 3 years
Invasive cervical cancer incidence per 100,000 women age 20+
Men age 75+ without prostate cancer who had a PSA test or digital rectal exam for prostate cancer screening within the past year
Lung cancer deaths per 100,000 population per year

Cardiovascular Care

Adults who received a blood pressure measurement in the last 2 years and can state whether their blood pressure was normal or high

Adult admissions for hypertension

Adult admissions for angina without cardiac procedure

Adult admissions for congestive heart failure

Hospital patients with heart failure and left ventricular systolic dysfunction who were prescribed angiotensin-converting enzyme inhibitor or angiotensin receptor blocker at discharge

Hospital patients with heart attack given percutaneous coronary intervention within 90 minutes of arrival

Hospital patients with heart attack given fibrinolytic medication within 30 minutes of arrival

Deaths per 1000 hospital admissions with acute myocardial infarction, age 18+

Deaths per 1000 hospital admissions with congestive heart failure, age 18+

Deaths per 1000 hospital admissions with abdominal aortic aneurysm repair, age 18+

Deaths per 1000 hospital admissions with coronary artery bypass graft, age 40+

Deaths per 1000 hospital admissions with percutaneous transluminal coronary angioplasty, age 40+

Substance Abuse

People age 12+ who received any illicit drug or alcohol abuse treatment in the last 12 months

People age 12+ who needed treatment for illicit drug use or an alcohol problem and who received such treatment at a specialty facility in the last 12 months

People age 12+ treated for substance abuse who completed treatment course

Diabetes

Adults age 40+ with diabetes whose condition was diagnosed

Adults age 40+ with diagnosed diabetes who received all four recommended services for diabetes in the calendar year

Adults age 40+ with diagnosed diabetes with hemoglobin A1c under control

Adults age 40+ with diagnosed diabetes with blood pressure under control

Mental Health

Adults who received mental health treatment or counseling in the last 12 months

Adults with a major depressive episode in the last 12 months who received treatment

Children 12–17 with a major depressive episode in the last 12 months who received treatment

Suicide deaths per 100,000 population

Infant Mortality and Maternity Care

Live-born infants with low birth weight (less than 2500 g)

Live-born infants with very low birth weight (less than 1500 g)

Infant mortality per 1000 live births

Maternal deaths per 100,000 live births

Birth trauma—injury to newborn per 1000 live births
Obstetric trauma per 1000 vaginal deliveries without instrument assistance
Obstetric trauma per 1000 instrument-assisted vaginal deliveries

Patient Safety

Healthcare-Associated Infections

Postoperative sepsis per 1000 adult discharges with an elective operating room procedure
Standardized infection ratios for central line-associated bloodstream infections and surgical site infections
Bloodstream infections per 1000 central-line days in neonatal intensive care units
Bloodstream infections per 1000 central-line days in adult intensive care units

Procedure-Related Events

Unadjusted mortality rate 30 days postoperation for colorectal surgeries among US hospitals participating in the American College of Surgeons–National Surgical Quality Improvement Program
Percentage of adult patients receiving hip joint replacement because of fracture or degenerative conditions who experienced adverse events
Percentage of adults with mechanical adverse events associated with central venous catheter placement

Nursing Home Setting

Nursing home residents experiencing urinary tract infections
Nursing home residents experiencing use of restraints
Pooled mean rate of healthcare-associated infections per 1000 resident days in Pennsylvania nursing homes

Home Health Setting

Home health patients with improvement in surgical wounds
Home health patients with improvements in their ability to take medications orally

Ambulatory Setting

Adults with a probable missed stroke in the emergency department
Adults age 65+ who received potentially inappropriate prescription medications during the calendar year

Culture

Average percent positive responses on the AHRQ Hospital Survey on Patient Safety Culture
Average percent positive responses on the AHRQ Medical Office Survey on Patient Safety Culture

Average percent positive responses for patient safety culture composite among participants in the National Center for Patient Safety High Reliability Team training

Percent change from baseline in observed annual mortality rate per 1000 procedures, by medical team training status of Veterans Health Administration facility

Organizations

Distribution of Patient Safety Organizations by category of event reports collected

Reduction in surgical site infections among Vascular Quality Initiative Centers that expanded from sporadic to routine chlorhexidine use

Person- and Family-Centered Care

Communications—Doctor's Office

Adults who had a doctor's office or clinic visit in the last 12 months who reported poor communication with health providers, by insurance, 18–64 and 65+

Adults who had a doctor's office or clinic visit in the last 12 months who reported poor communication with health providers, by ethnicity and education

Children who had a doctor's office or clinic visit in the last 12 months whose parents reported poor communication with health providers, by ethnicity and language spoken at home

Communications—Hospital

Adult hospital patients who reported poor communication with nurses and doctors, by age

Adult hospital patients who did not receive good communication about discharge information, by race

Communications—Home Health

Provider–patient communication among adults receiving home healthcare, by language spoken at home

Provider–patient communication among adults receiving home healthcare, by race/ethnicity

Engagement in Decision Making

Adults with a usual source of care whose health providers sometimes or never asked for the patient's help to make treatment decisions, by insurance and education

People with a usual source of care whose health providers sometimes or never asked for the patient's help to make treatment decisions, by number of chronic conditions and ethnicity

End of Life

Hospice patients who received care consistent with their stated end-of-life wishes, by age and ethnicity

Hospice patients who received the right amount of help for feelings of anxiety or sadness, by ethnicity and race

Hospice patients who received the right amount of medicine for pain, by sex and race

Rural Healthcare

Access to Healthcare
Patient Safety
Person- and Family-Centered Care
Communication and Care Coordination
Prevention and Treatment of Leading Causes of Morbidity and Mortality
Healthy Living
Affordability

Women's Healthcare

Access to Healthcare
Patient Safety
Person- and Family-Centered Care
Communication and Care Coordination
Prevention and Treatment of Leading Causes of Morbidity and Mortality
Healthy Living
Affordability

Sources:

2014 National Healthcare Quality & Disparities Report Chartbooks. Content last reviewed October 2015. Rockville, MD: Agency for Healthcare Research and Quality. *www.ahrq.gov /research/findings/nhqrdr/2014chartbooks/index.html*

2014 National Healthcare Quality & Disparities Report Data Query Tool. *Nhqrnet.ahrq.gov /inhqrdr/data/query*

2014 National Healthcare Quality and Disparities Report chartbook on access to health care. Rockville, MD: Agency for Healthcare Research and Quality; April 2015. AHRQ Pub. No. 15-0007-1-EF.

2014 National Healthcare Quality and Disparities Report chartbook on care affordability. Rockville, MD: Agency for Healthcare Research and Quality; June 2015. AHRQ Pub. No. 15-0007-6-EF.

2014 National Healthcare Quality and Disparities Report chartbook on care coordination. Rockville, MD: Agency for Healthcare Research and Quality; May 2015. AHRQ Pub. No. 15-0007-5-EF.

2014 National Healthcare Quality and Disparities Report chartbook on effective treatment. Rockville, MD: Agency for Healthcare Research and Quality; July 2015. AHRQ Pub. No. 15-0007-8-EF.

2014 National Healthcare Quality and Disparities Report chartbook on health care for Hispanics. Rockville, MD: Agency for Healthcare Research and Quality; September 2015. AHRQ Pub. No. 15-0007-11-EF.

2014 National Healthcare Quality and Disparities Report chartbook on healthy living. Rockville, MD: Agency for Healthcare Research and Quality; June 2015. AHRQ Pub. No. 15-0007-7-EF.

2014 National Healthcare Quality and Disparities Report chartbook on patient safety. Rockville, MD: Agency for Healthcare Research and Quality; April 2015. AHRQ Pub. No. 15-0007-2-EF.

2014 National Healthcare Quality and Disparities Report chartbook on person- and family-centered care. Rockville, MD: Agency for Healthcare Research and Quality; May 2015. AHRQ Pub. No. 15-0007-4-EF.

2014 National Healthcare Quality and Disparities Report chartbook on rural health care. Rockville, MD: Agency for Healthcare Research and Quality; August 2015. AHRQ Pub. No. 15-0007-9-EF.

2014 National Healthcare Quality and Disparities Report chartbook on women's health care. Rockville, MD: Agency for Healthcare Research and Quality; September 2015. AHRQ Pub. No. 15-0007-10-EF.

2015 National Healthcare Quality and Disparities Report and 5th Anniversary Update on the National Quality Strategy. Rockville, MD: Agency for Healthcare Research and Quality. AHRQ; April 2016. AHRQ Pub. No. 16-0015.

Appendix F: Health Plan Employer Data and Information Set (HEDIS) Measures for Physicians

Effectiveness of Care

Adherence to Antipsychotic Medications for Individuals with Schizophrenia

Adult BMI Assessment

Annual Monitoring for Patients on Persistent Medications

Antidepressant Medication Management

Appropriate Testing for Children with Pharyngitis

Appropriate Treatment for Children with Upper Respiratory Infection

Asthma Medication Ratio

Avoidance of Antibiotic Treatment in Adults with Acute Bronchitis

Breast Cancer Screening

Cardiovascular Monitoring for People with Cardiovascular Disease and Schizophrenia

Care for Older Adults

Cervical Cancer Screening

Childhood Immunization Status

Chlamydia Screening in Women

Colorectal Cancer Screening

Comprehensive Adult Diabetes Care

Controlling High Blood Pressure

Diabetes Monitoring for People with Diabetes and Schizophrenia

Diabetes Screening for People with Schizophrenia or Bipolar Disorder Who Are Using Antipsychotic Medications

Disease Modifying Anti-Rheumatic Drug Therapy for Rheumatoid Arthritis

Follow-Up after Emergency Department Visit for Alcohol and Other Drug Dependence

Follow-Up after Emergency Department Visit for Mental Illness

Follow-Up after Hospitalization for Mental Illness

Follow-Up Care for Children Prescribed ADHD Medication

Immunizations for Adolescents

Lead Screening in Children
Medication Management for People with Asthma
Medication Reconciliation Post-Discharge
Metabolic Monitoring for Children and Adolescents on Antipsychotics
Non-Recommended Cervical Cancer Screening in Adolescent Females
Non-Recommended PSA-Based Screening in Older Men
Osteoporosis Management in Women Who Had a Fracture
Persistence of Beta-Blocker Treatment after a Heart Attack
Pharmacotherapy Management of COPD Exacerbation
Potentially Harmful Drug–Disease Interactions in the Elderly
Statin Therapy for Patients with Cardiovascular Conditions
Statin Therapy for Patients with Diabetes
Use of High-Risk Medications in the Elderly
Use of Imaging Studies for Low Back Pain
Use of Multiple Concurrent Antipsychotics in Children and Adolescents
Use of Spirometry Testing in the Assessment and Diagnosis of COPD
Weight Assessment and Counseling for Nutrition and Physical Activity for Children/Adolescents

Access/Availability

Adults' Access to Preventive/Ambulatory Health Services
Children's and Adolescents' Access to Primary Care Practitioners
Initiation and Engagement of Alcohol and Other Drug Dependence Treatment
Prenatal and Postpartum Care
Use of First-Line Psychosocial Care for Children and Adolescents on Antipsychotics

Utilization

Adolescent Well-Care Visits
Frequency of Ongoing Prenatal Care
Well-Child Visits in the First 15 Months of Life
Well-Child Visits in the Third, Fourth, Fifth, and Sixth Years of Life

Source: HEDIS 2017 Measures Volume 1. *www.ncqa.org/hedis-quality-measurement/hedis-measures/hedis-2017.*

Appendix G: OASIS-Based Outcomes Measures

The following is a summary of the OASIS-based outcomes measure descriptions. See the *CMS Manual* for the complete measure, including details on the numerator and denominator, exclusions, and whether the measure is risk adjusted.

Percentage of home health quality episodes during which patient(s)

- Improved or stayed the same in ability to groom self
- Improved in ability to dress upper body
- Improved in ability to dress lower body
- Improved at bathing self
- Improved or stayed the same in the ability to bathe
- Improved in ability to get to and from and on and off the toilet
- Improved or stayed the same in ability to get to and from and on and off the toilet
- Improved or stayed the same in ability to manage toileting hygiene
- Improved in ability to get in and out of bed
- Improved or stayed the same in ability to get in and out of bed
- Improved in ability to ambulate
- Improved in ability to take their medicines correctly (by mouth)
- Improved or stayed the same in ability to take their medicines correctly (by mouth)
- Became less short of breath or dyspneic
- Frequency of pain when moving around improved
- Demonstrates an improvement in the condition of surgical wounds
- With Stage 2–4 pressure ulcers present at discharge that are new or worsened since the beginning of the quality episode
- Bowel control improves
- Are confused less often
- Needed urgent, unplanned medical care from a hospital emergency department, immediately followed by hospital admission
- Ended with the patient being admitted to the hospital
- Remained at home

Appendix H: Oasis-Based Process Measures

The following is a summary of the OASIS-based process measure descriptions. See the *CMS Manual* and related tables for the complete measure, including details on the numerator and denominator, exclusions, and whether the measure is risk adjusted.

Percentage of home health quality episodes in which

The start or resumption of care date was either on the physician-specified date or within 2 days of the referral date or inpatient discharge date, whichever is later.

Patients were screened for depression (using a standardized depression screening tool) at start/resumption of care.

Patients had a multi-factor fall risk assessment at start/resumption of care.

The physician-ordered plan of care includes regular monitoring for the presence of skin lesions on the lower extremities and patient education on proper diabetic foot care.

Diabetic foot care and patient/caregiver education were included in the physician-ordered plan of care and implemented (at the time of or at any time since the most recent SOC/ROC assessment).

Patient/caregiver was instructed on how to monitor the effectiveness of drug therapy, how to recognize potential adverse effects, and how and when to report problems (at the time of or at any time since the most recent SOC/ROC assessment).

Percentage of home health quality episodes

During which patients received influenza immunization for the current flu season.

During which patients were offered and refused influenza immunization for the current flu season.

During which patients were determined to have medical contraindication(s) to receiving influenza immunization.

During which patients were determined to have ever received pneumococcal polysaccharide vaccine.

During which patients were offered and refused pneumococcal polysaccharide vaccine.

During which patients were determined to have medical contraindication(s) to receiving pneumococcal polysaccharide vaccine.

In which a drug regimen review was conducted at the start of care or resumption of care and completion of recommended actions from timely follow-up with a physician occurred each time potential clinically significant medication issues were identified throughout that quality episode.

Source: Home-Health-Process-Measures-Table_OASIS-C2_02_03_17_Final-Revised-1.pdf, downloaded from *https://www.cms.gov/Medicare/Quality-Initiatives-Patient-Assessment-Instruments/Home HealthQualityInits/PBQIProcessMeasures.html*

Appendix I: NHS England Statistics (Measures)

The following summary of NHS Statistics, although developed for England, has potential applicability to a Performance Management Initiative in the United States or any other country that practices Western medicine. For example, a particular hospital in the United States may need to improve the performance of its ambulance service—an area that the NHS has addressed in detail. The NHS measures dealing with ambulance service performance might not be the perfect solution, but they will at least provide starting points upon which you can build.

What follows are highlights of the specific statistics. Fortunately, the open NHS system provides details of every measure, including excluded populations, all available through the *www .enghand.nhs.uk* website. Also, the source information from which the information listed below is excerpted is available through the Statistical Work Areas page of the NHS website, *www.england .nhs.uk/statistics/statistical-work-areas*.

Accident and emergency attendances and emergency admissions

Weekly and monthly accident and emergency (i.e., ER) attendances and admissions. Total number of attendances in the specified period for all A&E types, including Minor Injury Units and Walk-in Centers, and of these, the number of patients discharged, admitted, or transferred within 4 hours of arrival. Also included are the number of emergency admissions and any waits of over 4 hours and over 12 hours for admission following a decision to admit.

Ambulance systems indicators

The total number of Red 1 calls (i.e., top priority ambulance calls for cardiac/respiratory arrest victims) resulting in an emergency response arriving at the scene of the incident, the number of calls resulting in an emergency response arriving at the scene of the incident within 8 minutes, and the proportion of ambulances that responded to within 8 minutes.

The total number of Red 2 calls (i.e., second priority ambulance calls for life-threatening emergencies other than cardiac/respiratory arrest) resulting in an emergency response arriving at the scene of the incident, the number of calls resulting in an emergency response arriving at the scene of the incident within 8 minutes, and the proportion of ambulances that responded to within 8 minutes.

The total number of Category A calls (i.e., urgent, not life threatening) resulting in an emergency response arriving at the scene of the incident, the number of calls resulting in an emergency response arriving at the scene of the incident within 19 minutes, and the proportion of ambulances that responded to within 19 minutes.

Also, responsiveness of the switchboard to calls for an ambulance, by level of emergency/urgency.

Ambulance clinical outcomes quality indicators

Cardiac Arrest

The number of patients resuscitated by ambulance service following an out-of-hospital cardiac arrest, the number of these patients who had return of spontaneous circulation on arrival at hospital, and the proportion of those who were resuscitated who had return of spontaneous circulation on arrival at hospital.

The number of patients resuscitated by ambulance service following an out-of-hospital cardiac arrest, where the initial rhythm was ventricular fibrillation or ventricular tachycardia, the number of these patients who had return of spontaneous circulation on arrival at hospital, and the proportion of those who were resuscitated who had return of spontaneous circulation on arrival at hospital.

Acute ST-elevation myocardial infarction (STEMI)

The number of patients with STEMI who received primary angioplasty, where ambulance personnel performed the first diagnostic ECG and patient was transferred to a primary percutaneous coronary intervention (PPCI) center.

The number of patients with STEMI who received primary angioplasty, where ambulance personnel performed the first diagnostic ECG and patient was transferred to a primary percutaneous coronary intervention (PPCI) center, and primary angioplasty balloon inflation occurred within 150 minutes of emergency call.

The proportion of patients with suspected STEMI confirmed on ECG who received appropriate care.

Stroke

Measures of the number of patients potentially eligible for stroke thrombolysis, including those arriving at hospitals with a stroke center within 60 minutes of a call to the ambulance service. Measures of the number of suspected stroke or unresolved transient ischemic attack patients, including those who received appropriate care, as well as the resultant proportion of suspected stroke or unresolved transient ischemic attack patients who received appropriate care.

Cardiac Arrest

The number of patients who had resuscitation started or continued by the ambulance service following

- An out-of-hospital cardiac arrest, discharged from hospital alive
- An out-of-hospital cardiac arrest of presumed cardiac origin, where the arrest was bystander witnessed and the initial rhythm was ventricular fibrillation or ventricular tachycardia
- An out-of-hospital cardiac arrest of presumed cardiac origin, where the arrest was bystander witnessed and the initial rhythm was ventricular fibrillation or ventricular tachycardia, who were discharged from the hospital alive

Bed availability and occupancy

Occupancy rates and bed numbers.

Cancelled elective operations

The number of last-minute elective operations cancelled for nonclinical reasons, and the number of patients not treated within 28 days because of last-minute elective cancellation.

Cancer patient experience survey

Survey on patient experience with cancer treatment.

Cancer waiting times
>Waiting time by type of cancer.

Child immunization
>Child immunization statistics.

Combined performance summary
>Monthly summary of NHS 111, ambulance quality indicators, A&E attendances and emergency admissions, waiting times, and delayed transfers of care.

Consultant-led referral to treatment waiting times
>Median wait times for a referral, in weeks.

Critical care bed capacity and urgent operations cancelled
>Critical care capacity, including adult, pediatric, and neonatal available and occupied critical care beds, as a snapshot at midnight on the last Thursday of the month. Also, the number of urgent operations cancelled, including those cancelled for the second or more time throughout the month.

Delayed transfers of care
>Average daily rate of delayed transfers of care.

Dementia assessment and referral
>The number and proportion of patients 75+ admitted as an emergency for more than 72 hours who have been identified as potentially having dementia, who are appropriately assessed and, where appropriate, referred on to specialist services.

Diagnostic imaging data set
>Measures of diagnostic imaging tests, extracted from Radiology Information Systems (RISs), including referral source and patient type, type of test, GP registered practice, patient postcode, ethnicity, gender and date of birth, plus waiting times for each diagnostic imaging event.

Diagnostic test waiting times and activity
>A monthly measure of waiting times and activity for 15 key diagnostic tests and procedures, a quarterly measure of patients waiting over 6 weeks for a diagnostic test, and an annual measure of the number of imaging and radiological examinations or tests carried out during the year.

Direct access audiology waiting times
>Referral to treatment (RTT) times for completed pathways and incomplete pathways for direct access audiology. That is, how long a patient has to wait for care after a referral.

Early intervention in psychosis waiting times
>This measure is used to evaluate waiting time for patients who have started treatment for early intervention in psychosis, by week since referral.

Extended access to general practice
>This biannual (six monthly) statistic looks at a general practice's provision for pre-bookable appointments during extended hours on weekdays and weekends.

General practice (GP) patient survey
>This survey catalogs the overall patient experience with the GP, access to in-hours GP services, assessment of online GP services, waiting times, patient confidence and trust in the GP, the operating hours of the GP, the patient's overall health management, and the assessment of care planning.

General practice patient survey: dental results
>This survey includes the number of visits to dentists in last 2 years per patient, patient preference for a private dentist over an NHS dentist, and the patient's overall access to dental care.

Hospital activity

Monthly and quarterly reports of hospital inpatient and outpatient activity. Monthly reports include inpatient elective ordinary, elective day cases, elective ordinary planned, elective day case planned, and outpatient general practice written referrals made and seen. Quarterly reports include decisions to admit, patients admitted, patients failed to attend, outpatient number of general practice written referrals, first attendances seen, and subsequent attendances seen and did not attend.

Mental health community teams activity

A quarterly report on the number of patients on Care Program Approach followed up within 7 days of discharge from psychiatric inpatient care. Also, the number of inpatient admissions kept by Crisis Resolution Home Treatment teams.

Mixed sex accommodation breaches

The number of occurrences of unjustified mixing of sexes in relation to sleeping accommodation (i.e., mixing males and females in the same room/area).

National patient and staff surveys

A national patient survey on experience with primary care, secondary care, cancer, and overall satisfaction with the NHS system.

A national staff survey that includes an assessment of attitude, perceived discrimination, opportunities, and work versus home life.

NHS 111 minimum data set

Statistics on calls to "111" (roughly equivalent to "911" in the United States), including the number of calls, the average and maximum wait times, the number of calls transferred up the clinical hierarchy, the average length of calls, and whether an ambulance was dispatched in response to the call.

NHS staff survey in England

An extensive staff survey.

Overall patient experience scores

Patient views of care and services provided by the NHS. Constructed using results taken from the NHS Inpatient, Outpatient, Community Mental Health, and Accident & Emergency surveys.

Patient reported outcome measures (PROMs)

The quality of care delivered to NHS patients, from the patient perspective, on four clinical procedures: hip replacements, knee replacements, groin hernia, and varicose veins. PROMs calculate the health gains after surgical treatment using pre- and postoperative surveys.

Venous thromboembolism (VTE) risk assessment

The number of adults admitted as inpatients in the month who have been risk assessed for VTE on admission to hospital, the total number of adult inpatients admitted in the month, and the percentage of adult hospital admissions assessed for risk of VTE on admission.

Winter daily situation reports

Winter Accident and Emergency closures, cancelled operations, bed pressures, and ambulance delays.

Source: https://www.england.nhs.uk/statistics/statistical-work-areas

Appendix J: Highlights of the Australian National Safety and Quality Health Service (NSQHS) Standards

Governance

Establishes a governance system, including collecting and reviewing performance data, for safety and quality in health care. All of the subsequent standards are tied to governance in some way.

Partnering with Consumers

Establishes consumer partnerships for service planning, designing care, and the collection and evaluation of performance measures.

Infection

Aimed at preventing patients from acquiring infections, and when they do, manage the infections efficiently. Regular monitoring of policies, procedures, and protocols for waste management to antibiotic use. Surveillance system using dedicated workforce.

Medication Safety

Monitoring of patient medical history, including current medications, as well as subsequent prescribing and dispensing/administering of medications. Storing and compounding of medications are also monitored.

Patient ID and Procedure Matching

Standards are designed to ensure that the correct procedure is on the correct patient. A minimum of three patient identifiers are used when transferring patients or providing care.

Clinical Handover

Standards for transfer of care, whether by shift change, written orders, or transport to a new area, implemented primarily through governance.

Blood and Blood Products

Standards ensure safety and appropriateness of administering blood products to patients, via monitoring blood product prescribing and clinical use. Including clinical monitoring of blood product transfusion history and disposal of any products.

Pressure Injuries

Standards in place to ensure patients don't develop pressure injuries, and, when they do, how best to treat them.

Deterioration in Acute Health Care

Standards ensure patient deterioration—with the exception of mental deterioration—is detected and acted upon promptly and appropriately.

Falls

Standards attempt to prevent falls and the resulting harm to the patient.
Source: Australian Commission on Safety and Quality in Health Care, National Safety and Quality Health Service Standards (September 2012). Sydney. ACSQHC, 2012.

Acronyms

A&E	Accident & Emergency Department
AAA	Abdominal Aortic Aneurysm
AABB	American Association of Blood Banks
AAMC	Association of American Medical Colleges
AAPCC	Adjusted Average per Capita Cost
AAQHD	Australian Association for Quality Health Care
ABC	Activity-Based Costing
ABMS	American Board of Medical Specialties
ACA	Affordable Care Act/Allowance for Contractual Adjustments
ACC	American College of Cardiology
ACE	Angiotensin-Converting Enzyme
ACEI	Angiotensin-Converting Enzyme Inhibitor
ACHS	Australian Council on Health Standards
ACR	American College of Radiology
ACRRVS	American College of Radiology Relative Value Scale
ADA	Allowance for Doubtful Accounts
ADE	Adverse Drug Event
ADL	Activity of Daily Living
ADT	Admission Discharge Transfer
AERS	Adverse Event Reporting System
AES	Advanced Encryption Standard
AGC	Atypical Glandular Cells
AHA	American Heart Association
AHCPR	Agency for Health Care Policy and Research (now AHRQ)
AHD	American Hospital Directory
AHRQ	Agency for Healthcare Research and Quality
AI	Artificial Intelligence
AIAG	Automotive Industry Action Group
AIDS	Acquired Immune Deficiency Syndrome
ALOS	Average Length of Service; Average Length of Stay
AMA	American Medical Association
AMAP	American Medical Accreditation Program
AMI	Acute Myocardial Infarction
ANCC	American Nurses Credentialing Center
ANSI	American National Standards Institute
AOA	American Optometric Association

AONE	American Organization of Nurse Executives
AP	Anterior–Posterior
APC	Ambulatory Payment Classification
APD	Adjusted Patient Day
APhA	American Pharmaceutical Association
APSF	Anesthesia Patient Safety Foundation/Australian Patient Safety Foundation
ARB	Angiotensin II Receptor Blocker
ARRA	American Recover and Reinvestment Act of 2009
ART	Anti-Retroviral Therapy
ASC	Atypical Squamous Cells
ASHI	American Society of Histocompatibility and Immunogenetics
ASHP	American Society of Health-System Pharmacists
ASHRM	American Society for Healthcare Risk Management
ASPE	Assistant Secretary for Planning and Evaluation
ASQ	American Society for Quality
ASRS	Aviation Safety Reporting System
ASTM	American Society for Testing and Materials
AV	Arteriovenous
BBA	Balanced Budget Act (of 1997)
BBRA	Balanced Budget Refinement Act (of 1999)
BI	Business Intelligence
BIPA	Benefits Improvement and Protection Act (of 2000)
BMD	Bone Mineral Density
BMI	Body Mass Index
BNQP	Baldrige National Quality Program
BP	Blood Pressure
BPM	Business Performance Management
BRFSS	Behavioral Risk Factor Surveillance System
BSC	Balanced Scorecard
BSI	British Standards Institution
Ca	Calcium
CABG	Coronary Artery Bypass Graft
CAD	Coronary Artery Disease; Computer-Aided Dispatch
CAH	Critical Access Hospital
CAHMI	Child and Adolescent Health Measurement Initiative
CAHPS	Consumer Assessment of Health Plans
CAM	Complementary or Alternative Medicine; Confusion Assessment Method
CAMHS	Child and Adolescent Mental Health Services
CAP	Community-Acquired Pneumonia; College of American Pathologists
CC	Comorbidity or Complication
CDC	Centers for Disease Control and Prevention
CDCTB	National Tuberculosis Surveillance System
CEA	Carotid Endarterectomy
CEO	Chief Executive Officer
CERT	Centers for Education and Research in Therapeutics
CFO	Chief Financial Officer
CHAPS	Consumer Assessment of Health Plans

CHF	Congestive Heart Failure
CHI	Commission for Health Improvement
CHIN	Community Health Information Network
CHIPS	Center for Health Information Performance
CIO	Chief Information Officer
CITL	Center for Information Technology Leadership
CKD	Chronic Kidney Disease
CLIA	Clinical Laboratory Improvement Amendments
CMC	Correctional Managed Care
CME	Continuing Medical Education
CMI	Case Mix Index
CMR	Case Management Record
CMS	Centers for Medicare and Medicaid Services
CNST	Clinical Negligence Scheme for Trusts
COB	Coordination of Benefits
COGS	Cost of Goods Sold
COO	Chief Operating Officer
COPD	Chronic Obstructive Pulmonary Disease
COPPA	Children's Online Privacy Protection Act
CPA	Certified Public Accountant
CPM	Clinical Performance Measures
CPO	Chief Privacy Officer
CPOE	Computerized Physician Order Entry
CPT	Current Procedural Terminology
CRM	Customer Relationship Management
CSA	Canadian Standards Association
CSFII	Continuing Survey of Food Intake by Individuals
CSHCN	Children with Special Health Care Needs
CTV	Composite Time Value
CVD	Cardiovascular Disease
CY	Calendar Year
DFC	Dialysis Facility Compare
DFR	Direct Financial Reward
DHHS	Department of Health and Human Services
DHQP	Division of Healthcare Quality Promotion
DJD	Degenerative Joint Disease
DM	Disease Management; Diabetes Mellitus
DMO	Dental Maintenance Organization
DON	Diabetes Outreach Network
DPR	Drug Peer Review
DPU	Distinct Part Unit
DQIP	Diabetes Quality Improvement Project
DRG	Diagnosis-Related Group
DSM-IV	Diagnostic and Statistical Manual of Mental Disorders, Fourth Edition
DSS	Decision Support System
DTC	Direct to Consumer
DVT	Deep Vein Thrombosis

DWV	Dental Weighted Value
EBIT	Earnings before Interest and Taxes
EBITAR	Earnings before Interest, Taxes, and Rent
EBITDAR	Earnings before Interest, Taxes, Depreciation, Amortization, and Rent
ECHO	Experience of Care and Health Outcomes Survey (HEDIS)
ECRI	Emergency Care Research Institute
ED	Emergency Department
EDI	Electronic Data Interchange
EHR	Electronic Health Record
EKG	Electrocardiogram
EMR	Electronic Medical Record
EMV	Expected Money Value
EOC	Episode of Care
EPAD	Expenses per Adjusted Discharge
EPAPD	Expenses per Adjusted Patient Day
EPM	Enterprise Performance Management
ER	Emergency Room
ERM	Esophageal Resection Mortality
ERISA	Employee Retirement Income Security Act (of 1974)
ERM	Employee Relationship Management
ERP	Enterprise Resource Planning
ESRD	End-Stage Renal Disease
ESWL	Extracorporeal Shock Wave Lithotripter
EVA	Economic Value Added
FAA	Federal Aviation Administration
FACCT	Foundation for Accountability
FAP	Facility Admission Profile
FAQs	Frequently Asked Questions
FDA	Food and Drug Administration
FDASIA	Food and Drug Administration Safety and Innovation Act
FERPA	Family Educational Rights and Privacy Act
FHA	Federal Health Architecture
FIFO	First in, First out
FOBT	Fecal Occult Blood Test
FSA	Flexible Spending Account
FTE	Full-Time Equivalent
GAAP	Generally Accepted Accounting Principles
GAF	Global Assessment of Functioning
GDP	Gross Domestic Product
GFR	Glomerular Filtration Rate
GLB	Gramm–Leach–Bliley Act
GME	Graduate Medical Education
GP	General Practitioner
HAART	Highly Active Anti-Retroviral Therapy
Hb	Hemoglobin
HCFA	Health Care Financing Administration (now CMS)
HCPCS	Healthcare Common Procedure Coding System

HCSUS	HIV Cost and Services Utilization Study
HCUP	Healthcare Cost and Utilization Project
HDL	High-Density Lipoproteins
HEDIS	Healthcare Effectiveness Data and Information Set
HES	Hospital Episode Statistics
HF	Heart Failure
HFMA	Healthcare Financial Management Association
HHA	Home Health Agency
HHQI	Home Health Quality Initiative
HHS	Health and Human Services
HIC	Health Information Committee
HIM	Health Information Management
HIMA	Health Industry Manufacturers Association
HIPAA	Health Insurance Portability and Accountability Act
HIS	Hospital Information System
HITECH	Health Information Technology for Economic and Clinical Health
HIV	Human Immunodeficiency Virus
HMO	Health Maintenance Organization
HOPPS	Hospital Outpatient Prospective Payment System
HRSA	Health Resources and Services Administration
HSA	Health Savings Account
HSR&D	Health Services Research and Development Service
IADL	Instrumental Activity of Daily Living
IBM	International Business Machines
ICD	International Classification of Disease
ICD-9-CM	International Classification of Diseases, 9th Revision, with Clinical Modifications
ICD-10	International Classification of Diseases, 10th Revision
ICD-10-AM	International Statistical Classification of Diseases and Related Health Problems, 10th Revision, Australian Modification
ICS	International Classification for Standards
ICU	Intensive Care Unit
IDS	Integrated Delivery System
IHI	Institute for Healthcare Improvement
IIHI	Individually Identifiable Health Information
IMS	Indicator Measurement System
IOM	Institute of Medicine
IPA	Independent Practice Association
iPTH	Intact Parathyroid Hormone
IQA	Institute of Quality Assurance
IQI	Inpatient Quality Indicator
IRR	Internal Rate of Return
ISMP	Institute for Safe Medication Practices
ISO	International Organization for Standardization
IT	Information Technology
IV	Intravenous
IWA	International Workshop Agreement

JCAHO	Joint Commission on Accreditation of Healthcare Organizations
JCI	Joint Commission International
JIT	Just-in-Time
K/DOQI	Kidney Disease Outcomes Quality Initiative
KFSH&RC	King Faisal Specialist Hospital and Research Centre
KM	Knowledge Management
KPI	Key Performance Indicator
KPS	Karnofsky Performance Score
LAT	Lateral
LDL	Low-Density Lipoproteins
LHI	Leading Health Indicator
LIFO	Last in, First out
LMIP	Laboratory Management Index Program
LMWH	Low-Molecular-Weight Heparin
LOINC	Logical Observation Identifiers Names and Codes
LOS	Length of Stay
LTBI	Latent Tuberculosis Infection
LTC	Long-Term Care
LV	Left Ventricle
LVF	Left Ventricular Function
LVSD	Left Ventricular Systolic Dysfunction
M&M	Morbidity and Mortality
MADS	Maximum Annual Debt Service
MAR	Medical Administration Record
MBHO	Managed Behavioral Healthcare Organization
MBO	Management by Objective
MCO	Managed Care Organization
MDS	Minimum Data Set
MEC	Medical Executive Committee
MEPS	Medical Expenditure Panel Survey
MER	Medical Error Reporting
MERS-TM	Medical Event-Reporting System for Transfusion Medicine
MeSH	Medical Subject Headings
MI	Myocardial Infarction
MMR	Measles, Mumps, Rubella
MPSMS	Medicare Patient Safety Monitoring System
MQMS	Medicare Quality Monitoring System
MRP	Material Requirements Planning
MSO	Management Service Organization
MTBF	Mean Time before Failure
MTF	Monitoring the Future Study
NAEPP	National Asthma Education and Prevention Program
NAMCS	National Ambulatory Medical Care Survey
NASA	National Aeronautics and Space Administration
NCBD	National CAHPS Benchmarking Database
NCC-MERP	National Coordinating Council for Medication Error Reporting and Prevention

NCI	National Cancer Institute
NCPIE	National Council on Patient Information and Education
NCQA	National Committee for Quality Assurance
NCVS	National Crime Victimization Survey
NDEP	National Diabetes Education Program
NEMA	National Equipment Manufacturers Association
NESB	Non-English Speaking Background
NETSS	National Electronic Telecommunications System for Surveillance
NHA	National Health Accounts
NHAMCS	National Hospital Ambulatory Medical Care Survey
NHANES	National Health and Nutrition Examination Survey
NHDR	National Healthcare Disparities Report
NHDS	National Hospital Discharge Survey
NHHCS	National Home Health and Hospice Care Survey
NHIS	National Health Interview Survey
NHPF	National Health Policy Forum
NHQR	National Healthcare Quality Report
NHS	National Health Service
NHSDA	National Household Survey on Drug Abuse
NIDDK	National Institute of Diabetes and Digestive and Kidney Diseases
NIH	National Institutes of Health
NIOSH	National Institute for Occupational Safety and Health
NIS	National Immunization Survey
NIST	National Institute of Standards and Technology
NKF	National Kidney Foundation
NLHI	National Library of Healthcare Indicators
NNDSS	National Notifiable Disease Surveillance System
NNHS	National Nursing Home Survey
NNIS	National Nosocomial Infections Surveillance
NORA	National Occupational Research Agenda
NPLHD	National Profile of Local Health Departments
NPSF	National Patient Safety Foundation
NPV	Net Present Value
NQF	National Quality Forum
NQMC	National Quality Measures Clearinghouse
NSFG	National Survey of Family Growth
NSQHS	National Safety and Quality Health Service
NTBSS	National TB Surveillance System
NTSB	National Transportation Safety Board
NVSS	National Vital Statistics System
NVSS-I	National Vital Statistics System, Linked Birth and Infant Death Data
NVSS-M	National Vital Statistics System, Mortality
NVSS-N	National Vital Statistics System, Natality
NwHIN	Nationwide Health Information Network
NWHPS	National Worksite Health Promotion Survey
OASIS	Outcome and Assessment Information Set
OBQI	Outcome-Based Quality Improvement

OBRA	Omnibus Budget Reconciliation Act
OCR	Optical Character Recognition
OECD	Organization for Economic Cooperation & Development
OHA	Ontario Hospital Association
OIG	Office of Inspector General
OLAP	Online Analytical Processing
OMR	Optical Mark Recognition
ONC	Office of the National Coordinator for Health Information Technology
OPDIV	Operating Division
OPDRA	Office of Post-Marketing Drug Risk Assessment
OPPS	Outpatient Prospective Payment System
ORYX®	JCAHO's Quality Program
OSHA	Occupational Safety and Health Administration
PACS	Digital Picture Archiving and Communication System
PACU	Post-Anesthesia Care Unit
PBC	Prepared by Client
PBM	Pharmacy Benefit Manager
PC	Professional Component (of work)
PCI	Percutaneous Coronary Intervention
PCP	Primary Care Physician
PCWRVU	Professional Component Work Relative Value Unit
PE	Pulmonary Embolus
PECOS	Provider Enrollment, Chain and Ownership System
PET	Positron Emission Tomography
PHO	Physician–Hospital Organization
PHQ	Patient Health Questionnaire
PHR	Patient Health Record
PICU	Pediatric Intensive Care Unit
PM	Performance Management
PMPM	Per Member per Month
PN	Pneumonia
POS	Point of Service Organization
PPMC	Physician Practice Management Company
PPO	Preferred Provider Organization
PPS	Prospective Payment System
PQI	Prevention Quality Indicator
PR	Pregnancy and Related (Conditions)
PRM	Pancreatic Resection Mortality
PRO	Peer Review Organization
PSA	Prostate-Specific Antigen Test
PSI	Patient Safety Indicator
PTB	Preterm Birth
PTCA	Percutaneous Transluminal Coronary Angioplasty
QFD	Quality Function Deployment
QI	Quality Indicator
QIES	Quality Improvement Evaluation System
QIO	Quality Improvement Organization

QMS	Quality Management System
QuIC	Quality Interagency Coordinating Committee
QWL	Quality of Work Life
RBRVS	Resource-Based Relative Value Scale
RCM	Revenue Cycle Management
RDRG	Refined Diagnostic-Related Group
RFID	Radio-frequency Identification
RFP	Request for Proposal
ROA	Return on Assets
ROC	Receiver Operating Characteristic
ROE	Return on Equity
ROI	Return on Investment
RPQ	Request for Price Quotation
RRT	Renal Replacement Therapy
RVU	Relative Value Unit
SAMHSA	Substance Abuse and Mental Health Services Administration
SAS	Statistical Analysis System
SCC	Standards Council of Canada
SEER	Surveillance, Epidemiology, and End Results Program
SFAS	Statement of Financial Accounting Standards
SHPPS	School Health Policies and Programs Study
SIP	Surgical Infection Prevention
SMI	Service Mix Index
SMR	Subsidiary Medical Record
SMSA	Standard Metropolitan Statistical Area
SNF	Skilled Nursing Facility
SPC	Statistical Process Control
SPECT	Single-Photon Emission Computerized Tomography
SQL	Structured Query Language
SROM	Spontaneous Rupture of Membranes
STATE	State Tobacco Activities Tracking and Evaluation System
STD	Sexually Transmitted Disease
STDSS	Sexually Transmitted Disease Surveillance System
TASH	Total Available Staff Hours
TAT	Test Turnaround Time
TB	Tuberculosis
TC	Technical Component (of work)
TEP	Technical Expert Panel
TPO	Treatment, Payment, or Healthcare Operations
TQM	Total Quality Management
TRIP	Translating Research into Practice
TST	Tuberculin Skin Test
TTS	Text to Speech
UCR	Usual, Customary and Reasonable
UMR	Unit Medical Record
UNAIDS	United Nations Program on HIV/AIDS
URR	Urea Reduction Ratio

USC	Usual Source of Care
USP	US Pharmacopeia
USRDS	United States Renal Data System
UTI	Urinary Tract Infection
VA	Department of Veterans Affairs
VAP	Ventilator-Associated Pneumonia
VBAC	Vaginal Birth after C-Section
VHA	Veterans Health Administration
VTE	Venous Thromboembolism
VURI	Viral Upper Respiratory Infection
WACC	Weighted Average Cost of Capital
WHO	World Health Organization
WVS	Weighted Value Score
YRBSS	Youth Risk Behavior Surveillance System

Glossary

Access and Service: A measure of how well a health plan provides its members with access to care with good customer service.

Access to Care: Provision for timely and appropriate healthcare.

Accident: An event that involves damage to a defined system that disrupts the ongoing or future output of the system.

Accounts Payable: Total of all monies owed by the organization.

Accounts Receivable: Monies owed to the organization but not yet collected.

Accreditation: A decision awarded to a healthcare organization that is in compliance with established standards.

Accruals: Taxes or wages accumulated against current profits but not yet due to be paid.

Accuracy: The extent to which data are free of identifiable errors.

ACE Inhibitor: A drug that acts to widen the blood vessels and make it easier for the heart to pump blood through the body. Captopril, ramipril, and enalapril are commonly used angiotensin-converting enzyme inhibitors.

Active Error: An error at the level of the frontline operator whose effects are felt almost immediately.

Activity-Based Costing: An accounting method used to estimate costs of a service or product by measuring the costs of the activities it takes to produce that service or product.

Acuity: The degree of psychosocial risk of health treatment or the degree of dependency or functional status of the patient.

Acute Care Hospital: A hospital that provides acute care services. Excludes discharges to long-term and rehabilitation hospitals.

Acute Myocardial Infarction (AMI): Death of heart muscle resulting from insufficient blood supply to the heart.

Added Value: The additional tangible benefit derived by an organization through carrying out a business function or process.

Adjusted Average per Capita Cost (AAPCC): The amount of funding a managed care plan receives from the Health Care Financing Administration to cover costs.

Administrative/Billing Data: Patient demographics; information about the episode of care such as admission source, length of stay, charges, discharge status, and diagnostic and procedural codes.

Administrative/Financial Measures: Performance measures that address the organizational structure for coordinating and integrating services, functions, or activities across operational components, including financial management.

Admission–Discharge–Transfer (ADT) System: A computer-based system used to track the gross movement of patients from their arrival to their departure within a medical enterprise. ADT systems are concerned primarily with patient demographics and provider information.

Adult Day Care Program: A program providing supervision, medical and psychological care, and social activities for older adults who live at home or in another family setting, but cannot be alone or prefer to be with others during the day.

Adult Smoking Cessation Advice/Counseling: A measure that reports what percent of adult heart attack/heart failure/pneumonia patients are provided advice and/or counseling to quit smoking.

Advanced Practice Nurses: Graduates of an accredited school of nursing and licensed by state law to practice nursing, especially nurse administrators, nurse anesthetists, nurse clinicians, nurse practitioners, nurse psychotherapists, and nurse midwives.

Adverse Event: An injury resulting from a medical intervention.

Affordable Care Act (ACA): Also known as Obamacare, is the federal statute signed into law on March 2010 that is part of the healthcare reform agenda of the Obama administration.

Agency for Healthcare Research and Quality (AHRQ): The health services research arm of the US Department of Health and Human Services.

Aggregate: Measurement data collected and reported by organizations as a sum or total over a given time period or for certain groupings.

Algorithm: An ordered sequence of data element retrieval and aggregation through which numerator and denominator events or continuous variable values are identified by a measure.

Allied Health Personnel: Healthcare workers specially trained and licensed to assist and support the work of health professionals, such as dental assistants, dental technicians, medical record administrators, pharmacists' aides, and radiology technicians.

Allowable Value: The predefined range of alphanumeric values that are valid for a data element in a database.

Allowance for Doubtful Accounts: An estimated amount of bad debt subtracted from a balance sheet's accounts receivable. This is a reserve for doubtful and bad accounts.

Ambulatory Care: Healthcare services provided to patients on an ambulatory basis, rather than by admission to a hospital or other healthcare facility. Also called outpatient care.

Ambulatory Payment Classification (APC): A payment group under the Hospital Outpatient Prospective Payment System composed of procedures that are clinically similar and associated with similar resource requirements.

American Hospital Quest for Quality Prize: An American Hospital Association award that honors leadership and innovation in quality, safety, and commitment to patient care by hospitals and/or multi-hospital health systems.

American National Standards Institute (ANSI): A nonprofit organization that helps establish electronic data standards.

American Recovery and Reinvestment Act (ARRA): An economic stimulus package enacted in 2009 that included the HITECH Act.

Amortization: The gradual elimination of a liability in regular payments over a specified period of time. Alternatively, writing off an intangible asset investment over the projected life of the asset.

Ancillary Services: Tests, procedures, imaging, and support services provided in a healthcare setting.

Angioplasty: The reconstruction or restructuring of a blood vessel by operative means or by non-surgical techniques such as balloon dilation or laser.

Antibiotic Timing: Length of time from arrival at the hospital until antibiotics are given. This measure reports how long a pneumonia patient was in the hospital before they were given antibiotics.

Appropriateness: The degree to which the care provided is relevant to the patient's clinical needs, given the current state of knowledge.

Aspirin at Arrival: Heart attack patients receiving aspirin when arriving at the hospital. This measure reports what percentage of heart attack patients receive aspirin within 24 hours before or after they arrive at the hospital.

Aspirin Prescribed at Discharge: Heart attack patients who receive a prescription for aspirin when being discharged from the hospital. This measure reports how often aspirin was prescribed to heart attack patients when they are leaving a hospital.

Assets: Money, merchandise, land, buildings, and equipment that the organization owns and that have monetary value.

Assisted Living: A special combination of housing, supportive services, personalized assistance, and healthcare designed to respond to the individual needs of those who need help in activities of daily living and instrumental activities of daily living.

Assisted Living Facility: Assisted living residencies that provide or coordinate personal services, 24-hour supervision and assistance, activities, and health-related services.

Attestation: The part of the process to secure CMS EMR Incentive Program reimbursements that requires providers to prove (attest to) that they are meaningfully using a certified EMR.

Audit Trail: A software tracking system used for data security. An audit trail is attached to a file each time it is opened so an operator can trace who has accessed a file and when.

Auditability: Performance measure data obtained from enrolled healthcare organizations are traceable at the individual case level so that performance measurement systems can adequately assess the quality of data.

Authentication: Proving, with some degree of certainty, a user's identity.

Average Daily Census: The average number of inpatients, excluding newborns, receiving care each day during a reporting period.

Average Length of Service (ALOS): Number of years in continuous, full-time employment, or equivalent.

Backend Process: A process that doesn't represent a healthcare institution's unique skills, knowledge, or processes. Typical backend processes include payroll, billing, and accounts payable.

Bad Debt: Accounts receivable that will likely remain uncollectible and written off. Bad debts appear as an expense on the hospital's income statement, thus reducing net income.

Bad Debt Expense: Provision for actual or expected uncollectibles resulting from the extension of credit.

Bad Outcome: Failure to achieve a desired outcome of care.

Balance Sheet: A statement of the financial position of the enterprise at a particular time.

Balanced Scorecard: An integrated framework for describing strategy through the use of linked performance measures in four, balanced perspectives—Financial, Customer, Internal Process, and Employee Learning and Growth.

Baseline: The starting point for defining needs.

Behavioral Healthcare: Healthcare services organized to provide mental healthcare.

Benchmarking: The comparison of similar processes across organizations and industries to identify best practices, set improvement targets, and measure progress.

Beneficiary: A person eligible for coverage of healthcare services by either a public or private health insurance program.

Best of Breed: The service provider that is best in its class of services.

Best Practice: The most effective and desirable method of carrying out a function or process.

Beta Blocker at Arrival: Quality measure that assesses the percentage of heart attack patients who receive a beta blocker when they arrive at the hospital.

Beta Blocker Prescribed at Discharge: Quality measure that assesses the percentage of heart attack patients who have a beta blocker prescribed when they are discharged from the hospital.

Binary: A system of expressing numerical values as 0s and 1s.

Binary Outcome: Events or conditions that occur in one or two possible states, that is, 0 or 1. Such data are frequently encountered in medical research.

Bioinformatics: The use of computer-based methods, including large databases and related tools, to acquire, store, manage, and analyze biological data.

Biometrics: A method of verifying the identity of a user based on their fingerprints, facial features, retinal pattern, voice, or other personal characteristic.

Blood Cultures: A blood test for the presence of bacteria in the blood.

Boxplot: A graph in which thin lines connect the highest and lowest data points to boxes that represent the two center quartiles on the graph.

Break-Even Analysis: A calculation of the approximate sales volume required to just cover costs, below which production would be unprofitable and above which it would be profitable.

Browser: A software program that interprets documents on the Web.

Business Intelligence (BI): Information technology practices and products concerned with gathering and analyzing financial and operational indicators.

Business Process Management (BPM): A business improvement strategy based on documenting, analyzing, and redesigning processes for greater performance.

Bylaws: Self-imposed rules that constitute a contract between a corporation and its members to conduct business in a particular way.

CAHPS: A comprehensive and evolving family of surveys, funded and managed by AHRQ, that ask consumers and patients to evaluate the interpersonal aspects of healthcare. CAHPS initially stood for the Consumer Assessment of Health Plans Study, but as the products have evolved beyond health plans, the acronym now stands alone as a registered brand name.

Capital Budget: A summary of the anticipated purchases for the year.

Capital Expenditure: An expenditure on tangible and intangible assets that will benefit more than one year of account.

Capitation: A payment structure where a caregiver is paid a set amount per patient in advance, regardless of how many procedures are performed.

Cardiac Catheterization Laboratory: Facilities offering special diagnostic procedures for cardiac patients.

Cascading: The process of developing aligned scorecards throughout an organization.

Case Finding: The procedure for determining whether a case is potentially eligible for inclusion in the denominator of a measure.

Case Management: A system of assessment, treatment planning, referral, and follow-up that ensures the provision of comprehensive and continuous services and the coordination of payment and reimbursement for care.

Case Mix: The collective pool of patients in a health system, including data on age, gender and health status.

Case Mix Index (CMI): A severity statistic used as a weight for Medicare patients. CMI varies from 0.4 to over 16.0, with an average of 1.0.

Cash: Money the organization has control of and access to.

Cash Flow: A measure of a hospital's financial health, equal to cash receipts minus cash payments over a given period of time. Alternatively, net profit plus amounts charged off for depreciation, depletion, and amortization.

Cash Flow Statement: A report on the impact of an organization's operating, investing, and financing activities on the cash flow over an accounting period.

Categorical Variable: A categorical variable groups items into predefined discrete, noncontinuous classes.

Cause and Effect: A linkage between items on a Balanced Scorecard. Cause and Effect may be hypothetical.

Census Day: A period of service between the census-taking hours on two successive calendar days, the day of discharge being counted only when the patient was admitted the same day.

Central Tendency: A property of the distribution of a variable, usually measured by statistics such as the mean, median, and mode.

Change Management: The set of structures, procedures, and rules governing the adoption and implementation of changes in the relationship between the customer and the service provider.

Charity Care: Health services that were never expected to result in cash inflows.

Cheers Award: An award presented by the Institute for Safe Medication Practices (ISMP) that recognizes individuals, healthcare organizations, regulatory agencies, professional organizations, researchers, pharmaceutical, and other healthcare-related businesses that have set a superlative standard of excellence to following the prevention of medication errors during the award year.

Children: Individuals who have not reached the legal age for consent.

Children Wellness Program: A program that encourages improved health status and a healthful lifestyle of children through health education, exercise, nutrition, and health promotion.

Children's Online Privacy Protection Act (COPPA): The Federal law that regulates the Web-based collection and use of personal information gathered from or about children under age 13.

Chiropractors: Individuals specially trained and licensed to practice chiropractic.

Chi-square: A test for statistical significance, typically applied to data in contingency tables.

Choice Board: A Web-based, multi-user ordering system in which a customer's order is sent to suppliers along the entire supply chain.

Claim: A bill for healthcare service.

Clearinghouse: A service that manages the claims and other electronic data from providers, verifies the information, and forwards the proper forms to the payers.

Client-Server: A computer architecture in which the workload is split between desktop PCs or handheld wireless devices (clients) and more powerful or higher-capacity computers (servers) that are connected via a network such as the Internet.

Clinic Visit: A visit to a specialized medical unit that is responsible for the diagnosis and treatment of patients on an outpatient, nonemergency basis.

Clinical Data–Based Severity Adjustment Methods: Techniques that quantify risks of short-term outcomes based on clinical data.

Clinical Laboratory Improvement Amendments (CLIA): A congressional amendment passed in 1988 that established quality standards for all laboratory testing.

Clinical Laboratory Personnel: Those healthcare professionals, technicians, and assistants staffing a healthcare facility where specimens are grown, tested, or evaluated and the results of such are recorded.

Clinical Measures: Indicators designed to evaluate the processes or outcomes of care associated with the delivery of clinical services.

Clinical Outcome: A change in signs or symptoms as a result of clinical intervention.

Clinical Performance Measure: A quality measure reflecting the degree to which a provider competently and safely delivers clinical services that are appropriate for the patient in the optimal time period.

Clinical Performance: The degree of accomplishment of desired health objectives by a clinician or healthcare organization.

Clinical Survey: A tool used to collect data from clinicians who provide care.

Closed Formulary: A list of branded and generic prescription drugs that are approved for insurance coverage. Patients are required to pay more when they insist on brand-name drugs instead of less expensive generic drugs.

Closed Physician–Hospital Organization (PHO): A PHO that restricts physician membership to those practitioners who meet criteria for cost-effectiveness and/or high quality.

Cluster Analysis: One of several computationally efficient techniques that can be used to identify patterns and relationships in large amounts of patient data.

Cognitive Ergonomics: The applied science of equipment design, as for the workplace, intended to maximize productivity by reducing operator fatigue and discomfort.

Coinsurance: The portion of a covered claim that a patient must pay.

COLA: A nonprofit, physician-directed organization promoting quality and excellence in medicine and patient care through programs of voluntary education, achievement, and accreditation. COLA was established as a private alternative for physician office laboratories complying with the Clinical Laboratory Improvement Amendments of 1988.

Collusion: A fraudulent arrangement between two or more parties.

Commission: A type of finder's fee set by insurance brokers or agents for selling health plans.

Commission for Health Improvement (CHI): The National Health Service (NHS) inspectorate, responsible for reviewing clinical governance arrangements in NHS organizations.

Common Carrier: Licensed utilities that provide communications services for a fee, under nondiscriminatory terms.

Common Cause Variation: Random variation inherent in every process.

Communications Protocol: A set of standards designed to allow computers to exchange data.

Community Healthcare: Diagnostic, therapeutic, and preventive healthcare services provided for individuals or families in the community for the purpose of promoting, maintaining, or restoring health or minimizing the effects of illness and disability.

Community Health Information Network (CHIN): Providers and payers within a specific area who are networked to exchange medical and administrative information among them, eliminating redundant data collection and reducing paperwork.

Community of Practice: Groups whose members regularly engage in sharing and learning, based on common interests.

Comorbidities: Preexisting diseases or conditions.

Comparison Group: The group of healthcare organizations to which an individual healthcare organization is compared.

Comparison Level Data: Aggregation of healthcare organization level data to provide a standardized norm by which participating organizations can compare their performance.

Competitive Insourcing: A process where internal employees may engage in bidding to compete with competitive, third-party bidders for a defined scope of work.

Competitive Reward Model: A program that rewards relative performance.

Complications: Conditions arising after the beginning of healthcare observation and treatment that modifies the course of the patient's health or illness and the intervention/care required.

Composite Measure: A measure that combines the results of all process measures with a set into a single rating.

Computerized Physician Order Entry (CPOE): An electronic prescribing system that enables a physician to order through a computer rather than on paper.

Confidence Interval: A range of values containing the true value of the parameter being estimated with a certain degree of confidence.

Configuration: The operational characteristics of a performance measurement system.

Confounding Factors: Intervening variables that distort the true relationship between/among the variables of interest.

Consumer Informatics: Computer-based information available to the general public.

Continuity: The degree to which the care for the patient is coordinated among practitioners, among organizations, and over time.

Continuous Variable: A measure in which each individual value for the measure can fall anywhere along a continuous scale.

Contract: A binding agreement made between two or more parties, which is enforceable at law.

Contract Managed: General day-to-day management of an entire organization by another organization under a formal contract.

Contractor: A firm or person who has entered into a contract to supply goods and/or services.

Control Chart: A form of line chart that includes control limits based on plus or minus three standard deviations or sigma's from the centerline. There are heuristics for determining when an observed variation is statistically significant.

Controlled Vocabulary: A terminology system unambiguously mapped to concepts.

Convergence: The merging of all data and all media into a single digital form.

Coordination of Benefits (COB): A verification system used to make sure a claim is not paid twice.

Co-payment: The flat fee that a patient pays, usually at the time of service.

Core Competency: The healthcare organization's unique skills, knowledge, and processes.

Core Measure Set: A grouping of performance measures carefully selected to provide, when viewed together, a robust picture of the care provided in a given area.

Cost–Benefit Analysis: A technique designed to determine the feasibility of a project or plan by quantifying its costs and benefits.

Cost Shifting: A leveling method where one patient group is charged more to make up for another group's underpayment or inability to pay.

Cost-to-Charge Ratio: The ratio of hospital cost to what is charged to patients and third-party payers for services. Medicare has explicit guidelines for establishing cost-to-charge ratios.

Credentialing: The examination of a healthcare professional's credentials, practice history and medical certification or license.

Criteria: Expected levels of achievement or specifications against which performance or quality may be compared.

Critical Access Hospital: Hospitals with a patient census of less than 25 and that are located more than 35 miles from a hospital or another critical access hospital, or are certified by the state as being a necessary provider of healthcare services to residents in the area.

Critical Path: The shortest path to the final product or service in resource scheduling. The critical path represents the minimum length of time in which a project can be completed.

Current Assets: Cash, short-term investment, accounts receivable, inventory, prepaid expenses, and other assets that can be converted into cash within a year.

Current Liabilities: Liability that must be paid within a year, including accounts payable, wages and salaries, taxes, and mortgage payments.

Current Procedural Terminology (CPT): A uniform coding system for healthcare procedures developed by the American Medical Association (AMA) and used when submitting claims for healthcare to third-party payers. CPT coding assigns a five-digit code to each service or procedure provided by a physician.

Current Status of Development: The amount of work completed to date relative to the final implementation of a particular measure.

Current Use of the Measure: A measure is considered to be in current use if at least one health-care organization has used the measure to evaluate or report on the quality of care within the last three years.

Customer Perspective: One of the four standard perspectives used with the Balanced Scorecard.

Customer Relationship Management (CRM): The dynamic process of managing a patient–healthcare organization relationship. Patients are encouraged to continue mutually beneficial commercial exchanges and are dissuaded from participating in exchanges that are unprofitable to the organization.

Customer Segment: A homogeneous group of similar patients with similar needs, wants, lifestyle, interaction opportunities, profile, and purchase cycle.

Cycle Time: The time it takes to convert an idea into a new product or service or to improve an existing product or service.

Dashboard: A graphical user interface to key performance indicator data.

Data Collection: The act or process of capturing raw or primary data from a single or number of sources.

Data Editing: The process of correcting erroneous or incomplete *existing* data, exclusive of data entry input edits.

Data Element: A discrete piece of data, such as patient birth date or principal diagnosis.

Data Entry: The process by which data are transcribed or transferred into an electronic format.

Data Maintenance: The efforts required to keep database files and supporting documentation accurate.

Data Mart: An organized, searchable database system, organized according to the user's likely needs.

Data Mining: The process of studying the contents of large databases in order to discover new data relationships that may produce new insights on outcomes, alternate treatments, or effects of treatment.

Data Point: The representation of a value for a set of observations or measurements at a specific time interval.

Data Quality: The accuracy and completeness of measure data on performance in the context of the analytic purposes for which they will be used.

Data Repository: A database acting as an information storage facility. A repository does not have the analysis or querying functionality of a warehouse.

Data Sources: The primary source documents used for data collection.

Data Transmission: The process by which data are electronically sent from one organization to another.

Data Warehouse: A central database, frequently very large, that can provide authorized users with access to a cleaned, organized subset of the organizations data. A data warehouse is usually provided with data from a variety of noncompatible sources.

Database: An organized, comprehensive collection of variables and their values.

Database Management System (DBMS): A system to store, process, and manage data in a systematic way.

Day of Care: A period of service between the census-taking hours on two successive calendar days, the day of discharge being counted only when the patient was admitted the same day.

Days Hold: Number of accounts still within the specified number of days after discharge before billing.

Debt Service: The series of payments of interest and principal required on a debt over a given period of time.

Decision Effective Date: The date of the accreditation decision awarded to an organization following an accreditation survey.

Decision Support System (DSS): An application for analyzing large quantities of data and performing a wide variety of calculations and projections.

Decision-Tree Analysis: A graphical process used to select the best course of action in cases of uncertainty.

Defined Allowable Value: The predefined range of alphanumeric values that are valid for a data element in a database.

Defined Measure: A structured measure with defined populations that measure specific events or values.

Demand Management: A program administered by managed care organizations or provider organizations to monitor and process initial member requests for clinical information and services.

Denominator: The lower part of a fraction used to calculate a rate, proportion, or ratio.

Denominator Data Elements: Those data elements required to construct the denominator.

Denominator Event: The event or state that defines a case as eligible for inclusion in the denominator.

Denominator Excluded Populations: Detailed information describing the populations that should not be included in the denominator.

Denominator Included Populations: Detailed information describing the population(s) that the denominator intends to measure.

Denominator Sampling Frame: The list of all cases potentially eligible for inclusion in the denominator, from which a more highly specified selection of cases will be made.

Denominator Statement: A statement that depicts the population evaluated by the performance measure.

Denominator Time Window: The time period in which cases are reviewed for inclusion in the denominator.

Denominator Verification: The extent to which the entire population of interest, and only the population of interest, is identified through data collection.

Dentist: Individuals licensed to practice dentistry.

Depreciation: The decline in the value of a fixed asset over its useful life.

Diagnosis Hold: Number of accounts not yet coded in Medical Records.

Diagnosis-Related Group (DRG): A system of reimbursement by the Health Care Financing Administration based on a patient's primary diagnosis, length of stay, secondary diagnosis, surgical procedure, age, and types of services required. This case mix classification system is used primarily in the United States as a method of funding hospitals.

Diagnostic Mammography: The x-ray imaging of breast tissue in symptomatic women who are considered to have a substantial likelihood of having breast cancer already.

Dietitians: Individuals with a legally recognized qualification in nutrition and dietetics who apply the science of nutrition to the feeding and education of groups of people and individuals in health and disease.

Digital Signature: An encrypted digital tag added to an electronic communication to verify the identity of a customer. Also known as an electronic signature.

Direct Cost: That portion of cost that is directly expended in providing a service.

Disabled: Persons with physical or mental disabilities that affect or limit their activities of daily living and that may require special accommodations.

Discharge Instructions: A quality measure that reflects the percentage of patients with heart failure who are given information about their condition and care when they leave the hospital.

Discount Rate: The rate at which member banks may borrow short-term funds directly from a Federal Reserve Bank.

Discriminatory Capability: The extent to which an indicator demonstrates variation across multiple healthcare organizations.

Disease Management: A management approach that focuses on specific diseases, looking at what creates the costs, what treatment plan works, educating patients and providers, and coordinating care at all levels.

Disease Management: The development of an integrated treatment plan for patients with long-term illnesses or recurring conditions instead of viewing each physician visit as a separate event.

Disease-Specific Care: A certification program for disease management services, such as asthma or diabetes.

Disenrollment: The act of terminating the membership of a person or group in a health plan.

Disruptive Technology: A technology that causes a major shift in the normal way of doing things and that improves with time. The PC, digital camera, and cell phones are disruptive technologies.

DMADV: A Six Sigma strategy divided into five phases: Define, Measure, Analyze, Design, and Verify.

DMAIC: A Six Sigma quality improvement strategy described by five phases: Define, Measure, Analyze, Improve, and Control.

Downsizing: Reduction in employee headcount.

Drug Price Review (DPR): A monthly report that lists the average wholesale prices of prescription drugs.

Due Diligence: A thorough effort to intercept potential problems before they occur.

Ease of Use: Regarding a user interface, the ease or efficiency with which the interface can be used.

Economic Darwinism: Survival of the fittest; the most economically successful companies in the marketplace.

Economic Value Added (EVA): The after-tax cash flow generated by a business minus the cost of the capital it has deployed to generate that cash flow.

Economies of Scale: Reduction in the costs of production due to increasing production capacity.

Efficacy: The degree to which the care of the patient has been shown to accomplish the desired or projected outcome(s).

Electronic Data Interchange (EDI): An instance of data being sent electronically between parties, normally according to predefined industry standards.

Electronic Health Record (EHR): An electronic record of a patient's medical history, medications, and other pertinent health data. Need not be hospital-centric, as is the case with an EMR.

Electronic Medical Record (EMR): A hospital-centric, electronic record of a patient's hospital chart. This typically includes medical, social, and family histories, medications, lab results, and other data collected at the hospital.

Electronic Submission: The process whereby performance measure data are transferred electronically between information systems.

Eligibility: The ability to be part of a healthcare plan, with specific benefits for which a member qualifies and the time frame of coverage.

Emergency Care Research Institute (ECRI): An independent nonprofit health services research agency.

Emergency Medical Services: Clinical services specifically designed, staffed, and equipped for the emergency care of patients.

Emergency Medical Technicians/Paramedics: Personnel trained and certified to provide basic emergency care and life support under the supervision of physicians and/or nurses.

Emergency Room Visit: A visit to the emergency unit.

Employee Benefits: Social security, group insurance, retirement benefits, workman's compensation, and unemployment insurance.

Employee Contribution: The portion of health plan premiums paid by an employee to the company's contracted payer.

Employee Learning and Growth Perspective: One of the four standard perspectives used with the Balanced Scorecard. Employee skills, availability of information, and organizational climate are often measured in this perspective.

Employee Relationship Management (ERM): A dynamic process of managing the relationship between knowledge worker and enterprise such that knowledge workers elect to continue a mutually beneficial exchange of intellectual assets for compensation in a way that provides value to the enterprise and are dissuaded from participating in activities that are unprofitable to the enterprise.

Employee Retirement Income Security Act (ERISA): A federal outline for regulating employee benefit plans, including healthcare plans sponsored and/or insured by an employer.

Employer Mandate: For companies that provide health insurance for their employees, this stipulation forces the company to pay for at least part of the insurance premium for each employee.

Encryption: The process of encoding data to prevent someone without the proper key from understanding the data, even though they may have access to the data.

End-of-Life Care: Patient care related to those not expected to survive more than 6 months.

Enforceability: The conditions under which the terms, conditions, and obligations of the parties under an agreement will be adopted and confirmed by a court of competent jurisdiction.

Enrolled Organization: An organization contractually committed to participation in a performance measurement system.

Enrollee: A member of a health plan or a member's qualifying dependent.

Enrollment: In the context of the Affordable Care Act, enrollment is the act of selecting a particular coverage plan with a healthcare insurance provider.

Enrollment Assistance Services: A program that provides enrollment assistance for patients who are potentially eligible for public health insurance programs such as Medicaid, State Children's Health Insurance, or local/state indigent care programs.

Enterprise Resource Planning (ERP): The activities supported by software that helps an enterprise manage product planning, parts purchasing, maintaining inventories, interacting with suppliers, providing customer service, and tracking orders.

Episode of Care (EOC): Healthcare services provided for a specific illness during a set time period.

Equipment Management: The selection, delivery, setup, and maintenance of equipment to meet patients' needs, as well as the education of patients in its use.

Ernest A. Codman Award: An award given to organizations and individuals in the use of process and outcomes measures to improve organization performance and quality of care.

Error: Failure of a planned action to be completed as intended or use of a wrong plan to achieve an aim; the accumulation of errors results in accidents.

Established Patient: A patient who had received professional services within the past 3 years.

Excluded Populations: Detailed information describing the populations that should not be included in the indicator.

Executive Information System: A system that allows executives to analyze company data and reach management conclusions through decision-making tools, much as a physician might use a decision support system to narrow diagnosis options.

Expense: The cost of doing business.

Experience Rating: A method of determining a company's health insurance premiums by estimating the future healthcare risks of its employees.

Explanation of Benefits (EOB): A document that defines the portions of the service paid by insurance and the amount the patient has to pay.

External Comparison at a Point in Time: A comparison using the same measure for multiple comparable entities.

External Comparison of Time Trends: A comparison using the same measure for multiple comparable entities tracking change over time.

External Data Source: A repository for data that exists outside of the measurement system's control.

External Standards: Performance measurement systems developed by government entities, accrediting bodies, or any regulatory entities so that performance data are comparable across measurement systems.

Extracorporeal Shock Wave Lithotripter (ESWL): A device used for treating stones in the kidney or ureter through the transmission of acoustic shock waves directed at the stones.

Extranet: A private network using the Internet protocol to share business information or operations with vendors, customers, and/or other businesses.

Food and Drug Administration Safety and Innovation Act (FDASIA): Section 618 of the act directed development of risk-based regulatory framework for health IT.

Fee Schedule: A list of maximum fees, per service, a provider will be reimbursed within a fee-for-service payment system.

Fee-for-Service: A traditional method of paying for medical services. A physician charges a fee for each service provided, and the insurer or patient pay all or part of that fee.

Fertility Counseling: A service that counsels and educates on infertility problems and includes laboratory and surgical workup and management for individuals having problems conceiving children.

Financial Perspective: One of the four standard perspectives used with a Balanced Scorecard, often viewed as constraints within which the organization must operate.

Financial Statement: A written report that quantitatively describes the financial health of a company. This includes an income statement and a balance sheet, and often also includes a cash flow statement.

Firewall: A software and/or hardware security system that allows or denies access to information and the transfer of information from one network to another based on predefined access rules.

Fisher's Exact Test: A statistical test used on contingency tables, more accurate than the chi-square test.

Fixed Assets: Land and physical properties used in the creation of economic activity by the enterprise.

Fixed Cost: A cost that does not vary depending on production or sales levels, such as rent, property tax, insurance, or interest expense.

Focus: The activity or area on which a performance measure centers attention.

Forecasting: A mathematical method of extrapolating historical performance data to aid in planning. As with weather forecasting, the further into the future the forecast, the less certain the results.

Format: The specification of the character length of a specific data element.

Formulary: A list of pharmaceutical products and dosages deemed by a healthcare organization to be the best, most economical treatments.

Frail Elderly: Older adults or aged individuals who are lacking in general strength and are unusually susceptible to disease or to other infirmity.

Franklin Award of Distinction: Award for a case management system that demonstrates excellence in building collaboration among the various professional and technical staff in the hospital to focus on case management and performance measurement results having a positive effect on patient care.

Frequency Distribution: The division of a sample of observations into a number of classes, together with the number of observations in each class.

Full-Time Equivalent (FTE): A measure of employee time devoted to work, typically 8 hours per day.

Functional Specification: A document that incorporates and crystallizes the requirement specifications and specifies exactly what a software and/or hardware system will deliver.

Functional Status: A measure of an individual's ability to perform normal activities of life.

Gantt Chart: A graphical production scheduling method that shows lengths of various production stages.

Gatekeeper: A physician who manages a patient's various healthcare services, coordinates referrals, and helps control healthcare costs by screening out unnecessary services.

General Data Elements: The group of data elements used to link healthcare organization level to comparison group data.

Generally Accepted Accounting Principles (GAAP): The conventions, rules, and procedures that define accepted accounting practice, as defined by the Financial Accounting Standards Board.

Genetic Algorithms: Programs designed to mutate, breed, and spawn new, more fit algorithms, based on their success in solving a particular problem.

Geographically Defined: Persons located within a specified boundary.

Geriatric Services: The branch of medicine dealing with the physiology of aging and the diagnosis and treatment of disease affecting the aged.

Getting Better: Care related to acute illness or injury.

Governance: Activities and policies extended on behalf of senior management of the parent corporation.

Government Performance and Results Act (GPRA): Legislation that requires federally funded agencies to develop and implement an accountability system based on performance measurement.

Gross Profit: A financial indicator equal to profit before expenses, interest, and taxes have been deducted.

Gross Revenue: Total revenue less cost of goods sold.

Gross Sales: Total invoice value of sales, before deducting for customer discounts, allowances, or returns.

Group Model HMO: A form of HMO where a partnership or company provides services and pays for the facility and salaries.

Group Purchasing Organization: An organization whose primary function is to negotiate contracts for the purpose of purchasing for members of the group or has a central supply site for its members.

Half-Life: The time in which half of the devices or applications in a given population fail or become useless because of obsolescence.

Hamilton Depression Rating Scale: A 17-item scale that evaluates depressed mood, vegetative and cognitive symptoms of depression, and comorbid anxiety symptoms.

HCPCS: The HCFA Common Procedural Coding System.

Health Care Financing Administration (HCFA): The branch of the US Department of Health and Human Services that administers Medicare and the federal portion of Medicaid.

Health Care Network: An entity that provides, or provides for, integrated health services to a defined population or individuals.

Health Care Organization (HCO): Entity that provides, coordinates, and/or insures health and medical services for people.

Health Care System: A corporate body that owns, leases, religiously sponsors, and/or manages health provider facilities.

Health Episode Statistics (HES): A database containing details of all patients admitted to NHS hospitals in England.

Health Information Technology for Economic and Clinical Health (HITECH) Act: A component of the American Recovery and Reinvestment Act (ARRA) of 2009 that promotes the adoption and meaningful use of health information technology.

Health Maintenance Organization (HMO): An affiliation of independent practitioners that contracts with patients to provide comprehensive healthcare for a fixed periodic payment specified in advance.

Health Plan: A person's specific health benefits package or the organization that provides such a package.

Health Plan Employer Data and Information Set (HEDIS): NCQA's tool used by health plans to collect data about the quality of care and service they provide.

Health Risk State: Behavior associated with negative medical consequences.

Health Status Measures: Indicators that assess the functional well-being of specific populations, both in general and in relation to specific conditions.

Healthcare Informatics: The use of computer-based tools, applications, and communications to interact with and manage health-related data.

Healthcare Insurance Portability and Accountability Act (HIPAA): The US Government regulation that holds healthcare facilities responsible for bringing legacy IT systems into stringent compliance and ensuring the security of patient records.

Hemodialysis: Provision of equipment and personnel for the treatment of renal insufficiency on an inpatient or outpatient basis.

Heuristic: A rule of thumb.

HL7: A standard interface for exchanging and translating data between computer systems.

Holding Company: A corporation organized for the purpose of owning stock in and managing one or more corporations.

Home Care: Community health and nursing services providing coordinated multiple service home care to the patient.

Home Health Service Visit: A visit by home health personnel to a patient's home.

Home Health Services: Service providing nursing, therapy, and health-related homemaker or social services in the patient's home.

Home Healthcare Agency: An organization that arranges for and provides necessary healthcare services in a patient's home.

Homeless: Persons who have no permanent residence, including children and adolescents with no fixed place of residence.

Horizontal Analysis: The percentage change in indicator value from a previous year, that is, [(subsequent − previous)/previous] × 100.

Hospice Program: A recognized clinical program with specific eligibility criteria that provides palliative medical care focused on relief of pain and symptom control and other services that address the emotional, social, financial, and spiritual needs of terminally ill patients and their families.

Hospices: Facilities or services, which are especially devoted to providing palliative and supportive care to the patient with a terminal illness and to the patient's family.

Hospital: A healthcare organization that has a governing body, an organized medical staff and professional staff, and inpatient facilities and provides medical, nursing, and related services for ill and injured patients 24 hours per day, 7 days per week.

Hospital Alliance: Hospital groups that agree to buy equipment and services jointly rather than incurring the costs separately.

Hospital Information System (HIS): A computer-based system that usually includes patient tracking, billing and administrative programs and also may include clinical features.

Human Capital: Employee knowledge, skills, and relationships.

Human Factors: The study of the interrelationships between humans, the tools they use, and the environment in which they live and work.

Illiterate/Low-Literate Populations: Persons with low levels of education.

Immigrants: Persons coming into a country of which he or she is not a native for the purpose of setting up residence.

In Process: Indicates NCQA has reviewed the health plan for the first time and is in the process of making a decision on the accreditation outcome.

In Vitro Fertilization: Program providing for the induction of fertilization of a surgically removed ovum by donated sperm in a culture medium.

Incentive and Reward Program: A program that rewards and encourages providers to improve quality and efficiency.

Incidence: A rate, showing how many new cases of a disease occurred in a population during a specified interval of time, usually expressed as the number of new cases per unit time per fixed number of people.

Incident to Services: Those services furnished as an integral, although incidental, part of the physician's personal professional services in the course of diagnosis or treatment of an injury or illness.

Included Populations: Detailed information describing the population(s) that the indicator intends to measure.

Income Statement: An accounting of sales, expenses, and net profit for a given period.

Incurred but Not Reported (IBNR): When services have been delivered but the insurer has not processed the claim.

Indemnification: A method of shifting legal liability from one party to another by contract.

Indemnity insurer: An insurance company that pays for the medical care of its insured but does not deliver healthcare.

Independent Practice Association (IPA): A type of HMO that contracts with a group of associated physicians for services to its members.

Index: A type of composite measure that adds up individual scores on several items for an individual and divides this sum by the number of items scored.

Indicator: A measure used to determine performance of functions, processes, and outcomes over time.

Indirect Cost: A cost that is indirectly expended in providing a service.

Individually Identifiable Health Information (IIHI): Health information that can be associated with an individual.

Infrastructure: The system of servers, cables, and other hardware, together with the software that ties it together, for the purpose of supporting the operation of devices on a network.

Inhouse: Number of accounts for patients that have not been discharged.

Initiatives: The specific programs, activities, projects, or actions an organization will undertake in an effort to meet performance targets.

Inpatient Care: Services delivered to a patient who needs physician care for at least 24 hours, usually in a hospital.

Inpatient Day: A period of service between the census-taking hours on two successive calendar days, the day of discharge being counted only when the patient was admitted the same day.

Inpatient Mortality: Death of a patient with a heart attack during a hospital stay.

Inpatient Neonatal Mortality: A report of how often infants died before 28 days of birth, adjusted to reflect the fact that some babies are sicker than others at or shortly after birth.

Insourcing: The transfer of an outsourced function to an internal department of the customer, to be managed entirely by employees.

Institute of Medicine (IOM): A private, nonprofit institution that provides information and advice concerning health and science policy under a congressional charter.

Institutionalization: The care delivered in a hospital, rehabilitation hospital, nursing home, from admission to discharge.

Institutionalized Adults: Persons in long-term care or nursing homes.

Insurance Hold: Number of accounts waiting for insurance verification.

Intangible Asset: Something of value that cannot be physically touched, such as a brand, franchise, trademark, or patent.

Integrated Delivery System (IDS): A unified healthcare system that provides physician, hospital, and ambulatory care services for its members by contracting with several provider sites and health plans.

Integration: The process of bringing together related data from different sources to arrange it by customer.

Intellectual Property: Know-how, trade secrets, copyrights, patents, trademarks, and service marks.

Interface: The procedures, codes, and protocols that enable two systems to interact for a meaningful exchange of information.

Intermediate Care Facility: A place that provides medical care to patients who don't need to be in a hospital.

Internal Process Perspective: One of the four standard perspectives used with a Balanced Scorecard, used to monitor the effectiveness of key processes the organization must excel at in order to continue adding value for patients and shareholders.

Internal Standards: Performance measurement quality standards tailored to a specific healthcare organization.

Internal Time Comparison: A comparison using the same measure in the same organization at two or more points in time to evaluate present or prior performance.

International Classification of Diseases, 9th Revision, with Clinical Modifications (ICD-9-CM): A coding system developed in the United States, based on the ICD-9 code developed by the World Health Organization. ICD-9-CM codes provide a standard for comparison of birth, death, and disease data.

International Classification of Diseases, 10th Revision (ICD-10): A list that assigns codes to types of illnesses or conditions. Whereas CPT codes represent procedures and other services, ICD-10 codes represent diagnoses.

International Organization for Standardization (ISO): An international organization that establishes standards in a variety of areas, including quality management (see ISO 9000).

Invalid Data: Values for data elements that are required for calculating and/or risk adjusting a core measure that falls outside of the acceptable range of values defined for that data element.

Inventory: The stock of goods on hand that is for sale.

ISO 9000: The family of ISO standards concerned with quality management.

John M. Eisenberg Award for Patient Safety and Quality: An award that recognizes major achievements of individuals and organizations in improving patient safety and quality.

Joint Commission on Accreditation of Healthcare Organizations (JCAHO): A commission that defines standards concerning the content and quality of medical records, as well as requirements for organization-wide information-management processes that must be followed to qualify for participation in the Medicare and Medicaid programs.

Joint Venture: A contractual arrangement between two or more parties forming an unincorporated business.

Just in Time (JIT): A manufacturing philosophy in which raw materials arrive no earlier than they are required to reduce costs and inefficiencies associated with large inventory.

Kaizen: A Japanese quality improvement philosophy named after the phrase "continuous improvement."

Karnofsky Performance Score (KPS): A score used to quantify a patient's general well-being, often used to determine whether a cancer patient can receive chemotherapy. The score ranges from 0% (death) to 100% (normal, no complaints, no signs of disease).

Key Performance Indicators (KPIs): Core measures that gauge the performance of an organization in a particular area, in terms of how the organization has performed in the past and how it is currently performing.

Knowledge Engineering: The process of extracting knowledge from an expert with enough detail and completeness that the knowledge can be imparted to others or to an information system.

Knowledge Management: A deliberate, systematic business optimization strategy that selects, distills, stores, organizes, packages, and communicates information essential to the business of a company in a manner that improves employee performance and corporate competitiveness.

Knowledge Organization: An organization that creates, acquires, transfers, and retains information.

Knowledge Repository: A central location of information on best practices.

Knowledge Workers: Employees hired primarily for what they know.

Knowledgebase: A database that contains information about other data contained in the database.

Laboratory: Hospital-based main laboratories or Point of Care Testing, free-standing laboratories, embryology laboratories, reference laboratories, blood banks, and donor centers.

Lagging Indicator: A performance measure that represents the consequences of actions previously taken.

Latency: The delay inherent in a system.

Latent Error: An error in the design, organization, training, or maintenance that lead to operator errors and whose effects typically lie dormant in the system for lengthy periods of time.

Leading Indicators: Measures considered drivers of future performance. A predictive measure.

Lean Manufacturing: A quality methodology focused on eliminating all waste from the manufacturing process.

Legacy System: An existing information system in which an enterprise has invested considerable time and money.

Leverage: The degree to which an organization assumes a larger proportion of debt than the amount invested by its owners.

Liabilities: Everything a company owes a creditor. The sum of current liabilities and short-term debt.

Liquidity: Capacity to pay debts as they come due.

Living with Illness: Care related to chronic or recurrent illness.

Local Area Network (LAN): A network of computer and peripherals in close proximity, usually in the same building.

Localization: The process of adapting a website to a particular country or region.

Logical Observation Identifiers Names and Codes (LOINC): Universal identifiers for laboratory and other clinical observations.

Logistic Regression: A form of regression analysis used when the response variable is a binary variable.

Long-Term Care: The health and personal care services provided to chronically ill, aged, disabled, or retarded persons in an institution or in the place of residence.

Long-Term Care Pharmacy: Services that include the procurement, preparation, dispensing, and distribution of pharmaceutical products, and ongoing monitoring and assistance in managing the resident's clinical status and outcomes-related drug therapy.

Long-Term Debt: Financial obligations that come due more than 1 year from the date of the balance sheet statement.

Lost Opportunity Cost: The cost of not applying resources to toward an alternative investment.

Loyalty: A positive inner feeling or emotional bond between a patient and healthcare organization or provider.

LVF Assessment: A measure of the percentage of patients with heart failure who receive an evaluation of left ventricular function.

Magnet Hospital: An award presented by the American Nurses Credentialing Center (ANCC) to organized nursing services.

Magnetic Resonance Imaging (MRI): The use of a uniform magnetic field and radio frequencies to study tissue and structure of the body.

Malcolm Baldrige National Quality Award: An award established by Congress to promote quality awareness, to recognize quality and business achievements of US organizations, and to publicize the award winners' successful performance strategies.

Mammography Screening: The use of breast x-ray to detect unsuspected breast cancer in asymptomatic women.

Managed Behavioral Health (MBHO): A delivery system for behavioral health concerns that includes managed care services.

Managed Behavioral Healthcare Organization (MBHO): A system of behavioral healthcare delivery that manages quality, utilization and cost of services, and which measures performance in the area of mental and substance abuse disorders.

Managed Care: A healthcare system and ideology based on prepaid membership instead of fee-for-service payment each time service is delivered.

Managed Care: The assumption of responsibility and accountability for the health of a defined population and the simultaneous acceptance of financial risk.

Managed Care Organization (MCO): An insurer that provides both healthcare services and payment for services.

Managed Care Organization: A general term for health plans that provide healthcare in return for preset monthly payments and coordinate care through a defined network of primary care physicians and hospitals.

Managed Care Plans: Health insurance plans intended to reduce healthcare costs through a variety of mechanisms.

Management Services Organization (MSO): A corporation, owned by the hospital or a physician/hospital joint venture that provides management services to one or more medical group practices.

Margin of Safety: An excess of intrinsic value over market price.

Marginal Cost: The change in cost as the result of one more or less unit of output.

Marketing: The process associated with promoting products or services for sale, traditionally involving product, price, place, and promotion.

Mass Customization: Providing products as per customer specifications using traditional manufacturing techniques.

Master Patient Index: A database that collects a patient's various hospital identification numbers, perhaps from the blood lab, radiology, admission, and so on, and keeps them under a single, enterprise-wide identification number.

Material Requirements Planning (MRP): A strategy to increase manufacturing efficiency by managing the production schedule, reducing inventory, increasing cash flow, and delivering products in a timely manner.

Mean: The average value of a sample.

Meaningful Use: A Medicare and Medicaid program that awards incentives for using certified electronic health records (EHRs) to improve patient care.

Measure: A standard used to evaluate and communicate performance against expected results.

Measure Information Form: A tool used to provide specific clinical and technical information on a measure.

Measure-Related Feedback: Measure-related information on performance that is available, on a timely basis, to organizations actively participating in the performance measurement system for use in the organization's ongoing efforts to improve patient care and organization performance.

Median: The middle value when the numbers are arranged in order of magnitude.

Medicaid: A joint federal and state healthcare program for low-income or disabled persons.

Medical Informatics: The use of computer-based tools to assist with core clinical functions, decision support, and research functions.

Medical Record: Data obtained from the records or documentation maintained on a patient in any healthcare setting.

Medical Record Hold: Number of accounts not yet abstracted in Medical Records.

Medical Savings Account: A private equity fund, much like an individual retirement account, set up to help cover future healthcare expenses, forming medical financial security regardless of workplace health plans.

Medically Uninsured: Individuals or groups with no or inadequate health insurance coverage.

Medicare: The federal government's healthcare program for all persons over the age of 65 and for younger persons who have disabilities and cannot work.

Mentally Ill: Persons diagnosed as having a syndrome of emotional, cognitive, and/or perceptual problems leading to significant impairment of functioning or behavior.

Metadata: Data about data. How the structures and calculation rules are stored, information on data sources, definitions, quality, transformations, date of last update, and user access privileges.

Microsystems: The multiple small units of caregivers, administrators, and other staff who deliver care and services.

Minority Groups: A subgroup having special characteristics within a larger group, often bound together by special ties that distinguish it from the larger group.

Mirroring: Two identical files or databases created and updated simultaneously so an exact duplicate exists at all times.

Missing Data: When there are no values present for one or more data elements that are required for calculating and/or risk adjusting a core measure.

Mission Critical: Data relating to essential business operations.

Mission Statement: A mission statement defines the core purpose of the organization.

Mode: The most frequently occurring value for a data element.

Model-Based Approach for Risk Adjustment: A statistical technique that uses a mathematical model to describe the relationship between an outcome and a set of explanatory variables that are used to study and characterize the data.

Morbidity: A measurement of illness or accident risk, based on categories of age, region, occupation, and others.

Mortality: Statistical death rates, usually broken down by age or gender.

Mortgage: A legal document that pledges property to cover debt.

Multivariate Analysis: The analysis of the simultaneous relationships among variables.

Myocardial Infarction (MI): Heart attack.

National Committee for Quality Assurance (NCQA): A nonprofit organization that acts as a watchdog for the quality of care delivered managed care plans and physician organizations. Its accreditation process includes HEDIS and patient satisfaction surveys.

National Institute of Standards and Technology (NIST): A federal agency within the Commerce Department's Technology Administration whose primary mission is to develop and promote measurement, standards, and technology to enhance productivity, facilitate trade, and improve the quality of life.

National Library of Medicine (NLM): The largest medical library and a branch of the National Institutes of Health (NIH).

National Patient Safety Goals: The National Patient Safety Goals are a series of specified actions that accredited organizations are expected to take in order to prevent medical errors.

National Quality Forum (NQF): The independent, voluntary, consensus-based member organization that endorses standardized quality measures.

National Quality Improvement Goals: Standardized performance measures that can be applied across accredited healthcare organizations.

National Quality Measures Clearinghouse (NQMC): A public repository for evidence-based quality measures and measure sets sponsored by the Agency for Healthcare Research and Quality, US Department of Health and Human Services.

Neonate: A child under 28 days of age.

Net Earnings: The amount left over after deducting all due bills for the accounting period and paying off all due interest and federal taxes.

Net Income: Revenues less expenses.

Net Patient Revenue: Net revenue from patients, third-party payers, and others for services rendered.

Net Present Value (NPV): The total present value of all cash flows, discounted to present day dollars. Enables managers to evaluate investments in today's dollars.

Net Profit: Revenues minus taxes, interest, depreciation, and other expenses.

Net Revenue: Gross revenue adjusted for deductions and expenses.

Net Worth: Total assets minus total liabilities of an individual or company. Also called owner's equity, shareholders' equity, or net assets.

Network: A group of hospitals, physicians, other providers, insurers, and/or community agencies that voluntarily work together to coordinate and deliver health services.

Network Model HMO: A health maintenance organization that contracts with multiple groups of physicians for care delivery.

New Patient: One who has not received professional services from the physician, or another physician of the same specialty who belongs to the same group practice, within the past 3 years.

Non-Competitive Reward Model: A program that rewards absolute performance based on fixed targets or benchmarks.

Non-Operating Revenue: Investment income, extraordinary gains, and other non-operating gains.

Non-Weighted Score: A combination of the values of several items into a single summary value for each case.

Normalization: The process of reducing a complex data structure into its simplest, most stable structure. Normalization is often a prerequisite for an efficient relational database design.

Notes Payable: Money borrowed by the organization that is to be repaid within 1 year.

Numerator: The upper portion of a fraction used to calculate a rate, proportion, or ratio.

Numerator Data Elements: Those data elements necessary or required to construct the numerator.

Numerator Excluded Populations: Detailed information describing the populations that should not be included in the numerator.

Numerator Statement: A statement that depicts the portion of the denominator population that satisfies the conditions of the performance measure to be an indicator event.

Numerator Time Window: The time period in which cases are reviewed for inclusion in the numerator.

Objective: A concise statement describing the specific things an organization must do well in order to execute its strategy.

Observation Service: A service furnished on a hospital's premises that is reasonable and necessary to evaluate an outpatient's condition or determine the need for a possible admission to the hospital as an inpatient.

Occupied Bed Day: A period of service between the census-taking hours on two successive calendar days, the day of discharge being counted only when the patient was admitted the same day.

Office-Based Surgery: Small organizations or practices composed of four or fewer physicians performing surgical procedures.

Oncology Services: An organized program for the treatment of cancer by the use of drugs or chemicals.

Ongoing Data Quality Review Process: A data quality review process in operation and that is intended to continue for as long as data are accepted into the database.

Open Architecture: A network design that allows integration of various different types of computers and databases.

Open Heart Surgery: Heart surgery where the chest is opened and the blood is recirculated and oxygenated with equipment and the necessary staff to perform the surgery.

Open Physician–Hospital Organization (PHO): A joint venture between the hospital and all members of the medical staff who wish to participate.

Outcome Measure: A measure that indicates the result of the performance of a function or process.

Outcome of Care: A health state of a patient resulting from healthcare.

Outcomes: An assessment of a treatment's effectiveness by considering its success as a care solution as well as its cost, side effects and risk.

Outcomes Management: A program used to determine the clinical end results according to defined various categories and then promote the use of those categories that yield improved outcomes.

Outlier: A case in which costs far exceed those of a typical case within a Diagnostic-Related Group (DRG).

Outlier Payments: Supplements to prospective payments to defray some of the expenses in caring for the most costly cases.

Outpatient Prospective Payment System (OPPS): A prospective payment system established by the Balanced Budget Act of 1997 in which all services paid are classified into groups called Ambulatory Payment Classifications or APCs. A payment rate is established for each APC. Services in each APC are similar clinically and in terms of the resources they require.

Outpatient Surgery: Scheduled surgical services provided to patients who do not remain in the hospital overnight.

Outpatient Visit: A visit by a patient who is not lodged in the hospital while receiving medical, dental, or other services.

Outsourcing: Entrusting a business process to an external services provider for a significant period of time.

Out-tasking: A limited form of outsourcing in which a task is contracted out to a consultant or other service provider.

Overhead: The expense of running the business as opposed to the direct costs of personnel and materials used to produce the end result.

Oxygenation Assessment: A performance measure that reports how many patients with pneumonia had their blood/oxygen level measured.

Pain Management Program: A recognized clinical service or program providing specialized medical care, drugs or therapies for the management of acute or chronic pain and other distressing symptoms, administered by specially trained physicians and other clinicians, to patients suffering from an acute illness of diverse causes.

Palliative Care Program: An organized program providing specialized medical care, drugs, or therapies for the management of acute or chronic pain and/or the control of symptoms administered by specially trained physicians and other clinicians, and supportive care services, such as counseling on advanced directives, spiritual care, and social services, to patients with advanced disease and their families.

Parameter: Any characteristic of a population that can be inferred.

Parent Organization: The primary site of care for a healthcare organization. An organization may have multiple locations of care accredited under one parent organization.

Pathology and Clinical Laboratory Services: A service of a healthcare organization that is equipped to examine material derived from the human body to provide information for use in the diagnosis, prevention, or treatment of disease.

Patient Accounting System: Software that records charges to patients, creates billing forms, and maintains payment records.

Patient Day: A period of service between the census-taking hours on two successive calendar days, the day of discharge being counted only when the patient was admitted the same day.

Patient Demographics: Patient age, ethnicity, gender, and geographic location.

Patient Experience of Care: A patient experience is a report by a patient concerning observations of and participation in healthcare.

Patient Factor: A variable describing some characteristic of individual patients that may influence healthcare-related outcomes.

Patient Level Data: Collection of data elements that depict the healthcare services provided to a patient.

Patient Survey: Data obtained from patients and/or their family members/significant others.

Payer: A company or an agency that purchases health services.

Payroll Expenses: Payroll for all personnel including medical and dental residents, interns, and trainees.

Peak Debt Service: The largest annual interest expense and principal payments on existing debt.

Perception of Care: Satisfaction measures that focus on the delivery of clinical care from the patient's/family's/caregiver's perspective.

Percutaneous Coronary Intervention (PCI): Coronary angioplasty, a procedure used to open up a blocked artery of the heart and restore blood flow to the heart muscle.

Performance Management: The skillful accomplishment of business through the effective use of resources.

Performance Measure: A quantitative tool that provides an indication of an organization's performance in relation to a specified process or outcome.

Performance Measurement System: A system of automated databases that facilitates performance improvement in healthcare organizations through the collection and dissemination of process and/or outcome measures of performance.

Performance Measurements: The collected results of a healthcare organization's actual performance over a specified time.

Personal Digital Assistant (PDA): A handheld electronic organizer that may have Internet access and e-mail functions.

Perspective: In Balanced Scorecard vernacular, a category of performance measures. The standard four perspectives are Financial, Customer, Internal Process, and Employee Learning and Growth.

PERT Chart: A method for project planning by analyzing the time required for each step.

Pervasive Computing: The anytime, anyplace access of computational power and data, in an unobtrusive form.

Pharmaceutical Services: Those services provided directly or through contract with another organization that procure, prepare, preserve, compound, dispense, or distribute pharmaceutical products, and monitor the patient's clinical status.

Pharmacists: Those persons legally qualified by education and training to engage in the practice of pharmacy.

Physician Group Practices/Clinics: Any groups of three or more full-time physicians organized in a legally recognized entity for the provision of healthcare services, sharing space, equipment, personnel, and records for both patient care and business management, and who have a predetermined arrangement for the distribution of income.

Physician Hospital Organization (PHO): A system where a hospital and its physician groups jointly own the organization. The PHO as an entity then assumes the responsibility of arranging contracts with managed care plans and care facilities.

Physician Practice Organization (PPO): A system where insurance companies, employers, and other healthcare buyers arrange lower fees with select physicians and facilities.

Physicians: Individuals licensed to practice medicine.

Picture Archiving and Communications System (PACS): A system that uses an image server to exchange x-rays, CT scans, and other medical images over a network.

Pneumococcal Vaccination: A measure that reports how many patients 65 years and older were screened and vaccinated to prevent pneumonia.

Point of Service (POS): An indemnity-type option offered by HMOs in which members can refer themselves outside the plan and still get some coverage.

Point-of-Sale (POS): The device that is the first point in a financial transaction.

Point-of-Service Collections as a Fraction of Goal: Percentage of target monies collected at time of service.

Population: A complete set of actual or potential observations.

Portal: A website that offers a broad array of resources and services, from e-mail to online shopping. Most of the popular search engines have transformed themselves into Web portals to attract a larger audience.

Positron Emission Tomography (PET): A nuclear medicine imaging technology used to produce composite pictures based on metabolic activity or blood flow.

Poverty Populations: Persons living below the standard level of living of the community.

Practice Sanctions: Penalties, ranging from practice limitations to nonrenewal of contract, for failure of contracted providers to perform above minimum standards.

Practitioner: Any individual who is qualified to practice a healthcare profession.

Precision: The ability of an instrument to resolve small differences. Also known as resolution.

Predicted Value: The statistically expected response or outcome for a patient after the risk adjustment model has been applied and the patient's unique set of risk factors have been taken into account.

Predictive Modeling: The use of a software program to predict, with quantifiable accuracy, future indicator values, based on past data. These past data typically include data not directly related to the data used to calculate the indicator.

Preferred Provider Organization (PPO): A form of managed care that has contracts with physicians, hospitals, and other providers of care who offer medical services to enrollees on a fee-for-service basis.

Prescriptive Standard: A standard set as a goal that ought to be achieved, or as a threshold that defines minimum performance. This standard may be derived from studies using different measurement methods.

Prevalence: The proportion of people in the entire population who have a disease at a certain point in time without regard to when they first got the disease.

Prevention: The degree to which appropriate services are provided for promotion, preservation, and restoration of health and early detection of disease.

Primary Care Department: A unit or clinic within the hospital that provides primary care services through hospital-salaried medical and/or nursing staff, focusing on evaluating and diagnosing medical problems and providing medical treatment on an outpatient basis.

Primary Care Network: A group of primary care physicians who contract among themselves and/or with health plans.

Prisoners: Individuals involuntarily confined in a penal institution.

Process: An interrelated series of events, activities, actions, mechanisms, or steps that transform inputs into outputs.

Process Management: An evaluation and restructuring of system functions to make certain processes are carried out in the most efficient and economical way.

Process Map: A graphic description of a process, showing the sequence of process tasks, which is developed for a specific purpose and from a selected viewpoint.

Process Measure: A measure that focuses on a process that leads to a certain outcome.

Process Optimization: The removal or re-engineering of processes that don't add significant value to product or service, impede time to market, or result in suboptimal quality.

Profiling: The process of taking a few key customer data points, such as name, occupation, age, and address, and generating best guesses about their other characteristics.

Profit: The positive gain from business operations after subtracting all expenses.

Profit Center: A segment of the healthcare enterprise for which costs, revenues, and profits are separately calculated.

Profit Margin: Net profit after taxes divided by sales for a given 12-month period, expressed as a percentage.

Proprietary: Owned, copyrighted, or for which exclusive legal rights are held.

Prospective Payment: Any advance payment to a provider or facility for future healthcare services. Capitation is a form of prospective payment.

Prospective Payment System (PPS): A reimbursement program in which Medicare pays a predetermined amount for each inpatient discharge.

Protected Health Information (PHI): Individually identifiable health information (HIPAA).

Protocol: A way of doing things that has become an agreed-upon convention. Alternatively, a set of standards that defines communications between computers.

Provider Data: Provider-generated data not necessarily contained in the medical record.

Provider Profile: An examination of services provided, claims filed, and benefits allocated by healthcare facilities, physicians, and other providers to assess quality of care and cost management.

Proxy for Outcome: A process of care used as an indicator of health status, such as an admission to hospital used as an indication of increased severity of illness.

Psychologist/Non-Physician Behavioral Health Clinicians: Persons legally qualified by education and training to practice in the field of mental health.

Public Domain: Belonging to the community at large, unprotected by copyright, and subject to appropriation by anyone.

Public Health Professionals: Persons educated in public health or a related discipline who are employed to improve health of populations.

Push Technology: The automatic delivery of Web news and other information without a request from the user.

Qualified Providers: NCQA accreditation measure that verifies each physician in a health plan is licensed and trained to practice medicine and that the health plan's members are happy with their service.

Quality: A standard of service established by the healthcare enterprise, patients, or credentialing body.

Quality Assurance: An assessment of the delivery portion of healthcare plans to make sure patients are receiving high-quality care when and where they need it.

Quality Bonus: Monies for performance improvement.

Quality Function Deployment (QFD): Prioritizing and translating customer needs into technical requirements and then delivering a quality product or service that aims to satisfy the customer.

Quality Management: The process of ensuring care is accessible and available, delivered within community standards; and that there is a system to identify and correct problems and to monitor ongoing performance.

Quality Measure: A mechanism to assign a quantity to quality of care by comparison to a criterion.

Quality of Care: Degree to which health services for individuals and populations increase the likelihood of desired health outcomes and are consistent with current professional knowledge.

Quality of Life Measure: A score based on a patient's overall well-being.

Quality Tools: A clearinghouse for quality assessment indicators sponsored by the Agency for Healthcare Research and Quality.

Radiation Therapy: The branch of medicine concerned with radioactive substances and using various techniques of visualization, with the diagnosis and treatment of disease using any of the various sources of radiant energy.

Random Sample: A subset selected in such a way that each member of the population has an equal opportunity to be selected.

Randomization: A technique for selecting or assigning cases such that each case has an equal probability of being selected or assigned.

Range: The difference between the largest and smallest number in a set. A measure of the spread of a data set.

Rate: A score derived by dividing the number of cases that meet a criterion for quality by the number of eligible cases within a given time frame where the numerator cases are a subset of the denominator cases.

Rate of Return: The annual return on an investment, expressed as a percentage of the total amount invested.

Rate-Based: An aggregate data measure in which the value of each measurement is expressed as a proportion or as a ratio.

Ratio: A relationship between two counted sets of data, which may have a value of zero or greater. In a ratio, the numerator is not necessarily a subset of the denominator.

Rationale: An explanation of why an indicator is useful in specifying and assessing the process or outcome of care measured by the indicator.

Real Time: Computer communications or processes that are so fast they seem instantaneous.

Receiver Operating Characteristic (ROC): A graph obtained by plotting all sensitivity values on the y axis against their equivalent values for all available thresholds on the x axis.

Re-Engineering: The process of analyzing, modeling, and streamlining internal processes so that a company can deliver better quality products and services.

Referred Visit: A visit to a specialty unit of the hospital established for providing technical aid used in the diagnosis and treatment of patients.

Refined Diagnostic Related Group (RDRG): A version of the DRG program that classifies cases into levels of severity and complexity based on the impact they are likely to have on use of hospital resources.

Registry Data: Those data obtained from local, regional, or national disease or procedure-related registries.

Regression: A mathematical method of forecasting using line equations to explain the relationship between multiple causes and effects.

Regression Coefficient: For a linear relationship, the constant that represents the rate of change of one variable as a function of changes in the other.

Rehabilitation Centers: Facilities that provide programs for rehabilitating individuals with mental illnesses, drug or alcohol addictions, or physical disabilities.

Rehabilitation Service: An organization service providing medical, health-related, social, and vocational services for disabled persons to help them attain or retain their maximum functional capacity.

Reimbursement: Payment for medical services delivered.

Relational Database: A database where all information is arranged in tables containing predefined fields.

Relative Value Unit (RVU): A composite measure of the time, difficulty, and resources associated with a procedure or service, used to establish fees, reimbursement levels, and physician incentives.

Relevance: The applicability and/or pertinence of the indicator to its users and customers.

Reliability: The degree to which the measure is free from random error.

Reliability, Availability, Serviceability (RAS): An evaluation method weighs a system's performance and maintenance/repair record to determine whether or not the productivity of the system is worth the cost to maintain it.

Remittance Advice: A notice of payment due, either in paper form or as a notice of an electronic data interchange financial transaction.

Repeatability: The ability of an instrument or system to provide consistent results.

Reporting Period: The defined time period that describes the patient's end of service.

Request for Proposal (RFP): A document that requests prospective service providers to propose the term, conditions, and other elements of an agreement to deliver specified services.

Requirements Specification: A description, in operational terms, of what management expects the vendor's product or service to do for the company.

Residential Care Facilities: Long-term care facilities, which provide supervision and assistance in activities of daily living with medical and nursing services when required.

Residual Value: The value remaining in a device, as a function of time. The longer the time from the original purchase date, the lower the residual value.

Resolution: The ability of an instrument to resolve small differences.

Respect and Caring: The degree to which the patient or a designee is involved in his or her own care decisions and to which those providing services do so with sensitivity and respect for the patient's needs, expectations, and individual differences.

Respiratory Care Practitioners: Individuals trained and certified in the field of respiratory therapy.

Retained Earnings: The portion of an organization's net earnings not paid to shareholders in the form of dividends.

Retention: The result when members remain on a health plan from 1 year to the next. Alternatively, the percentage of a premium that a health plan keeps for internal costs or profit.

Return on Assets (ROA): The ratio of operating earnings to net operating assets. The ROA is a test of whether a business is earning enough to cover its cost of capital.

Return on Equity (ROE): The ratio of net income to the owner's equity. The ROE is a measure of the return on investment for an owner's equity capital invested in the organization.

Return on Investment (ROI): Profit resulting from investing in a process or piece of equipment. The profit could be money, time savings, or other positive result.

Revenue: The inflow of assets from providing services to patients.

Risk-Adjusted Measures: Those measures are risk adjusted using statistical modeling or stratification methods.

Risk-Adjusted Rate: A rate that takes into account differences in case mix to enable valid comparisons between groups.

Risk Adjustment: A statistical process for reducing, removing, or clarifying the influences of confounding factors that differ among comparison groups.

Risk Adjustment Data Elements: Those data elements used to risk adjust a performance measure.

Risk Adjustment Model: The statistical algorithm that specifies the numerical values and the sequence of calculations used to risk adjust performance measures.

Risk Factor: A variable describing some characteristic of individual patients that may influence healthcare-related outcomes.

Risk Factor Value: A specific value assigned to a risk factor for a given episode of care (EOC) record.

Risk Model: The statistical algorithm that specifies the numerical values and the sequence of calculations used to risk adjust performance measures.

Risk Sharing: An arrangement that combines the risk of financial losses for all care providers in a business entity such as a hospital or physician group. One provider's losses are shared by all, but gains also are shared.

Rollout: The process of introducing a new technology-based service.

Root Cause Analysis: A step-by-step approach that leads to the identification of a fault's first or root cause.

Rural Healthcare: Healthcare services, public or private, in rural areas.

Rural Populations: Persons inhabiting rural areas or small towns classified as rural.

Safety: The degree to which the risk of an intervention and the risk in the care environment are reduced for the patient and others, including the healthcare provider.

Sales: Total dollar amount collected for services provided.

Salvage Value: The estimated price for which a fixed asset can be sold at the end of its useful life.

Sample: A subset of the population selected according to some scheme.

Sample Size: The number of individuals or particular patients included in a study.

Sampling: The process of selecting a group of units, portions of material, or observations from a larger collection of units, quantity of material, or observations that serve to provide information that may be used as a basis for making a decision concerning the larger quantity.

Sampling Design: The procedure for selecting a subset of a population to observe or estimate a characteristic of the entire population.

Sampling Method: The process used to select a sample. Possible approaches to sampling include simple random sampling, cluster sampling, systematic sampling, and judgment sampling.

Satisfaction Measures: Indicators that assess the extent to which the patients/enrollees, practitioners, and/or purchasers perceive their needs to be met.

Satisfaction Survey: A survey sent to members of a health plan to allow feedback on the organization's service and quality.

Scheduled Survey Date: The date an organization is to begin its full survey.

Score: A rating, usually expressed as a number, and based on the degree to which certain qualities or attributes are present.

Scorecard: A table of the key performance indicators tracked by an organization. A Balanced Scorecard is a particular type of scorecard.

Self-insured: A company that creates and maintains its own health plan for its employees instead of contracting with an outside insurance provider. Also called self-funded.

Sensitivity: In statistics, the percentage of actual positives that are counted as positive.

Sentient Computing: A computing system in which computers, telephones, and everyday objects track the identity, location, and predict the needs of users.

Sentinel Event: Relatively infrequent, clear-cut events that occur independently of a patient's condition that commonly reflect hospital system and process deficiencies and result in unnecessary outcomes for patients.

Server: A computer that controls access to the network and net-based resources.

Service Level Agreement (SLA): An agreement between the parent corporation or other customer and the shared services unit in which the unit agrees to provide services to a specified performance level.

Service Mix Index (SMI): The average relative weight of the procedures billed for a service.

Severity: The degree of biomedical risk, morbidity, or mortality of medical treatment.

Shared Risk Payment: A payment arrangement in which a hospital and a managed care organization share the risk of adverse claims experience.

Shareholders' Equity: What the owners of the organization have left when all liabilities have been met. The difference between total assets and total liabilities.

Sigma: In statistics, the unit of standard deviation.

Simple Random Sample: A process in which a predetermined number of cases from a population as a whole is selected for review.

Single-Photon Emission Computerized Tomography (SPECT): A nuclear medicine imaging technology that combines existing technology of gamma camera imaging with computed tomographic imaging technology to provide a more precise and clear image.

Six Sigma: A statistically driven quality management methodology designed to reduce defects and variation in a business process, thereby increasing customer satisfaction and business profits. The stated goal is to reduce defects to a level equal to six standard deviations (sigma) from the mean.

Skilled Nursing Facility (SNF): An institution primarily engaged in providing skilled nursing care and related services for residents who require medical or nursing care, or rehabilitation services for the rehabilitation of injured, disabled, or sick persons, and is not primarily for the care and treatment of mental diseases.

Slack: In the context of project management, the time in which a minor process or activity can be completed in advance of the next major operation or activity that depends on it.

Social Capital: The sum of the resources embedded within, available through, and derived from the network of relationships possessed by an individual or social unit.

Social Workers: Individuals trained and certified in the field of social work.

Sourcing: The process of identifying potential suppliers of specified services or goods.

Special Cause Variation: Variation due to specific factors, and not due to random error.

Special or Unique Data Source: A data source that is unique to an organization and inaccessible to outside entities or persons.

Specificity: The percentage of actual negatives that are rejected.

Speech–Language Pathologists: Individuals trained and certified in the field of speech–language pathology, a field dealing with the diagnosis and treatment of speech or language disorders.

Sports Medicine: Provision of diagnostic screening and assessment and clinical and rehabilitation services for the prevention and treatment of sports-related injuries.

Stability: The ability of an instrument or device to provide repeatable results over time.

Staff Model HMO: A Health Maintenance Organization variation where the staff physicians work only for a single HMO and have no private practices.

Staffing Ratios: Clinical hospital staff to patient ratios.

Standard: A process, format or transmission protocol that has become convention by agreement of a group of users.

Standard Deviation: A measure of dispersion in the sample, calculated by taking the square root of the variance.

Standard Industry Code (SIC): Codes assigned to various industries and jobs.

Standard of Quality: A generally accepted, objective standard of measurement against which an individual's or organization's level of performance may be compared.

Standards: Agreed principles of protocol set by government, trade, and international organizations that govern behavior.

Statement of Retained Earnings: A report on how much of the organization's earnings were not paid out in dividends.

Statistic: A number resulting from the manipulation of sample data according to specific procedures.

Statistical Process Control (SPC): A method of differentiating between acceptable variations from variations that could indicate problems, based on statistical probability.

Staying Healthy: Care related to healthy populations or the general health needs of non-healthy populations.

Strategic Management System: The use of the Balanced Scorecard in aligning an organization's short-term actions with strategy.

Strategic Resource Allocation: The process of aligning budgets with strategy by using the Balanced Scorecard to make resource allocation decisions.

Strategic Services: Processes that directly affect an enterprise's ability to compete.

Strategy: The differentiating activities an organization pursues to gain competitive advantage.

Strategy Map: The interrelationships among measures that weave together to describe an organization's strategy.

Stratification: A form of risk adjustment that involves classifying data into subgroups based on one or more characteristics, variables, or other categories.

Stratified Measure: A performance measure that is classified into a number of subgroups to assist in analysis and interpretation.

Structure Chart: A graphic description of a process that shows the modular structure of a system, the hierarchy into which the modules are arranged, and the data and control interfaces among modules.

Structure Measure: A measure that assesses whether organizational resources and arrangements are in place to deliver healthcare, such as the number, type, and distribution of medical personnel, equipment, and facilities.

Structured Query Language (SQL): A standard command language used to interact with databases.

Subacute Care: Medical and skilled nursing services provided to patients who are not in an acute phase of illness but who require a level of care higher than that provided in a long-term care setting.

Subrogation: An agreement by which the primary insurer can collect funds from a patient's other benefits sources as reimbursement for claim costs.

Subsidiary: A company that is wholly controlled by another or one that is more than 50% owned by another organization.

Subsidiary Medical Record (SMR): A medical record maintained by a specific department.

Sunk Cost: Investments made in the past that have no bearing on future investment decisions.

Supply Chain: The flow of materials, information, and finances as they move in a process from supplier to manufacturer to wholesaler to retailer to consumer.

Supply Chain Management: Managing the movement of goods from raw materials to the finished product delivered to customers.

Swing Bed: Temporary nursing home care in a hospital setting. Hospitals offering swing beds have fewer than 100 beds, are located in a rural region, and provide 24-hour nursing care.

Synergy: The benefit derived from the cooperation between two business entities.

Syntax: The ordering of and relationship between the words and other structural elements in phrases and sentences.

Systematic Random Sampling: A process in which one case is selected randomly, and the next cases are selected according to a fixed period or interval.

Systematized Nomenclature of Human and Veterinary Medicine (SNOMED): A standardized vocabulary system for medical databases.

Systems Integration: The merging of diverse hardware, software, and communications systems into a consolidated operating unit.

Tacit Knowledge: Unspoken or implied knowledge.

Tangible Asset: Assets having a physical existence, such as cash, equipment, and real estate, as well as accounts receivable.

Target: The desired result of a performance measure. Targets make meaningful the results derived from measurement and provide organizations with feedback regarding performance.

Taxonomy: The classification of concepts and objects into a hierarchically ordered system that indicates relationships.

Telemedicine: A segment of telehealth that focuses on the provider aspects of healthcare telecommunications, especially medical imaging technology.

Telemonitoring: Monitoring patient physiologic parameters, images, or other data from a distance.

Terminally Ill: Persons with an incurable or irreversible illness at the end stage that will result in death within a short time.

Tertiary Care: Care that requires highly specialized skills, technology, and support services.

Test Cases: Fictitious patient-level data composed of clinical data elements that yield an expected result for a specific core measure algorithm.

Third- or Fourth-Degree Laceration: A measure of how often patients have significant vaginal tears during delivery.

Third-Party Administrator: A company independent of a healthcare organization that handles claims and/or other business services.

Third-Party Payer: An insurance company, health maintenance organization, or government agency that pays for medical services for a patient.

Tiering: A cost-sharing model used by purchasers and health plans to encourage selection of better-performing, more effective and efficient providers.

Time to PCI: Length of time before a clogged artery in the heart is opened via percutaneous coronary intervention.

Time to Thrombolysis: Length of time before thrombolytic therapy is initiated.

Timeliness: The degree to which care is provided to the patient at the most beneficial or necessary time.

Tobacco Treatment/Cessation Program: Organized hospital services with the purpose of ending tobacco-use habits of patients addicted to tobacco/nicotine.

Total Cost of Ownership (TCO): The cost of owning a device or technology, including operating expenses.

Total Expenses: All payroll and non-payroll expenses as well as any non-operating losses.

Total Quality Management (TQM): A customer-centric philosophy based on constant improvement to meet customer demands.

Touch Point: The point of contact between a patient and a healthcare enterprise.

Transients/Migrants: Mobile, short-term residents who move, usually to find work.

Transmission Schedule: The schedule of dates on which performance measurement systems are expected to be transmitting data.

Transplant Services: The branch of medicine that transfers an organ or tissue from one person to another or from one body part to another to replace a diseased structure or to restore function or to change appearance.

Trend Analysis: The percentage change in indicator value from a reference or base year, that is, [(subsequent − base year)/base year] × 100.

Trended: The application of trend analysis on a performance indicator.

Triage: A means of guiding patients to proper services by using an intermediary person to gather preliminary information and answer patients' questions.

Ultrasound: The use of acoustic waves to visualize internal body structures.

Uniform billing code: The procedural rules on patient billing, including what information should appear on the bill and how it should be coded.

Urgent Care Center: A facility that provides care and treatment for problems that are not life threatening but require attention over the short term.

Useful Life: The time, usually expressed in months or years, that a device can perform a useful function.

User Interface: The junction between the user and the computer.

Usual and Customary: An insurance industry term for a charge that is usual and customary and made by persons having similar medical conditions in the county of the policyholder.

Utilization Management: A review process used to make sure a patient's hospital stay, surgery, tests, or other treatment is necessary.

Vaginal Birth after a Cesarean Delivery (VBAC): A measure that reports how often patients had a vaginal birth after previously having a Cesarean section.

Validity: The degree to which the measure is associated with what it purports to measure.

Value Chain: The sequence of events in the process of delivering healthcare.

Value Proposition: A description of how an organization will differentiate itself to customers, and what particular set of values it will deliver.

Value-Added Network (VAN): An information exchange network between a healthcare site and its business operations such as billing and supply offices.

Values: The deeply held beliefs within the enterprise that are demonstrated through the day-to-day behaviors of all employees.

Variable: A phenomenon that may take on different values.

Variable Cost: A unit cost that depends on total volume.

Variance: A measure of dispersion in a sample, calculated by taking the average of square differences between observations and their mean.

Virtual Knowledge Management: A Knowledge Management model in which knowledge workers and management work and communicate through the Web and other networks.

Vision: A shared mental framework that helps give form to the often-abstract future that lies ahead.

Vulnerable Populations: Groups of persons who may be compromised in their ability to give informed consent, who are frequently subjected to coercion in their decision making, or whose range of options is severely limited, making them vulnerable to healthcare quality problems.

Wage Index: A measure of the relative differences in the average hourly wage for the hospitals in each labor market area compared to the national average hourly wage.

Warranty: A contractual undertaking given by the supplier, to provide a specified level of product or service support.

Web Service: A tool or capability that can be accessed through the Web, rather than being run locally on a desktop.

Weighted Index: An index adjusted to reflect the differential importance of variables relative to other values.

Weighted Mean: The sum of the mean of each group multiplied by its respective weights, divided by the sum of the weights.

Weighted Score: A combination of the values of several items into a single summary value for each case where each item is differentially weighted.

Women: Adult females, including pregnant women.

Workflow: A process description of how tasks are done, by whom, in what order and how quickly.

Working Capital: The funds available for current operating needs. Computationally, it is current assets less current liabilities.

Zero Defects: A management strategy practice that aims to reduce defects in products or services as a way to increase profits.

Index

Page numbers followed by f and t indicate figures and tables, respectively.

9781138104532